REDS & RAMS

David Marples

REDS & RAMS

The Story of the
East Midlands Derby

First published by Pitch Publishing, 2022

Pitch Publishing
9 Donnington Park,
85 Birdham Road,
Chichester,
West Sussex,
PO20 7AJ
www.pitchpublishing.co.uk
info@pitchpublishing.co.uk

© 2022, David Marples

Every effort has been made to trace the copyright.
Any oversight will be rectified in future editions at the
earliest opportunity by the publisher.

All rights reserved. No part of this book may be reproduced,
sold or utilised in any form or transmitted in any form or by
any means, electronic or mechanical, including photocopying,
recording or by any information storage and retrieval system,
without prior permission in writing from the Publisher.

A CIP catalogue record is available for this book
from the British Library.

ISBN 978 1 80150 182 8

Typesetting and origination by Pitch Publishing
Printed and bound in Great Britain by TJ Books, Padstow

Contents

Introduction. 9

1. Railways and Robin Hood 13
2. And so it begins: 1892–1899 35
3. End of a century; end of an era: 1899–1915 . 64
4. Between the wars: 1919–1939 86
5. The see-saw years: 1945–1973 103
6. The pendulum swings this way: 1967–1973 . 132
7. The pendulum swings that way: 1973–1980 . 159
8. Empires crumble and walls come tumbling down: 1980–1993. 198
9. The short-lived Premier League years: 1993–2005 258
10. Hopelessly intertwined: 2005-2014. 294
11. Local heroes and villains: 2014-2022. . . . 346

Acknowledgements 427

Bibliography 428

For anyone who has ever
loved one football club but
loathed another.

Introduction

BEYOND THE nuance, facades, and emotional concealments, two very base emotions drive human beings: love and hate. The more love we feel for someone or something, the deeper the hate we feel towards any threat to that precious someone or something. Despite our protestations, we are quite simple creatures.

The story of the East Midlands derby is – like any derby – one that is propelled by these two powerful forces: love and hate. Unconditional love for one team; unadulterated hate for the other. This particular derby isn't unique in that sense, but that doesn't mean it isn't special.

The festering resentment between the two clubs – between the two cities – has been simmering since the late-Victorian era, bubbling over into blind fury and violence every so often. Since the first league meeting in 1892, the clubs have rarely been out of each other's orbit, irritating, needling and annoying the other simply by existing. This is not a derby featuring teams from the same town or city, but one experienced by clubs who occupy spaces 16 miles from each other.

As such, the rivalry occupies its own Goldilocks zone: close enough for fans of each club to have regular interaction, yet far enough away for the others to seem utterly alien, different and indeed 'other'.

This is the story not just of Nottingham Forest and Derby County, or even Nottingham and Derby, but also the story of the evolution of English football. From footballers wearing caps, playing on cricket or racecourse grounds and possessing wonderful Edwardian moustaches, through to heavy footballs, long shorts and boots drenched in dubbin to the present day of social media banter, huge fan displays and multicoloured boots, this fixture shows us how football has changed and adapted over the course of 130 years or so. It is also the story of how two East Midlands cities and their residents have strived to retain a sense of identity through wars, desperately bleak economic times, high rates of unemployment and civil unrest.

In truth, the season just finished – 2021/22 – was the gift that kept giving in terms of the subject of this book. After 14 consecutive seasons spent locked in the second tier, the clubs were like two irritated and tired toddlers constantly squabbling with each other and desperate for some relief. At times, the very future of the fixture in its current iteration looked in doubt as Derby County faced severe existential threat. The fortunes of each club ebbed and flowed throughout the campaign, and anything seemed possible at one stage or other, from both clubs suffering relegation to both clubs staying in the same division or indeed each club leaving the division through very different doors.

Temporarily separated, they will one day meet again and, just like in 1892, two football clubs – one wearing red, the other white – will continue to battle for arguably the sweetest feeling in football: that of having vanquished the

Introduction

other lot down the road. Each fixture is a carnival and a battle for identity and meaning all wrapped up in a chaotic bundle of football. Each game is both the most eagerly anticipated yet the most dreaded at the same time. A derby game is a pure distillation of contradiction: love and hate, joy and despair. They are the games that can provide the most, but leave you with the least.

These are the games that create heroes and villains whose deeds echo down through generations, which are the pulse of the respective communities at either end of the A52 – the Brian Clough Way. This is the story of the East Midlands derby.

1
Railways and Robin Hood

NOTTINGHAM AND Derby are locked in a perpetual struggle to assert authority, dominance and, ultimately, the cultural and moral high ground over the other.

Derby boasts of its status as the birthplace of the Industrial Revolution, thus precipitating Nottingham's booming lace market. It developed its reputation for engineering excellence by establishing itself at the heart of the British railways system, then carried this high on its shoulders into the 20th century with Rolls-Royce and Bombardier maintaining this fine tradition. It is the home of Joseph Strutt, the revolutionary ideas of Erasmus Darwin, the altruism of Florence Nightingale, the art and vision of Joseph Wright and Joseph Pickford and the famous nails of Belper. It is the self-styled underdog of middle England.

Nottingham was not immune to the industrial era factories but forged its reputation on rebellion, or at least, being the centre and home for those who wished to kick and push at the boundaries. The most famous of these types is Robin Hood, the socialist sympathising rebel who made it his business to get right up the noses of the ruling gentry by redistributing wealth from rich to poor.

Nottingham Castle, home of Robin Hood's antagonist the Sheriff of Nottingham, was the focal point for the beginning of the English Civil War in August 1642 and was soon commandeered by the Roundheads who opposed Charles I. The king came to Nottingham Castle and raised his royal standard to demonstrate his authority, thus setting off a chain of events that effectively started the civil war. The castle repeatedly came under attack from forces loyal to the king but remained in rebel hands until the end of the war in 1646 when Charles surrendered at Southwell, Nottinghamshire.

In his revolutionary footsteps followed the Luddites: not the backward and resistant-to-change conservatives they are often made out to be but the protectors of artisan craftsmanship. The trailblazing Eric Irons, fighting for justice and equality by becoming the first black magistrate in England and Helen Watts, founder of the Women's Freedom league, both found a home in Nottingham. Writers Alan Sillitoe and D.H. Lawrence challenged traditions by telling the stories of the children of the Industrial Revolution – the angry young men of the working class.

Derby and Nottingham: similar but different. Made of the same cloth but cut, styled and modelled into different garments. Yet for all this, they remain tethered to each other, persistently agitating to define themselves as distant and different to the other while forever remaining a mere 16 miles from each other. Served by different rivers but appropriately linked by Brian Clough Way, they are two teenage brothers kicking and screaming at each other, desperately wanting to assert their independence while refusing to acknowledge their many similarities. To understand their differences in spite of their close geographical proximity, we need to understand how each evolved, what ties and binds them and what powers each to define the other as just that – 'other'.

* * *

Derby expanded rapidly once the kindling of the Industrial Revolution started smouldering. Having visited Piedmont in Italy in 1717 and returned armed with knowledge of Italian silk-throwing machines, John Lombe established Lombe's Mill by the side of the River Derwent in the middle of Derby. Soon afterwards, hosiery became big business thanks to Jebediah Strutt's Derby Rib Attachment, which enabled mass production of stockings. When Strutt paid off his previous partners in 1762, he teamed up with a prominent hosier and spinner from Nottingham called Samuel Need and established Need, Strutt and Woollatt – a successful and prosperous partnership. The Nottingham connection continued when Messrs Wright, bankers of Nottingham, pointed Richard Arkwright in the direction of Strutt and Need to obtain finance for his revolutionary cotton-spinning mill, the first of which opened in Nottingham in 1770. A year later, the three combined to build the world's first commercially successful water-powered, cotton-spinning mill in Cromford, Derbyshire. The Industrial Revolution gathered pace as mills sprung up around the county, most notably in Belper where the North Mill still stands today. It was one of the world's first fireproof buildings owing to Strutt's use of cast iron instead of timber for the internal structure.

Nottingham got busy too. Arkwright established a cotton mill in Hockley in 1768, leading to the development of terraced housing for its workers. Lace production started with William Lee and was enhanced by John Heathcote and John Levers, developing lace into a major international export over the coming years. But the working class of Nottingham wanted a different type of revolution. Taking their cue from the Luddites, named after Ned Ludd, a young apprentice who was rumoured to have wrecked a textile apparatus in 1779, the first major Luddite riot broke out in Arnold, Nottingham in 1881. Mills were set alight and factory equipment destroyed as an expression of frustration at the increasingly challenging working conditions in the factories and mills, but perhaps more significantly as a protest against the rising popularity of automated textile equipment, replacing an artisan skill and leaving the door wide open to cheaper and unskilled workers.

The movement took hold and unrest spread throughout England, weakening the economy over the next two years. It was a turbulent time as Napoleon was nipping at Empire's heels and across the Atlantic, President James Madison signed into law a declaration of war as the United States sought to rid itself of its British ties. Civil unrest reached a crescendo when the army was deployed to quell the riots. Some were hanged, others sent to Australia and the rebellion dissipated. Yet the Luddites' point remained: the workers powering the Industrial Revolution would not go cheaply into the night and both Nottingham and Derby were at the heart of the rise of workers' rights. Derby provided the work; Nottingham defended their rights.

The people of Nottingham had developed a taste for rebellion now. The Whig Party sought to introduce a Reform Bill to ensure constituencies better reflected their growing population, yet the Duke of Newcastle sought to oppose it. All hell broke loose, and the citizens of Nottingham rioted, setting fire to his residence on the site of the castle. It was a constitutional crisis, prompting the resignation of prime minister Charles Grey and a period of political upheaval. Britain was on the brink of full-blown revolution. Riots occurred in Derby, too, reminding us that our two protagonists in this tale haven't always been on the opposite ends of the scale; they are cut from the same textile or lace cloth.

Despite this upheaval, life and the Industrial Revolution continued apace, shaping and defining each. In 1836, Derby elected Joseph Strutt mayor and, three years later, Nottingham opened its first railway station on the west side of Carrington Street on 20 May. Naturally, a station requires a service and a destination and, on 4 June, the Midlands Counties Railway opened the first railway service between Nottingham and Derby. They were now bound together. The first public train left for Derby at precisely 12.30pm on the opening day and took 40 minutes to get there, stopping once to take on water. A year later, the Midland Counties Railway merged with the Birmingham and Derby Junction Railway to form Midland Railway and it established headquarters in Derby, meaning that the town was effectively the centre of the British rail industry. Its population boomed from 14,000 in 1801 to 48,000 in 1850 and a further staggering growth to 118,000 by 1901. The railways had most certainly got Derby on the move.

The big bang of the first organised football league emerged from the silk mills of Derbyshire and the lace factories of Nottingham, providing each area with a growing population, eager to indulge in some well-earned leisure activities. At first stumbling from a Victorian sporting soup before clambering into existence and the solid ground of the Football League, it was from the cricket, racecourse, baseball and shinney fields that Nottingham Forest and Derby County were born, emerging from a series of meetings held in smoky, wood-panelled rooms.

Everything was in place: the working classes were gathered together in rapidly expanding towns, while the railways were starting to link these provincial out posts together. In addition, the proletariat required some kind of release from all those long and hard hours labouring in a mill or factory – a reason to shout or cheer, a receptacle for that simmering anger at their working conditions. There was a gap in the market.

In 1846, those boffins at Trinity College, Cambridge, made an initial attempt to formulate some sort of rules to codify the rather wild and erratic game that had existed in many different guises depending on which part of the country a ball was kicked on to a field. The concept stalled as rugby still ruled among the elite of Eton, Winchester and Shrewsbury. The idea was not dead, though, and those up north had not only the determination to get some rules in place but also the teams to put them into practice. This was football only: no concessions to the notion of picking the ball up or any such nonsense. Thus, Sheffield FC and Hallam got down to the business of playing the first football match under such rules. These were football clubs too – not an offshoot of a cricket or shinney or baseball club, but pure football. Somewhat poetically, this game took place amid a snowstorm on Boxing Day in 1860 on the east bank of the

River Sheaf. Sheffield FC beat Hallam 2-0 and football – as we know it – was born, alive and very much kicking.

From that moment, things moved fast. The boffins, specifically J.C. Thring, went back to the drawing board and came up with some revised laws in 1862 that everyone could get onboard with. These were published with the title *The Simplest Game* and would lead to the birth of the Football Association.

In Nottingham, the young men of the lace industry, although happily indulging in shinney – a form of hockey, its winter cousin known as bandy – were becoming better disposed towards football. Yet although industry and especially lace had brought jobs and a degree of prosperity to the city, it wasn't a case of it being a utopian haven. Work was hard, poorly paid and life was short. Although the population was only 80,000, the place was hugely overcrowded, especially around the Narrow Marsh area. One government official even went as far as calling it the worst town in England. Gangs roamed the streets looking to take advantage of the poor and dispossessed, perhaps the most infamous being the Nottingham Lambs who followed and supported the legendary local boxer William 'Bendigo' Thompson. After winning the heavyweight championship of England, Bendigo slipped into alcoholism and in the 1860s joined his former supporters in drunken rampages, resulting in imprisonment before sobered up and turned his life around.

This was also the year that the Riot Act was literally read in Nottingham on 26 June owing to riots in the Market Square after a rally by Liberals Samuel Morley and Charles Paget descended into scuffles. Despite this, the impressive and imposing Theatre Royal was built at the top of Market Street in 1865.

Over in Derby, Midland Railway, now one of the largest railway companies in Britain and the town's largest employer, purchased the beautiful red-brick Midland Hotel and Posting House, built in 1841 to reflect the meeting of three important railway lines in Derby: the Midland Counties from Leicester and Nottingham, the Birmingham and Derby Junction from Birmingham and the north Midland from Leeds. Its function from here on was solely to cater for the increasing number of travellers via rail to and through Derby, following in the footsteps of Queen Victoria and Prince Albert who stayed there overnight while travelling back from Balmoral Castle to Osborne House in the Isle of Wight. The importance of Derby in terms of Midland Railway was illustrated by the distance from Derby becoming the measurement of the Midland Railway Empire in the form of mileposts across the network which recorded the distance from Derby station. The first of these can still be seen at the end of Derby station platform and it is marked D 0, meaning 0 miles from Derby.

All the while, football was growing. On 2 January 1865, Sheffield FC played their first fixture outside South Yorkshire, in Nottingham. Notts County had formed in 1862 and they fancied trying their hands – or feet – at this increasingly popular sport. So, in 1865, just a few months after Robert E. Lee surrendered the last major Confederate army to Ulysses S. Grant, signalling the end of the America Civil War, a group of young sportsmen in Nottingham formally switched from shinney to football and Forest Football Club came into being. This was formally marked by a meeting at the Clinton Arms in Sherwood Street. It was another two years before shinney was dropped as an activity of the club and Nottingham was added to the name, thus amending it to Nottingham Forest Football Club. A plaque commemorating the birth of Nottingham Forest now hangs proudly on the walls of this pub. One of the founders, William Brown, was tasked with purchasing red-coloured shirts, along with matching caps and tassels. Inspired by Giuseppe Garibaldi, who successfully led a revolt against the Spanish Bourbon rulers in southern Italy and; in doing so, unified the country by championing nationalism, freedom and romance, the embryonic football club was swept up in the popularity of this figure of radicalism and like the biscuit, honoured him by wearing not just any old red, but Garibaldi red.

Like many football clubs emerging at this time, Forest Football Club evolved from a wider sports club yet shinney was a most unusual sport from which a football club emerge from. In its preview of the 1898 FA Cup Final, *Sporting Life* praised Nottingham and its sporting history, 'Certainly, they have always had leather chasers amongst them, but they have always devoted a great deal of attention to athletics and even to cricket. The club was the outcome of the enthusiastic love of all sport which is inherent in the bosoms of all Nottingham people, and in the days when the old dribbling games was played, a section of the members fancied the new style football, and the team was got together.' It all seems quite simple really: they loved sport, they loved football, they formed a football club.

Within a year, on 22 March 1866, Forest played their first game against, naturally, Notts County, at The Forest, now known as the Recreation Ground and site of the renowned Goose Fair. After all, 'It was necessary that the Notts club [Notts County], an even still older organisation, should be met and a decision come as to which was the champion.' It turns out that the upstarts of Forest were to be the new champions as the 'Foresters won a goal to nil'. In fairness, the veracity of this scoreline is debatable: it is rumoured that Forest might have played with 17 players. But this was a very sound start, even if the next five years or so would be spent scouring the area for meaningful opposition beyond local cup competitions. Not even the oldest football competition in the world – the FA Cup – had been born yet. That was still five years away. A picture painted by John Holland, *Nottingham Races*, depicting scenes on The Forest in 1865, pays attention to the boisterous antics of the crowd in which skirmishes have broken out and the police are making arrests. It is not documented whether Forest and Notts supporters clashed and brawled during the original game played at the same venue, but one suspects probably not.

Until then, though, not only were teams restricted to their locality when it came to actually playing a game, but even if they did travel further afield, the rules might well need to be negotiated before a ball was kicked in anger. Simply put, a northern club might well have played by different rules to a midlands or southern club. This needed sorting out and the launch of the FA Cup in 1871 went some way towards ironing out regional variations in the rules. Initially a purely amateur competition, the first Association Cup was contested between 16 teams from across Britain. A glance at some of the teams competing reflects football's emergence not from the belching factories populated by the proletariat, but the educated elite: Harrow Chequers, Donington School, Reigate Priory and Civil Service indicate that the FA weren't quite ready to open it up to scruffy northern and midlands football clubs just yet. The first FA Cup was won by Wanderers, whose team was comprised of former pupils from leading public schools. They beat Royal Engineers 1-0 at Kennington Oval in front of a reported 2,000 fans. Competitive football was off and running.

In between Forest playing their first game against their city rivals and the launch of the FA Cup, the first recorded reference to the famous folk song, 'The Derby Ram', was made. This would later provide Derby County with their nickname and mascot. Llewellyn Jewitt wrote *The Ballads and Songs of Derbyshire*. In it, he stated that he thought 'The Derby Ram' had been sung for at least half a century. It has been reported that George Washington sang it to his friend's children in 1796.

All the while, football continued its evolution. Something was definitely stirring as clubs specialising solely in football continued to spring up the length and breadth of the country. Although still an amateur game, a sense of professionalism started to creep in, if not in the form of payment (although clubs did and would find a way to entice players, usually in the shape of guaranteed jobs in, for instance, a factory around the corner from the ground), but certainly in competitive spirit. Crowds gathered in increasing numbers and, where there are crowds, there is money to be made. And with competitive spirit comes a desire to be better than the other lot down the road, a factor which meant that the better players – northerners and Scots – started dominating the team lists of many clubs. And this was all before the notion of a competitive league was even a twinkle in the eye of an administrator.

The FA Cup was a huge success and although dominated by Wanderers, Royal Engineers and Old Etonians – between them accounting for nine of the first 11 winners – its reach and popularity were growing. Even the likes of Sheffield and Notts County were invited to the party and, in 1879, Forest got their invitation. In between times, they had been busy as not only had they relocated to Trent Bridge, but also made their first major contribution to the development of football as we know it. Perhaps sick of coming home from games with bruised shins, Sam Widdowson had the simple but bright idea of cutting down a pair of cricket pads and strapping them to his shins, outside his socks. He might have looked unusual – maybe a bit daft even – but he would be the one credited with inventing shin pads. What's more, his legs were significantly less bruised.

A similar story and evolution of the game was playing out in the United States as with the end of the civil war and the American frontier experience over, the young male intellectual in an Ivy League school required a new means by which to prove this masculinity and, as in England's private schools, it was at Harvard and Yale that a game similar to but more violent and military in style with an emphasis on taking land evolved. In 1879, a former captain in the civil war, Richard Henry Pratt, founded the Carlisle Indian Industrial School, a boarding school for Indian American children with the motto 'kill the Indian, save the man', the notion being to teach assimilation skills to the Native Americans in order to survive and thrive in the new America. With American football still in its infancy, a teacher and dormitory master who formerly taught at an Ivy League school turned up at Carlisle and felt that playing football would toughen the students up. It caught on.

After many injuries, Pratt put a stop to this seemingly barbaric game as his intention was to civilise the students. But not to be deterred, a group went to petition Pratt to reinstate it. 'While they stood around my desk, their black eyes intensely watching me, the orator gave practically all the arguments in favour of our contending in outside football and ended up requesting the removal of the embargo,' wrote David Wallace Adams in *More than a Game: The Carlisle Indians Take to the Gridiron*. The 'Pirates' team was established and a challenge game was organised against a powerful and renowned Yale team in October 1896 at the old polo ground in New York in front of around 4,000 fans. Predictably, it was billed as a battle between the refined, civilised and best of the modern American male versus the barbaric natives. Despite a highly dubious call that went against Carlisle, they maintained their cool and, at the behest of Pratt, won the crowd's hearts and minds. The game took an evolutionary leap forward.

And so to Forest's first participation in the FA Cup, shin pads and all. In the first round, they would face none other than their city rivals and promptly beat them 3-1 away from home before progressing all the way to the semi-finals, beating Old Harrovians and Oxford University, then succumbing to Old Etonians. It was a highly creditable maiden performance, one that they repeated again the very next year. Again, they faced Notts County in the first round and, again, beat them, this time 4-0 at home. They progressed against Turton, beating Blackburn Rovers 6-0 (a notable result since a period of sustained cup success lay just around the corner for Blackburn), Sheffield and enjoyed a fifth-round bye before bowing out again at the semi-final stage to Oxford University. Intriguingly, Forest were the first club to progress in the FA Cup owing to their opponents' disqualification. After a 2-2 draw at Trent Bridge, Sheffield were expecting a replay, but the FA rules dictated that a replay would only be forthcoming if the scores were still locked after extra time. Sheffield weren't having that and refused to play the extra 30 minutes. It is said that, regardless of the lack of opposition, Widdowson dribbled the ball into an empty net just to make sure. After Widdowson's shin pads, this was another first for Forest.

Despite Widdowson's smart thinking, he would not have a permanent home ground on which to parade his bruise-free shins. The Nottinghamshire Cricket Club secretary Edwin Browne took on the same role at Notts County and, in 1882, Forest lost their winter tenancy at Trent Bridge to Notts. This stoked the flames of the city rivalry, which had been simmering along quite nicely after County had dropped Forest from their fixture list, taking exception to the revolutionary associations with the Garibaldis. Forest went off to play at Parkside on Derby Road and then the Gregory Ground, while County turned professional and enjoyed big crowds at Trent Bridge. Perhaps County were still a little bitter about their FA Cup first-round defeats to their neighbours.

The FA Cup itself experienced its first shock in 1883 when the first northern team, Blackburn Olympic, lifted the trophy. They were arguably the first proletaran team to claim the cup when they beat Old Etonians after extra time after preparing by having a pre-match holiday in Blackpool. Theirs was a team composed of machine operators, weavers and spinners and it meant a bloody nose to the toffs who had up to now dominated it. This was seismic as the cup was wrestled from the clutches of southern elite clubs and would consequently be won by northern or Midlands-based clubs up until 1901 when Tottenham Hotspur would beat Sheffield United and wrestle it back. From then on though, right up until 1936, the cup would be dominated by the north and Midlands with only Tottenham, Arsenal and Cardiff breaking the run.

The power balance in football was shifting from the wide green fields of public schools and the educated elite to the working classes as they seemed to be taking the competitive side of the game to new heights and blurring the line between amateur status and professionalism. In 1884, Preston North End were disqualified from competing after an FA committee decreed that they had been offering financial inducements to Scottish players. It is likely that Preston were not the only club to be offering such incentives as the growing popularity of the game meant bigger attendances, which meant more pressure to compete, which meant playing hard and fast with what amateur status meant when it came to improving the team.

Derby was certainly not immune to all of this excitement. The county already boasted of some kind of football game being played in Ashbourne as far back as the 12th century. The Royal Shrovetide Football Match requires one set of villagers, the Up'Ards, to get the ball to Sturston Mill, while the other set, the Down'Ards, to Clifton Mill. The game was a whole town affair, contested between Shrove Tuesday and Ash Wednesday and was frequently violent. Such mob football evolved and branched off into various forms of modern football, such as Australian Rules, Gaelic, rugby football and public-school football. The spirit of football ran deep in Derby. Some see this as the origins of the term 'derby' to denote a game between two local teams, yet a more widely received theory is it derives from the Derby Stakes run at Epsom, or in other words, the Epsom Derby, on account of the huge popularity and interest it provoked.

The town had already had Derby Town and Derby Midland, whose formation in 1881 signalled the end of the former. But what goes around comes around and the formation of another football club posed a threat to the short but promising lifespan of Midland. In September 1884, after a meeting of Derbyshire County Cricket Club, which was on a sticky wicket and undergoing some financial issues both on and off the field, at the Bell Hotel in Sadler Gate in May, the *Derby Daily Telegraph* announced, 'The Derbyshire County Cricket Club has decided on the formation of a football club under Association Rules and desires to render football worthy of the patronage bestowed upon it by the public by endeavouring to arrange matches with first-class clubs which will enable the public to witness matches of a higher order than have hitherto been played in Derby. The subscription for the Derbyshire County Football Club is fixed at five shillings, which we think will be thought sufficiently moderate.' The popularity of football had been well and truly noted by the cricket club, especially W.M. [William] Morley, and after some tinkering with and abbreviation of the name, Derby County Football Club was born.

This newly formed club wasted no time in getting started and enjoyed a fast and meteoric rise, perhaps as a result of the conditions surrounding its birth. According to *Sporting Life*, 'The County was, so to speak, "born with a silver spoon in its mouth" for it was from its inception associated with the Derbyshire County Cricket Club and has valuable aid granted to it by that body. Up to the season 1895/96, the games of the club were played on a portion of the cricket ground so that there was not struggling for money for a capital ground, and as the cricket pavilion was already on the spot, there was no initial costs of stands, dressing rooms, etc. But in addition to the great advantage, the club has always had the support of well-known men of the town, including the honourable W.M. Jarvis, Mr Morley and a number of others.'

Either way, Derby got down to business. They went straight into the FA Cup, yet went out at the first round to Walsall Town, 7-0 at home in their very first competitive match. This took place at the Racecourse Ground, which is now the cricket club's County Ground, and was unsurprisingly (given its name) originally enclosed inside a racecourse, with racing ceasing in 1939. A couple of years later, the Racecourse Ground held the distinction of being the first ground to stage an FA Cup Final outside London: the 1886 final between Blackburn and West Brom, albeit it the game was a replay. This would have been mightily pleasing for the cricket committee in terms of the monetary income it generated.

With no organised league system and only a humbling FA Cup experience under their belts, it was with a certain inevitability that the first Derby County versus Nottingham

Forest game would be contested. Accordingly, the game took place amid a bit of a gale on Tuesday, 3 February 1885. Derby not only won the toss and decided to play with the strong wind behind them, but they won the game too and, handsomely, 6-1. After only ten minutes, John Barrington Trapnell Chevallier put Derby in front and it only got progressively worse for the Foresters from then on. Cooper, Smith, Hickinbottom and Chevallier again made it 5-0 by half-time. Forest improved in the second half – could they have got any worse? – but could make no real impact on the scoreline until five minutes before the end when they pulled one back. But Derby promptly went and scored another.

Forest would argue that they were missing key players in Thomas Danks and Tinsley Lindley and, furthermore, this was effectively a friendly game. Regardless, the rivalry was under way. *The Sportsman* published the teams, 'Derby County: Hill (goal), Flower and Morley (backs), Williamson, F.H. Sugg and Kelsall (half-backs), Cooper, Bakewell, J.B.T. Chevallier, Hickinbottom and Smith (forwards). Notts Forest: Beardsley (goal), Hancock and Caborn (backs), Ward, Billyeald and Norman (half-backs), Fox, Leighton, Widdowson, Unwin and Davis (forwards).'

Although few knew it at the time, Nottingham would soon be able to console itself with the birth of the world-famous Raleigh bike, as in the spring of that same year Raleigh started advertising in the local press. The *Nottinghamshire Guardian* of 15 May 1885 printed what was possibly the first Woodhead and Angois classified advertisement. Raleigh would grow exponentially into a worldwide name over the next five years.

Undeterred by their underwhelming first appearance in the FA Cup and taking heart from their dismantling of a Forest side, Derby achieved a notable success in the cup against Aston Villa, knocking them out in the first round on 14 November 1885. Villa were a highly regarded team who would go on to take the mighty Blackburn Rovers' trophy two years later. At the final whistle, the delirious home fans invaded the pitch, high on this new elixir known to some as cup fever; Derby County had stuck a large flag in the ground and marked their arrival. Perhaps this result went some way towards Derby being invited to be part of the Football League, about which ideas were forming in Aston Villa's boardroom.

* * *

The final piece of the football jigsaw puzzle was finally found and positioned neatly into place when Villa board member William McGregor proposed some kind of organised fixture list and on 17 April 1888, the Football League was formed. As the response of those not invited, the Football Combination was created but it lacked the organisation of the Football League. Perhaps reminded of his side's humbling in the FA Cup three years previously, McGregor invited Derby County to be founder members, cementing the meteoric rise of a club in only their fourth year of existence. *Sporting Life* provided a rather more mundane reason for Derby's involvement, 'For the seasons prior to the formation of the Football League, four seasons after the foundation of the club, the success which attended the players was not any means phenomenal, but still to avoid selecting two clubs in some towns, it was found necessary to invite Derby to take place.'

Despite Samuel Widdowson having hung up his boots and now representing Forest as chairman, Forest's request in a meeting with the Football League to be included was turned down, along with The Wednesday (later Sheffield Wednesday) and Halliwell FC of Greater Manchester. With only 22 dates for fixtures, the league could only cope with 12 teams and perhaps Forest's desire to maintain strict amateur status and reject professionalism counted against them.

The FA Cup Final that year provided not only a bit of a shock, but also a neat preview of the 1898 Final, at least in terms of pre-game photographs. Going into the final, Preston were favourites but that was ended by West Bromwich Albion in front of 19,000 at the Kennington Oval. In a breathtaking exhibition of hubris, Preston manager William Suddell demanded his team's picture be taken with the cup before kick-off in order to capture their pristine white shirts. They lost 2-1. What was established for Victorian photographers was that white shirts were definitely preferable when it came to taking pictures of football teams, a custom that caused a bit of a stir when Derby and Forest would meet at the same stage ten years later.

But back to the formation of the Football League and Derby's first league game, which saw them win 6-3 at Bolton Wanderers, especially impressive since they were 3-0 down at one stage. They finished a respectable tenth in a 12-team division. This was the era of the Preston 'Invincibles' who won the title and the FA Cup and did so without losing a game. The bottom four clubs did not suffer the indignity of relegation but were all successfully re-elected to have another go the following season. Forest's invitation was presumably lost in the post.

The Football Alliance launched for 1888/89, which was a bit like the Football League but less organised. This mattered not to Derby who in their sophomore season in the Football League improved by finishing seventh, while the mighty Preston romped to the title again. They weren't quite so invincible this time, though, and lost four games while seeing their north-west rivals Blackburn Rovers reclaim their FA Cup dominance of the mid-1880s.

The summer of 1890 saw a rather curious development in the town of Derby: the arrival of a baseball pitch. Local factory owner and general businessman Francis Ley returned from the States, having had his eyes widened by baseball and set about developing a patch of land near to his foundry with the intention of not only offering his workers some recreational facilities but of developing a national league. On 3 May, Derby beat a team from Erdington, Birmingham, 23-11 to win the first game of baseball with the home plate in the corner of the Columbo Street Railway Terrace (latterly the Baseball Ground's Popside terrace) junction which became known as Catcher's Corner. Amid much controversy, Derby Baseball Club claimed to be the winners of the title on three separate occasions, yet Aston Villa strongly protested on the grounds of them playing too many Americans and of generally playing fragrant with various bylaws. Derby were stripped of their title and Villa took it from them. Perhaps more significantl, though, was a young Derby striker by the name of Steve Bloomer and Forest goalkeeper Danny Allsopp on the roster for the Derby team. Bloomer would appear intermittently for the Derby baseball team, right up until 1898.

The following season was less successful as Derby County finished 11th out of 12. However, they did chalk up the season's biggest win: a 9-0 home victory against Wolves on 10 January 1891. This was no mean feat, considering Wolves finished fourth that season.

Forest, meanwhile, maintained their reputation as pioneers after some bright spark introduced the idea of a crossbar and goal nets in a north v south game at their new home, the Town Ground. Clearly somebody got tired of having to fetch the ball every time a goal was scored and of the incessant debate about whether a shot could be deemed to be over or under. Forest too took a huge lurch towards professionalism by signing their first paid players and it showed as they hammered Clapton 14-0 in the first round of the FA Cup on 17 January 1891. Forest were on the rise as they won the final Alliance league and, along with The Wednesday and Combination winners Newton Heath (later Manchester United), joined the Football League, now the First Division. Derby improved slightly by finishing in tenth place and, perhaps more significantly, absorbed Derby Midland to become the town's sole football club. To mark this, a change of colours was adopted, when they ditched the cricket club colours of chocolate, amber and pale blue for black and white. The stage was set for regular competitive meetings between these two rivals. The crossbars were in place, shins were suitably protected and, in the event of any illnesses or injuries, a new shop opened on Pelham Street in Nottingham by the name of Boots.

2

And so it begins: 1892–1899

FAR AWAY in Ambala, India, the counties of Nottinghamshire and Derbyshire were already locking horns on a football field. On a British army base, established in 1842, soldiers whiled away a hot sunny evening on 22 August 1892 by staging their own East Midlands derby. The two regiments – Sherwood Foresters (representing Notts) and Left Wing 2nd Battalion Derbyshire Regiment (representing Derbyshire) – played out a 1-0 win to Forest, two months before the two football teams would meet for the first time in the newly formed First Division. In fact, this was a replay of the same game a year previous, when Forest had beaten Derby 2-0 in Jabalpur. The Derby team again faced an uphill task as 'the Derby men not having sufficient talent to represent them, Notts allowed them to pick four of the best men of the wing from other counties as substitutes', according to *Football News*. Private Baines kicked off at 6.30pm and the Notts team were nearly two goals up after two minutes. Private Green scored the deciding goal after an assist by Private Edwards, eliciting much hollering and 'with the Trent Bridge cry of "Play up, Notts" ringing in their ears' as they sought a second goal.

Back in England, the 1892/93 season meant the first competitive meeting between Derby County and Nottingham Forest. Derby were still playing at the seemingly perennially windswept Racecourse and it was here that the fixture was played out. The Rams were yet to make any real impact on the higher league positions in the First Division, while Forest were perhaps a bit of an unknown quantity in their maiden campaign, having gained entry as champions of the Alliance. But their run to the semi-finals of the FA Cup and only losing out to eventual winners West Bromwich Albion after a replay suggested they would cope. The division consisted solely of teams in the Midlands and north, the furthest south being Aston Villa and, discounting the reigning champions Sunderland as an outlier, the furthest north being Burnley.

As it was, Forest went and promptly posted a tenth-placed finish, above founder members Derby who finished 13th, one place above the perforated lines that back then didn't mean automatic relegation but a test match against teams in the division below. Of the three teams new to the league, Forest performed the best, finishing two places above The Wednesday and comfortably above Newton Heath, who came in bottom of the pile yet remained in the league as they defeated Small Heath (later Birmingham City) in their test match. Sunderland retained their title, finishing 11 points clear of nearest challengers Preston. Wolverhampton Wanderers lifted the FA Cup.

Going into the game on 1 October, Forest were not in great shape. They had managed a draw in their opening match against Everton, but since then had been unable to field their preferred team and had lost three in succession.

Derby were a mixed bag, having beaten Stoke on the opening day, then lost to Preston, but followed that up with successive draws against Notts County and West Bromwich Albion.

For the very first league meeting between Derby and Forest the teams lined up like this: Derby County – J.W. Robinson, J. Methven, J. Staley, J. Cox, A. Goodall, W. Roulstone, G. Ekins, J. McLachlan, J. Goodall, S. Bloomer, S. McMillan. Nottingham Forest – W. Brown, A. Ritchie, A. Scott, K. Hamilton, A. Smith, P. McCracken, N. McCallum, 'Tich' Smith, A. Higgins, H. Pike, T. McInnes.

Rather predictably and setting the template for the majority of games between the two, an eventful encounter in front of 8,000 fans unfolded. Although quite even, Forest were by all accounts slightly more effective and thought they had opened the scoring through Alex Higgins, only for it to be ruled out for offside. As it was, it was Derby that had the pleasure of scoring the first competitive goal between the two East Midlands rivals, the honour falling to Steve Bloomer whose shot was misjudged by William Brown in the Forest goal. Not to be denied though, Higgins scored a legitimate goal five minutes later meaning the honours were even come half-time.

After the break, Forest took the lead in a somewhat peculiar manner when Danny Robinson, in the Derby goal, appeared to have a long shot under control, but *Athletic News* reported, 'his two half-backs did not afford him the slightest protection, and just as he tipped the ball, he was unceremoniously bundled through, and the Forest chalked up a second point'. Untidy and perhaps powered by brute force the goal may well have been, but Forest were in front.

The game continued to ebb and flow, and Frederick George Ekins thought he had equalised until it was chalked off owing to an offside decision. Then with ten minutes to go, poor play from Derby let Tom McInnes in on goal and he kept his composure to give Forest a 3-1 lead. That wasn't quite the end of the matter, though, as Archie Goodall promptly went up front and pulled one back almost immediately to make it 3-2 to the visitors, and that is how it ended. A match high on drama and excitement perhaps, but according to *Athletic News*, '[It was] not a particularly brilliant game. Notts Forest were certainly the better team, for the forwards showed superior combination and the defence was clearly in front of that of Derby, who made many blunders.' Yet, 'they appeared to get on the ball much quicker than their opponents, who worked with little or no system'.

A personal dissection of individual performances followed in the match report, with Thomas Hamilton of Forest identified as having 'a nasty habit of sliding at his opponents with his leg outstretched'. Brown, in goal for Forest, was 'evidently not in form', while Derby's Archie Goodall was singled out for praise as being 'exceedingly clever and useful' while 'Bloomer and [Stuart] McMillan were the best wing, and the former should develop into a good man'. The journalist's instincts proved to be right on the nose as Bloomer, having only made his debut a month earlier, did indeed evolve from a useful person to have on second base in a baseball game into not only a fine player of international renown, but also a Derby County and footballing legend.

In terms of the game being a derby or particularly spicy, defeat certainly seems to have provoked strong feeling among the home crowd as 'the spectators are evidently adept at yelling, and the referee was also a recipient of their compliments and other things, and these chiefly came from persons in the pavilion attired in the garb of gentlemen'. One wonders about the nature of these 'other things' that were loudly articulated towards the referee. It is logical to draw the conclusion that it was not polite or helpful advice. Despite a penchant for exhibiting dignity and restraint, the Victorians could swear with the best of them. It seems logical to deduce that enmity between the Derby and Nottingham camps was tangible. After all, Notts County were referred to as 'Lambs' by Derby folk, meant as derogatory in comparison to their own forceful and masculine ram.

The return fixture took place on 28 January 1893, with both sides making five changes from the previous meeting. Perhaps most notable was Harry Daft, once of Derby Junction, making his debut for Forest when the teams met again at the Town Ground in The Meadows, Forest's home since 1890 after a stint playing at first the Parkside Ground and then, adjacent to it, the Gregory Ground, in Lenton on Derby Road, close to the Savoy Theatre. A crowd estimated at 9,000 attended. One of the biggest gates of the season, it was swollen by many Derby supporters taking advantage of special trains to take them to the 'lace city', conjuring up scenes from a very modern derby game. It seems too that the rivalry between these two clubs had already been established despite precious little history between them on the pitch. 'Excitement, as is always the case in these engagements, ran extremely high and the game throughout was vigorously contested,' claimed *Sporting Life*. 'At times the play was very rough and two of the players, Shaw and Roulstone, were cautioned by the referee. Several slight injuries were the outcome of foul tactics.' Again, this all sounds very modern, and one could substitute Harry Shaw and Walter Roulstone with, say, Stuart Pearce and Mick Harford or Kenny Burns and Francis Lee and the description would be timeless.

After a goalless first half, Higgins pounced on a poor pass and capitalised to put Forest ahead 'amid great cheering'. Derby pressed for an equaliser but came up short, leaving the home side to celebrate a double over their rivals in their debut season in the First Division and nudging them up to fifth, with Derby glancing nervously over their shoulders in 12th. Sunderland sat top and would go on to win the title, while Forest would slip to tenth and Derby to 13th, narrowly escaping the test match that faced the bottom three: Notts County, Accrington and Newton Heath. Notts County lost to Darwen and were invited to join the Second Division, Accrington resigned from the Football League after losing to Sheffield United in a test and Newton Heath remained in the First Division after winning their match against Small Heath.

All of which represented a pleasing if unspectacular debut campaign in the Football League First Division for Forest. For Derby, this was a slight drop from the previous season's tenth-placed finish (albeit there were only 14 clubs in the league that season).

1893-1895

The Forman saga

The season after, 1893/94, Forest maintained their stranglehold over Derby by beating them twice in December: 4-3 at the Racecourse Ground and 4-2 in Nottingham. They improved their league position too with a highly creditable seventh-placed finish and a run to the quarter-finals of the FA Cup (although losing 4-1 to their city rivals rather took the gloss off the achievement). Derby went even better, and not only matched Forest's cup run before going out to Blackburn Rovers but also posted an impressive third-placed finish, thanks in no small part to the blooming of Steve Bloomer who was hitting his stride. He scored 19 goals in 27 games that season, raising the eyebrows of the England selectors. The prolific Jack Southworth, formerly of Blackburn and now of Everton, was top scorer that season but Bloomer's time would come – he was waiting in the wings.

The following season was one of struggle for Derby although they did chalk up their first competitive win against Forest. Yet it was off the field where events further shaped this rivalry. Come the end of the season, Forest found themselves comfortably mid-table, while Derby finished 15th in a division of 16. They would beat Notts County 2-1 in the test match and thus clung on to their First Division status, but it was a close-run thing. Such test matches were initially play-offs between the champions of the Second Division and bottom of the First Division, which then evolved into a mini league, but not in a straightforward way as teams faced sides from the other division twice without playing opponents from their own division. This gave way to the more straightforward system of automatic promotion and relegation in 1898.

Derby's campaign got off to a miserable start with an 8-0 hammering at the hands of the previous season's runners-up Sunderland, who would go one better and become champions. But their next game, their first at home of the season, saw Forest travel to Derby's Racecourse Ground for one final time since, come the following season 1895/96, Derby would relocate to the Baseball Ground. Forest themselves kicked their season off with a 2-1 home win against a decent Burnley side, all of which makes their 4-2 reverse a little surprising, especially when it turned out to be Derby's only win in the opening ten games.

The rivalry seems to have evolved into an established entity now, with *Football News* reporting that 'matches between Derby and either of the Nottingham clubs are always exciting, so keen is the rivalry between the two towns in matters of football'. The article refers to Derby County as the sadly underused 'Peakites', who were yet to vanquish their rivals in competitive games. Yet from the period of 31 January 1865 to April 1895, the reporter calculated, 'Forest have 25 goals against Derby and Derby have 31.' Even so, Forest remained unbeaten in league games in Derby.

For their first home game of the season, after their unfortunate experience in Sunderland, 6,000 souls turned up and were rewarded for their efforts by a heavy rainfall before the game. Derby started well as their 'forwards danced round the Forest goal'. Chances came and went at both ends and Sam Raybould, a local lad who was playing particularly well and, no doubt fired up for this one, put Derby ahead after 12 minutes. Bloomer added another on the half-hour mark to give his side a comfortable and deserved lead, and Stuart McMillan bagged a third after a cross by Raybould. The first half had gone as badly as it could possibly go for Forest and those of a Derby persuasion were particularly enjoying this one, as reported in *Football News*, 'The Derby spectators who go up like toy balloons when the team is winning and burst like them when fortune ceases to befriend their club, roared their loudest.' Just before half-time, Forest struck back and came out an improved team for the second half, so much so that 'the not too impartial spectators on the pavilion were constrained to remark upon it'. However, McMillan extended Derby's lead after a scrimmage before Bloomer thought he had made it 5-2, but his effort was ruled out for offside. Regardless, the damage had been done and Derby had recorded their first league victory against their rivals.

This sent Forest into a bit of a tailspin as they lost their next four games. In a remarkable act of symmetry, Derby did precisely the same too, yet while Forest recovered their form as the season unfolded, the Rams' struggles continued for the duration. Forest's form improved enough to exert some revenge when they beat Derby 2-1 in November and then in December, the Forman affair added a new dimension to the East Midlands rivalry.

Fred Forman had made only four appearances for Derby before leaving to join Forest. His brother Frank, also with Fred at Derby and boasting eight appearances, joined him in December 1895. The saga encapsulated the growing tension between amateurism and professionalism. The Forman brothers cost Forest nothing and left willingly in search of more first-team opportunities, the problem being that Derby were reluctant to release them. Yet the lure of football and professional wages was strong. The *Lancashire Evening Post*, in previewing the 1898 FA Cup Final between the two sides, felt it appropriate to raise the matter again, presumably to emphasise the nature of the deep rivalry between the two clubs, 'Derby County did not release them willingly, but you can't hold amateurs. For amateurs, the brothers played until they could no longer afford the time necessary for football without incurring too serious a pecuniary loss. Then, rather than desist from playing, they accepted the alternative – and the renumeration.'

In turn, Forest were accused of being underhand and poaching the players, hence the brouhaha. Fred was injured and so wouldn't face his former club in the 1898 final, yet Frank would. So upset was Frank at the extent of ill feeling surrounding the transfer, he was moved to defend both himself and Forest against such accusations by penning a letter that was published in the *Nottinghamshire Guardian* on Saturday, 26 January 1895. In it, he accused the Derby County committee of acting in an 'unsportsmanlike manner' and of 'deliberately broken promises made' in refusing his transfer. He stated, 'The Forest Club have never approached me in any way, but, on the contrary, I asked them to find me a place in their team so that I could play with my brother. I believe the League were misled when they refused to interfere.' At the thought of the League getting involved in the saga, he added, 'I intend to ask the League to reconsider the case and hear me personally. I must say it seems to me a great shame I cannot be allowed to play with whatever club I choose, and I am sure that amateurs will in future be very careful how they sign any form for Derby County Club.'

Footballers have always agitated to play first-team football it seems, regardless of where that may be. The transfer of the Forman brothers was the first in a long list of controversial switches between the two clubs, causing ill feeling and rancour.

Despite, or more likely as a result of, their poor season and flirtation with relegation, Derby moved from the

Racecourse Ground to the Baseball Ground as tenants. Back in 1892, they had to make alternative arrangements for a fixture against Sunderland owing to a clash with a race meeting and, when this happened again on Easter Monday in 1895 regarding a game against Corinthians, this left them in little doubt as to where they lay in the pecking order between cricket and football. They had occasionally taken Francis Ley, owner of the Baseball Ground, up on his offer and used the stadium for fixtures due to clashes, but with professionalism on the rise and football taking off, it seems fair to assume they wanted to have a place they could call home. The move was formalised after a special meeting at the Derwent Hotel in April. Derby would have to pay 100 shillings a year for the privilege, but in return, Ley would provide funds to renovate the ground to increase capacity.

Ley had built a complex of sports grounds for workers at his foundry, Ley's Malleable Castings Vulcan Ironworks. Initially, Derby County were merely co-tenants there since Ley's Derby Baseball Club enjoyed fleeting success as their owner sought to launch baseball on the unsuspecting English masses. It was short-lived though. The baseball club managed to last until 1900, with Steve Bloomer occasionally popping up on second base, but football was taking hold. And Derby, with Bloomer about to enter his pomp, were determined to avoid another season like the deeply unsatisfactory previous one.

1895-1897
Old Mallender

All of this spurred Derby on to great things and the 1895/96 season was a memorable one for them, with a double over

Forest, a run to the semi-finals of the FA Cup, the division's biggest home and away win and the league's leading goalscorer in Steve Bloomer. This would be the first of 12 consecutive seasons in which Bloomer would end up as the club's top scorer. For Forest, a struggle against relegation meant that their season highlight was their Town Ground being used for the FA Cup semi-final between Bolton Wanderers and Sheffield Wednesday.

Derby christened their new home with a 2-0 win against Sunderland, Bloomer helping himself to a couple of goals. Fears that attendances would be affected by the move proved unfounded as the workers at Ley's factory and on the railway flocked from their terraced houses to make the very short walk to see Derby County play. The story goes that since Ley had to move a gypsy community on in order to develop his sporting complex, a curse was subsequently put on the club, possibly gaining credence since the grass was apparently cut and rolled by a gypsy by the name of 'Old Mallender'. If there was, it didn't seem to have any impact on Bloomer, although Derby's terrible record in securing the FA Cup gave the rumour legs until 1946 when club captain Jack Nicholas apparently crossed a gypsy's palm with silver ahead of the final for the benefit of the press. Derby promptly won the cup, beating Charlton Athletic 4-1 and laying to rest the disappointment of their three previous cup final defeats.

Derby would have to wait to receive Forest at their new home since the first fixture between the two that season took place in Nottingham, where the sides met on 5 October 1895 with both in patchy form. Both Frank and Fred Forman were in the team to face their rivals at the Town Ground in what turned out to be a miserable experience for them. *Football News* talked up the rivalry in a thinly concealed reference to the Formans, reminding its readers, 'They invariably bring over an exceedingly large contingent of footballers from Derby.' Furthermore, this fixture was now an occasion for the supporters, especially when the famous Nottingham Goose Fair was in town. 'There was no exception to this on the present occasion, the Fair, of course, being an additional attraction for Derby people to come to Nottingham,' wrote the newspaper.

In front of 10,000 fans, Fred Forman had an early chance, but his weak shot was easily saved. From then on, Derby were the better team and were 3-1 up by half-time. Bloomer had a blinder and Derby came away with a 5-2 win. Inspired by the victory, Derby lost only one game in their next 13 before losing to Bolton on 1 January 1896. They promptly went on a nine-game unbeaten streak. In among this was a 4-0 win over Forest at the Baseball Ground on 7 December, a resounding way to christen their new home in terms of the East Midlands derby.

Going into this game, Forest were struggling for form, having won only three from eight since losing at home to Derby. They lost the other five. Derby smelled blood and went for the jugular. Everything pointed to a Derby win and, according to *Football News*, confidence was low among the Forest fans, 'Not in the ten years during which Forest have been meeting Derby County, and certainly not since both club's token part in the League competitions, have the supporters of the "reds" felt more doubt about the issue than they did of the contest at Derby today. Whilst Forest have been going very badly this season their opponents have been carrying everything before them.'

The game panned out as most thought it would. Bloomer bagged a brace, both goals came when he converted a cross from the wing, and John Miller weighed in with another to put the Rams three goals up by half-time. This being a derby, it meant more and the 'Derby supporters yelled themselves hoarse with delight'. Bloomer helped himself to another after the break to claim his first hat-trick of three against Forest. It could have been more but for the sterling defensive work of Frank Forman.

In the year that Derby asserted their superiority over Forest on the pitch, a grocer from Nottingham produced a hugely significant culinary development. A recipe invented and developed by David Hoe of Bottesford, Leicestershire, was sold to Frederick Gibson Garton, a Nottingham grocer, who registered the name H.P. Sauce, after reportedly hearing that a restaurant in the Houses of Parliament had begun serving it.

Derby were irresistible from that point onwards and their second-placed finish might well have been supplemented by an FA Cup Final appearance were a Bloomer goal hadn't been contentiously chalked off in their semi-final against Wolves. Bloomer tied with Johnny Campbell of Aston Villa as top scorer with 20 goals and he, as well as his club, might well have had more had they not lost his services through injury for the last half a dozen games or so. Derby, and Bloomer in particular, were enjoying life at the Baseball Ground.

Their good form continued into the next season when they finished third in the table and reached another FA Cup semi-final, this time losing 3-2 to Everton, who would go on to lose to Aston Villa in the final. They also avoided losing to Forest, who themselves improved slightly on the previous season by finishing two places higher in 11th. On the opening day of the season, Forest managed a creditable 1-1 draw at the Baseball Ground, yet in November they succumbed 2-1 to the high-flying Rams. Frank Forman was starting to find the net although Adrian Capes was their top scorer, while in Derby, Bloomer was hitting top form and was the outright top goalscorer, finding the net 22 times.

1897/98
The FA Cup Final

The 1897/98 season was a momentous one for both clubs since although progress in the league was steady with both trundling along in mid-table, they met in the FA Cup Final, the rivals reaching this stage for the first time. This was a fitting way to mark the occasion of Nottingham being granted its city charter as part of Queen Victoria's Diamond Jubilee celebrations on 18 June 1897. Before cup fever took hold though, the teams met in the league on 30 October. As if further evidence of this fixture being established as a grudge match was required, the *Sheffield Evening Telegraph* confirmed the matter by describing the second half as 'brimful of incident and characterised by bad feeling on the part of players and spectators'. Around 12,000 fans gathered to see the game, including a large contingent from Derby.

Derby went in with a full-strength team, while Forest's Fred Spencer made way for Tom McInnes and it was he who was tripped by Jack Cox, resulting in a penalty for the home side, which John McPherson converted. Archie Goodall equalised with a lovely curling shot from 30 yards and Derby took the lead when a splendid centre by Hugh McQueen was converted by Bloomer. The Rams went into half-time 2-1 ahead. Spencer equalised for Forest early in the second half, but Alex Maconachie nudged Derby ahead again. Almost immediately, Arthur Capes brought Forest back level with a disputed goal as the away side claimed offside. Not to be denied, Jimmy Stevenson grabbed a winner to make it 4-3 and take the points back home to Derbyshire after a breathless encounter.

This was a much-needed win for the Rams as, although they enjoyed an excellent run of three successive victories early in the season, they had stuttered since then and had gone five without one. Forest had only won two games all season and, now in 11th position, were starting to look over their shoulders while Derby climbed to seventh.

The first round of the FA Cup took place on Saturday, 29 January. Derby had a difficult tie yet squeezed past Aston Villa 1-0 at the Baseball Ground thanks to a Hugh McQueen goal, while Forest eased to a 4-0 home win against Second Division Grimsby Town. Derby's route to the final didn't get any easier in the next round as they travelled to high-flying Wolves and defeated them with a John Leonard goal. Forest's fortunes continued with another home tie against Second Division opposition, this time Gainsborough Trinity. They made light work of it with another 4-0 win – Charlie Richards bagging another brace to go along with the one he got in the previous round.

The third round took place on Saturday, 26 February and both clubs were handed tricky First Division opposition. Forest travelled to West Bromwich Albion and squeezed through 3-2 in front of 16,500 fans thanks to goals from Frank Forman, Alf Spouncer and another one for Richards, taking his cup tally to five in three games. Spouncer would later go on to manage Barcelona for the 1923/24 season where he won the Campionat de Catalunya (Spain's first football league, preceding La Liga which was established in 1929) with ten wins out of ten. Derby faced Liverpool at home and, with Bloomer still missing from the side, drew 1-1 with a goal from Jimmy Stevenson. The replay took place a week later and, with Bloomer back in the team, Derby won 5-1 with a hat-trick from John Boag and a couple from their star striker. Cup fever hit as the semi-finals loomed.

Derby faced Everton at Molineux on 19 March and prevailed 3-1 thanks to goals from Goodall and another brace from Bloomer. Forest's progression to the final was far more complicated. They faced Southampton of the Southern League but were no pushovers, having won 13 of their 16 league games so far and seen off First Division Bolton Wanderers in the previous round. Forest went ahead after only five minutes thanks to Len Benbow, but Southampton hadn't come this far to give in so easily. Despite striker Jack Farrell getting injured and being reduced to merely limping around the pitch, they conjured an equaliser through Harry Haynes, meaning a replay at Crystal Palace five days later.

With a blizzard raging throughout, the first half was goalless and Forest were thankful for that after Joe Turner missed a penalty for the Saints. Not to be deterred, Southampton were the better team in the second half, up until the moment that referee John Lewis stopped the game owing to the inclement weather. When the match recommenced, the blizzard redoubled its efforts and conditions became farcical. Goals from Tom McInnes and Charlie Richards in the last few minutes put Forest through, but Southampton protested that the game should never have restarted and claimed that their goalkeeper George Clawley's eyes were 'choked with snow' when the goals flew past him. The Southampton board protested long and loudly, but to no avail – the FA wouldn't budge, and their decision was final. Besides, referee John Lewis also happened to be on the FA board, a fact that probably didn't help Southampton's cause. Despite some anti-Forest feelings as a result of events at Crystal Palace and Southampton's cup exploits bringing them to national prominence, Forest went through to the final to meet their rivals Derby, and that was that.

Before Forest returned to Crystal Palace to contest the final, there was the small matter of the return league fixture against Derby at the Baseball Ground on Monday, 11 April, just five days before the showpiece. Forest's form was still limping along, while Derby came into this game on the back of three successive defeats after their semi-final success. Most other teams had already completed their fixtures and Sheffield United had secured the title while Derby sat in tenth. Apart from local pride and the forthcoming final, the smart money was on this being a low-key and somewhat cagey game. It turned out to be anything but.

A heavy downpour in the morning didn't deter a big bank holiday crowd of 14,000 turning out, including a strong contingent from Nottingham, who no doubt wanted to wish their team success for the big day on Saturday. The *Sheffield Daily Telegraph* reported how the Forest team was below full strength 'partly due to injuries and partly, it was said, owing to a couple of members failing to turn up'. This set the tone for the game between these 'old and keen rivals'.

Forest won the toss and decided to defend the Osmaston Road goal. Despite their weakened line-up, Forest started brightly and had an early goal ruled out for offside, while Fred Forman, returning to his former team, shot just over. But after only five minutes Bloomer did what he did best and scored for the Rams against Forest. Bloomer sent a cross to Jimmy Stevenson whose shot was saved by Allsopp in the Forest goal, but 'only partially, however, and a scrimmage ensued in the goal mouth, and Bloomer rushing in, scored with a rattling shot'.

Excitement among the fans grew as the game became even more frantic before Derby went 2-0 up, Stevenson's corner converted by McQueen in the tenth minute. Bloomer almost made it three with a brilliant overhead kick before he did get the third goal, 'dashing long by himself in brilliant style' before unleashing 'one of the best shots ever seen on a football field' after 20 minutes. Predictably, tempers flared. After Goodall went close and a flare-up occurred between John Boag and Albert Iremonger, the game was stopped owing to McCracken getting an accidental blow in the face. Despite this being a so-called dress rehearsal for the FA Cup Final, nobody told the players who battled as if it was just another full-blooded East Midlands derby.

After half-time, more heavy rain and, three goals down, Forest had to do something. Frank Forman and Benbow changed places, like they had the previous Saturday in their win against Bury, in an attempt to get Forman in the game and repeat his three assists and two goals. That was struggling Bury though, and this was fierce rivals Derby who were not about to let an advantage like this slip away. Bloomer was kicked in the side by Iremonger yet, in a foretaste of Chris Cohen and Jamie Ward at the City Ground in 2011, Forest played on and scored, or at least thought they had, but the goal did not stand as the referee had already blown.

Boag made it four for Derby with a fine overhead shot and, although Forest kept creating opportunities, they weren't going in. Iremonger continued to give Bloomer the special attention a centre back has for a free-scoring striker and the two came to blows again. Bloomer promptly cracked a shot against the post before he made it five and claimed the first of three hat-tricks against Forest. Although Forest fielded a weakened side, there could be no doubting the quality of Derby's performance and they headed to Crystal Palace with a spring in their step. The venue was not in fact an actual crystal palace but a ground in a bowl in the shadow of the magnificent Crystal Palace built for the Great Exhibition in 1851. Within the grounds were acres of gardens, a maze, a landscaped park and huge fountains.

In preparation for the Cup Final, both teams spent a few days in Matlock Bath to prepare, while supporters plotted their routes to London. It has been estimated that slightly more Derby supporters made their way south on the big day. An early version of a special away day train service was seemingly laid on as many, according to the *Derbyshire Advertiser and Journal,* travelled to London 'glad to take advantage of the facilities afforded by the railways companies of spending a day in town at a reasonable rate'. Thousands of fans hopped on a variety of services towards Crystal Palace, affording travellers, especially those from Derby, an opportunity to learn more about their passion: railways, as the newspaper continued, 'Some walked but the larger number chose one of the several railway routes, and ether going or returning, probably got a few new notions as to the holding capacities of a third-class compartment and were able to compare the rate of travel on the southern lines to that which they were accustomed at home.'

Irrespective of whether there were more Derby or Forest fans, it was noted that the air was thick with an accent unfamiliar to that of the locals and by 2pm there were about 50,000 present, swelling higher once the game commenced. Composed of spectators of all grades and professions, the crowd was so huge that some climbed up the trees on the Penge side of the enclosure to secure a view. Officially the crowd is recorded as 62,017, with gate receipts of £2,312.

Apparently, just before kick-off, Derby's Archie Goodall was still outside among the crowd seeking to offload his surplus tickets: hardly ideal preparation for a cup final, especially one against your biggest rivals. There's no doubt about it, the game had captured the imagination of the wider public, intrigued to see how two Midlands rivals would fare on the national stage. *Sporting Life* noted, 'A comparison shows Notts Forest to be a much superior team to the County, but outside Nottingham it would be difficult to find many followers of the game who could back the Notts Forest for even a draw.'

The general feeling was that Derby would atone for their past failures in losing twice in the previous two seasons at the semi-final stage. Furthermore, given that just five days previously, Derby had walloped the Foresters 5-0 and, simply put, had Steve Bloomer in their side, it is easy to see how the consensus was that Derby's name was on the cup. After all, Forest's route to the final seemed gentler and, along the way, they had acquired the tag of the villains for controversially dumping the minnows of Southampton out at the semi-final stage.

Derby fielded the same side that mauled Forest 5-0, while their opponents, to confirm the notion that the team which lost so miserably was far below full strength, made five changes, most notably with captain John McPherson, second top scorer Arthur Capes and reputedly one of the finest left-backs in the country, Adam Scott, all returning to the side. This was no league fixture; this was the FA Cup Final, and it would be very different.

The player profiles in *Sporting Life* made for interesting reading. Forward John Goodall was described as 'without doubt, one of the best footballers who ever donned the jersey'. Bloomer was singled out for special praise too, possessing 'a shot the like of [a better one in the country] it would be difficult to find'. For Forest, Scott, the club captain up until the previous season, played 'in as creditable a manner as any man in any other team in the country', while incumbent captain John McPherson was afforded high praise indeed, 'Too much cannot be said of his play, as he is as near perfection as they make 'em.'

This was also a big game for Frank Forman, having left Derby with his brother to sign for Forest and causing a degree of consternation four years previously. Since doing so, he had made great strides, vindicating his decision to leave, having 'played twice for England, first against Wales and then against Scotland in the second half. In the latter game, he acquit himself so well that he was spoken of as one of the best men in the field.' Indeed, Frank and Fred Forman were the only brothers to play for England in all their home international fixtures in one season, up until the Charlton brothers came along. A year later, the Formans would both make the score sheet for England in their 13-2 win against Ireland at Roker Park. Fred scored two, Frank scored one and Bloomer bagged a brace too.

A glance at the birthplaces of those on the team sheets confirms the notion that football had evolved from the elite-educated classes of Eton and Oxford to the proletarians of the Midlands, the north and Scotland. Both teams were constituted exclusively of midlanders and Scots. Indeed, Derby had five Scots in their team and Forest four, with the Englishmen hailing from Derbyshire, Staffordshire, West Midlands, Burton-on-Trent and Gainsborough.

Forest won the toss and defended the Palace goal. They quickly found their stride and it came as little surprise when they took the lead on 19 minutes through Capes, after his shot went through a forest of legs. Unsurprisingly, Bloomer got his name on the score sheet with a header that went in off the bar. From then on, Forest allowed little concession to Derby and played 'with irresistible dash and showed far more of the valuable quality than did their opponents all through the game. Dash and plonk won the day and finesse was nowhere.' Just before half-time, Forest took the lead again when Derby keeper John Fryer could only parry a shot and Capes pounced on the loose ball.

In the second half, Derby saw more of the ball, but did little with it despite Forest's Willie Wragg clearly struggling with injury and being reduced to little more than an observer. With time running out and Derby a spent force, Forest secured the win when McPherson held off two challenges and got off a shot that found the net. It was Forest's name that was etched not only on the cup, but into history. Somewhat fittingly, the day also happened to be Sam Widdowson's birthday, the shin guard pioneer.

The 5-0 hammering in the league just five days previously counted for nothing and despite scoring, 'Bloomer was not the Bloomer of old'. Indeed, Derby's key players simply underperformed on the day and it was agreed that the best team undoubtably won what would 'long be remembered as one of the keenest contests ever seen on a football field'. Keeping abreast of the score back in the Midlands was a difficult affair, yet in Derby, a shopkeeper displayed updates at various stages as best he could via wires from London. Apparently, a rumour spread that Derby were ahead at one stage, leading to what the *Derbyshire Advertiser* described as 'enthusiastic cheering'. One can only imagine their disappointment and frustration when the actual score was relayed.

In Nottingham, the scenes were quite different, even if the expectant crowds gathered in Parliament Street echoed those in Derby. 'The enthusiasm was contagious,' reported *Football News,* 'for tiny urchins, the youth of both sexes, young men and maidens, and even people of mature age were observed beaming with gladness. Particularly was there noticed several young ladies smartly dressed in costumes of string whose thoughts one would have fancied would have been all with cycling and tennis – exuberant as they could be with girlish glee, tugging joyously at the arms of companions of the sterner sex (possibly brothers) and chirping every now and then a happy "Dear old Forest!" So as the result was all and everything, and there was really little more than it was desirable to know until after tea, bit by bit the crowd melted away and Parliament Street again assumed its quiet and sober aspect.'

The Forest players stayed overnight in London, but on their return were greeted by the city's delighted public in great numbers. According to the *Nottingham Evening Post*, 'The train by which they travelled from St Pancras was not timed to arrive until ten minutes past eight but long before that hour eager spectators began to take their positions on elevated platforms along the line of the route. The whole locality seemed to "see red". Flags, neckerchiefs, ties, sashes, ribbons, hatbands – all manner of appendages flaunted the familiar colour and not only the average football enthusiast was there. Even the usually sober and sedate citizen appeared to be consumed with a desire to honour those who had done honour to the city.'

As for Derby, there was a degree of sympathy for the team, which seemed to be destined not to lift the trophy, and especially for Bloomer, as expressed by *Sporting Life*, 'For the captain of the team one is genuinely sorry that such a fitting crown to his long and honourable career as a player has been denied him, but he at least will have the satisfaction of knowing that no carelessness or neglect of duty on his part contributed to the results which has occasioned the supporters of the club with so much disappointment.'

A rather curious photograph of Forest's FA Cup-winning team exists. It shows the players posing with the trophy in the foreground. Two things seem to jar though. Firstly, the faces are oddly unsmiling for a team that has just won the cup. Secondly – and very likely related to the lack of smiles – the team is wearing white shirts and dark shorts, not the established Garibaldi red. A simple explanation exists: it was conventional to take official team photographs before the game, with and without the cup, and then destroy the picture of the losing team with the trophy. In this instance, so the story goes, Forest's red shirts and blue shorts provided too little contrast on a dull day and so the victorious Forest players were asked to wear the white shirts of the close rivals they were to vanquish in the final. Taking a photograph wasn't simple back then. What is also clearly visible is Sam Widdowson's brainchild: shin guards, being worn by the team on the outside of their socks.

1898/99

Bloomer's revenge

On 3 September 1898, buoyant from their cup success and perhaps mindful of the upturn in Derby's fortunes since they acquired a home of their own, Forest moved for the final time to the City Ground. Funds were required to bring it up to scratch and so bearer bonds of £5 each were issued in an effort to raise money. They were fortunate in that one of their members, William Bardill, happened also to be a nurseryman and he had the foresight to dig out a cellar stretching the length and breadth of the field and filled it with a drainage shelf, a most useful design given the ground's close proximity to the River Trent. To celebrate their cup success, Forest flew a flag from the main stand proclaiming their status as cup-winners. Their previous home, the Town Ground, took its name from the nearby Town Arms pub and although officially the ground now sits in West Bridgford rather than the city of Nottingham, at the time of moving there, the strip of land upon which the ground is built remained within the city boundary until a redrawing in 1951 shifted Forest outside and into West Bridgford. Thus, a shift from Town Ground to City Ground seemed appropriate, especially in the light of Nottingham being granted city status the previous year.

With the First Division expanded to 18 teams now, new challenges were there to be faced and both clubs consolidated their status over the next four years with a sprinkling of cup success – and heartache – along the way. Forest especially found settling into their new home hard going as it took them until the eighth league game to win there, a 2-1 victory over Stoke City.

December 1898 saw the two clubs meet for the first time since the FA Cup Final and thereby christen the City Ground with its first East Midlands derby. Perhaps appropriately, it was a humdinger of a game too. As was the norm, special trains were laid on to carry Derby supporters to Nottingham, contributing to a considerable crowd of approximately 12,000. It was Derby who scored first in the seventh minute as Frederick Richards latched on to a brilliant pass from Henry Allen. Yet barely two minutes later, Forest equalised through their own Richards. Not to be outdone, Derby went and took the lead again before Capes levelled again before half-time.

The second half was 'full of excitement', according to *Sporting Life*, with 'The fast pace being well kept up, especially by the forwards. The Forest front rank quite excelled, while for Derby Bloomer and Harry Allen were generally conspicuous.' Bob Norris nudged Forest ahead thanks to a clever assist by Frank Forman, but it was short-lived as Bloomer sped past Wragg and Iremonger, and scored the best goal of the game, allowing him some sense of satisfaction after the disappointment of losing the final. All in all, 'It was universally admitted that the match was one of the finest and best-played on the city enclosure this season.'

Although both clubs were firmly ensconced in mid-table, Derby desperately wanted to atone in the FA Cup and, just like the previous season, once again made it to Crystal Palace for the final where they would meet fellow First Division side Sheffield United. With the Blades struggling in the league (they finished 16th out of 18), the stars were aligned for Derby to put things right, especially after they took an early lead through Boag in front of a then record attendance. Everything was in place until midway through the second half when the wheels fell off spectacularly as the Yorkshire side scored three times in nine minutes and added another in the final minute to confirm a 4-1 win. Derby must have been sick of the sight of the Crystal Palace ground.

Although a small consolation, Derby could take some form of revenge as their final two league fixtures were against Forest and Sheffield United, both at the Baseball Ground. Bloomer was clearly not in the mood for messing around and scored all of Derby's goals in their 2-0 and 1-0 wins respectively, ensuring he topped the scoring charts with 23 goals.

For the derby at the Baseball Ground, the *Nottingham Journal* noted that the game 'would attract considerable attention owing to the rivalry between the two clubs'. The travelling Forest supporters left Nottingham on a 4.05pm train for a 5.30pm kick-off, yet initially the attendance was low, perhaps unsurprising given the deflation Derby supporters must have been feeling, just five days after their FA Cup Final defeat.

There were very few spectators present when the teams ran out, probably not more than 500. Frank Forman was excellent throughout a first half and, although it was goalless at half-time, the crowd had swollen from around 500 to 3,000. In the second half, Boag set up Bloomer who scored with a signature wallop into the bottom corner and, although Forman almost immediately equalised, Bloomer added another to make it 2-0, eliciting much enthusiasm from the home supporters. Capes thought he'd pulled one back but it was judged to be offside, and Forman blotted his copybook when he blazed over from close range. Bloomer thought he'd claimed a hat-trick but his strike was, rather controversially, ruled to have come after the final whistle and did not stand.

Derby finished in ninth and Forest 11th, but there were reasons to be optimistic for both clubs going into a new century. Forest finally had a settled home and Derby proved to be an excellent cup team, despite successive defeats in the final, and they also had Steve Bloomer, who scored a magnificent six goals in one game against the hapless Wednesday in a 9-0 win.

3

End of a century; end of an era: 1899–1915

THE VICTORIAN era was in its final throes as a period of conflict and turmoil loomed on the horizon. In October 1899, the Second Boer War was triggered by the discovery of diamonds and gold in the Boer states in what is now the country of South Africa and the people of Derby were welcomed to the new century by the *Derby Daily Telegraph* speaking of 'Boer arrogance and misrule' on the front page. They were informed of an update on progress in the war from a rising Conservative politician by the name of Mr Winston Spencer-Churchill. In Forest's Boxing Day game against Notts County at Meadow Lane, gate receipts were donated to the Boer War effort, while in August of that year, Alma Lucy Reville was born in Nottingham – she would later marry a young film director in 1926 by the name of Alfred Hitchcock.

Football and principality rivalries continued regardless, of course. Both clubs improved slightly in the 1899/00 season by posting solid mid-table placings – Derby in sixth and Forest in eighth – while the latter reached the semi-finals of the FA Cup but went out to similarly mid-table Bury after a replay at Bramall Lane. The teams could not be separated at the first time of asking, with a 1-1 result taking place at the Victoria Ground in Stoke, and Arthur Capes scoring in both games. Bury eventually prevailed and faced Southampton in the final, who were no doubt still smarting and aggrieved by a blizzard and Forest's semi-final antics of 1898. Yet there was no redemption for them as they were roundly beaten 2-0 by Bury.

In the league games, Forest and Derby played out a 2-2 draw at the Baseball Ground in October, with Frank Forman and Jack Calvey (who would earn a solitary England cap in 1902) scoring for the Reds and Dick Wombwell and Steve Bloomer for the Rams. In the return fixture, Forest ran out comfortable 4-1 winners with Fred Forman among the scorers and, naturally, Bloomer getting Derby's goal. That season Billy Garraty of league champions Aston Villa outscored Bloomer with 27 goals while Forest's new signing from Swindon Town, Grenville Morris, enjoyed a promising first campaign, scoring 14 league and cup goals. These were the first 14 of a career total 217 for the Reds, and he remains the club's highest scorer.

From then on, it was the usual tale for both clubs of middling league finishes with the odd cup run until a slide towards relegation. Forest enjoyed the better season of the two in 1900/01, with a 1-0 win in Nottingham (Calvey the scorer), which came amid six consecutive victories, including an impressive 6-1 away scoreline at West Bromwich Albion, in which Morris scored a hat-trick.

On 22 January the Victorian era ended as Queen Victoria died at Osborne House on the Isle of Wight.

The Edwardian era thus began. All football matches were cancelled that weekend.

In March, Derby and Forest played out a goalless draw at the Baseball Ground while Liverpool claimed the title, but it was in the FA Cup where a shift in the pendulum swing was to be found as Tottenham Hotspur became the first southern club to lift the trophy since Old Etonians in 1882, thus challenging the Midlands and northern hegemony. What's more, they weren't even in the First or Second Division at the time but the Southern Division. Steve Bloomer claimed his top goalscoring title back from Villa's Garraty with 23 goals, despite his team finishing in an unspectacular 12th, while Forest, buoyed by the goalscoring prowess of Calvey and Morris, finished fourth, a point behind Notts County.

The 1901/02 season was a curious one in that both clubs enjoyed strikingly similarly successful outcomes. Forest ended up in fifth with Derby in sixth, split only by goal average. Both reached the semi-final stage of the FA Cup, yet both lost out. Forest lost to their old cup rivals and competition specialists Southampton at White Hart Lane in the midst of a smallpox epidemic in Nottingham, meaning that fewer than 200 fans took the train to support their team. Derby finally succumbed to Sheffield United after two stalemates, with the second replay taking place at the City Ground where they lost to a single goal. Unsurprisingly, the games between Derby and Forest were tight, with a 1-1 draw at the Baseball Ground in November (predictably, Morris scored for Forest and Bloomer for Derby) in a match that left the *Derby Daily Telegraph* reporters thoroughly unimpressed, decrying the general lack of quality in Derby's play and football in general, 'In these days we cannot count with any certainty on the ball being retained by the same set of forwards beyond the second or third pass and this circumstance in itself illustrates the lamentable loss of accuracy that has latterly come over the forward work of nearly all the great teams.'

Forest did gain some small claim of superiority for the season with a 3-1 at the City Ground on 1 March, Spouncer, Calvey and Fred Forman finding the net for the home side and, naturally, Bloomer for Derby. By the end of March, Derby would lose again in Nottingham in their cup semi-final, no doubt making them thoroughly miserable at the sight of the City Ground that season.

The following season was a familiar tale of similarity in terms of league positions: Derby in ninth and Forest in tenth, yet for Derby, it was another case of an FA Cup slipping away as they once again reached the final, played once again at Crystal Palace, yet once again lost. Actually, putting it bluntly, they were hammered by Bury, with whom they finished level on points in the league. Going into the final, Bloomer was a fitness concern, and he didn't start owing to injury. Bury's 6-0 score remained the record winning margin in FA Cup finals until 2019 when Manchester City equalled that tally against Watford. In fairness to Derby, there was something about Bury in the cup that season as they went through their whole successful cup campaign without conceding a goal, the first team to do so since Preston North End in 1889. This cup final defeat spelled the end of manager Harry Newbold's reign.

If Derby were looking for further excuses for their miserable Cup Final display, they could point towards how their world was literally rocked less than a month before as, on 24 March, an earthquake struck Derby and the surrounding area. This was not uncommon as seismic activity stuck in 1886, but back then, it occurred at 5.30am while this one struck in the middle of the day. The *Derbyshire Advertiser and Journal* reported that it 'commenced with a rumbling noise, followed by a heaving motion of the ground, and the shaking of the walls of the houses'. There would be further activity on 3 May, perhaps an aftershock of the 6-0 cup final defeat. Meanwhile, over in Nottingham, the Midlands Industrial Exhibition opened in May with its centrepiece building the Ivory Palace, not unlike the Brighton Pavilion built in 1893, taking pride of place at the city end of the Trent Bridge. The complex featured an Industrial Hall and, rather implausibly yet excitingly, a Mexican toboggan and a Fairy River. Sadly, a fire burned the whole complex down in July 1904.

In terms of the derby, honours were even as each side chalked up an away win: Forest by a single Morris goal away and Derby finally experiencing some joy at the City Ground after some recent painful visits there with a 3-2 win, thanks to a brace from Bloomer.

The season after brought some joy for both clubs, despite humdrum league form. Forest finished ninth out of 18 in the First Division with Derby a little lower in 14th. However, the Rams continued to excel in the FA Cup and once again reached the semi-finals. Although perhaps driven by the pain of the previous year's final, they were unable to make amends as they lost 1-0 to Bolton Wanderers at Molineux.

If that was painful, then their two performances against Forest that season offered no consolation, succumbing 6-2 at home and 5-1 away. Derby went into the 6-2 defeat on 14 November in miserable form, having not won in nine games, despite starting the season well with two wins. An expectant crowd of 8,000 was in attendance and, according to the *Yorkshire Post and Intelligencer*, 'Some remarkable football was witnessed.' Forest shot into a two-goal lead thanks to Sid Sugden and breakout star Billy Shearman, who would joint top score with Morris for Forest that season. As expected, Bloomer pulled one back before Morris extended the lead to make it 3-1 to Forest at half-time. Despite Derby penning Forest back in the second half, Shearman broke away and added another before William Whittaker in the Derby goal had what could only be described as a calamitous half as he apparently 'put a screw shot from Spouncer through his own goal' and then 'repeated the error'. One can only be thankful for poor Whittaker that social media was a century away.

The return fixture in Nottingham in March offered little solace for the Rams, losing 5-1 and prompting *Football News* to declare 'A DARK DAY FOR DERBY, BUT ONE OF REJOICING FOR THE REDS'. It was a crucial game for the Rams as despite their cup run, they went into it looking over their shoulders at the relegation zone, even after a promising run of eight unbeaten. An insight into the visit of Derby and the rivalry from a Nottingham perspective was offered by the reporter in *Football News*, 'The Rams are our neighbours and we don't want to see them go into the Second Division. But when clubs are fighting for existence it is a case of a certain gentleman not mentioned in polite society capturing the hindmost ["Devil take the hindmost": The idea is that if everyone is running away, the devil will capture those who are farthest from the front. Therefore, if someone uses this expression, it means that those in the rear of a group are at risk], and the "reds" who this morning were not over safe, had a lot at stake in the present match.'

The odd thing about such rivalries is that although for many, relegation for rivals is a gleeful occurrence to be celebrated with vim and vigour, there comes a point when absence makes the heart, if not grow fonder, then at least yearn for those derby days, that nail-biting, stomach-churning experience of a game against the other lot.

Forest wasted no time in dismantling their opposition with Spouncer's opener and apparently 'charged over and through the Derby lines, like a cavalry brigade over raw volunteers'. A somewhat jarring description given the Boer War lingered strong in the memory, having ceased less than a year previously. Perhaps more poetic is the description of Forest's play after going four goals ahead, 'It was if the "reds" has been dosed with elixir vitamin and the "rams" with some stupefying mixture.' The reporter could not hide their disappointment in a Derby side without Bloomer, 'As for Derby, I really could not understand them. Their defence seemed to crack up wretchedly.' Five days later, Derby lost to Bolton in the semi-final of the cup. One could forgive Derby for being truly sick of the sight of the City Ground by now.

As if a double loss to their rivals and a painful semi-final defeat were not enough to take for Derby, they were also enduring a period of financial worries. In July, the *Burton Chronicle* reported on the annual meeting of the directors and shareholders of the club being held on Tuesday evening at the Royal Hotel in which, 'Working expenses showed a decrease on previous seasons.' The losses were cited as a result of increases in players' wages: £200 had been spent on re-turfing the Baseball Ground and a considerable sum of money on strengthening the stands. Match receipts were down by £900 and, owing to the semi-final loss, there was no FA Cup Final to boost income. Mr H.F. Morton pointed out that the wage bill was up on the previous year and thought they might have expected better performances for the money. He also criticised the increase in travelling expenses, while vice-president William Morley simply put it down to a case of the team having bad luck. If there was a silver lining, it was that Bloomer, despite missing games through injury, reclaimed his title as the league's top goalscorer, yet although he wasn't to know it at the time, this would be the last time he would do so.

Despite Derby's miserable season, it was Forest who would spiral downwards over the next two years while the Rams posted a couple of lower mid-table finishes. In the 1904/05 season, Derby exacted some form of revenge for their recent hapless form in Nottingham by chalking up a 1-0 win at the City Ground. The *Nottingham News* proudly proclaimed that it was 'Derby Day again! The whirling of time brings round these meetings between the Nottingham clubs and our friends of Railwayopedia very frequently, but never too often.' Again, the paradoxical feelings of wanting your rivals to fail yet wanting them around to fail is captured neatly here, with a dash of friendly light mockery thrown in the use of the curious word 'Railwayopedia', playing on Derby's established reputation as the centre of railway engineering.

Bloomer was back for Derby, who came into the game in encouraging form. After a goalless first half, the attendance swelled to around 15,000 and judging by the vocal support for the away team the Rams apparently did not lack a big following. As usual, physical violence was evident on the pitch in such a game as Ben Warren of Derby and Tom Niblo of Forest had a contretemps, with the latter sustaining some 'damage to his countenance'. A minute later, Derby scored as Frederick Barker smashed one in to take the spoils back to Derbyshire, despite Bloomer apparently not having one of his better days.

The teams met back in Derby on 25 February and, with Forest on a miserable run of form, they lost 3-2. Even without Bloomer, Derby were able to inflict a double on their rivals, just as they had been on the receiving end of one the previous season. Although Forest started and ended the scoring, they were unable to prevent the three goals in between for the home side. Derby's first goal was a curious one, as described in the *Nottingham Journal*, 'The home team equalised in a very fortunate manner. Davies headed in a centre from the right, and everyone, [Harry] Lineacre included, thought the ball might go yards wide. But instead it struck the post and rolled into the net.' The description of the second goal, to take Derby into the lead, also mentioned the Forest keeper specifically again, 'In some extraordinary way, the ball found its way through a crowd of legs into the net without Lineacre (who had a bright sun in his eyes, and his view obstructed by players) seeing it at all.'

Perhaps it is this game to which a mocking postcard – an early meme – refers, exaggerating the demise of Forest. Under a picture of a horse-drawn carriage, upon which sits a robed figure, the text reads, 'In loving memory of Notts Forest. After the ball was rolling, after the whistle blew, many a heart was acheing (sic), Till Derby banged it through. All the crowd was cheering, You should have heard them all, When Lineacre was knocked, Through the goal post after the ball. R.I.P. No flowers by request.' Of course, it could just as easily be that the meaning is not tied to a specific game, but more generally directing scorn in Forest's general direction – understandable given their struggles over the course of this season and the next.

Forest finished in 16th and narrowly escaped relegation as the bottom two went down while the top two from the Second Division replaced them. Derby fared only slightly better in 11th but took a huge degree of satisfaction by exacting some revenge on their rivals for the previous season's two defeats. Yet the final places in the table hinted at an unfolding story of slide for both clubs, with Forest sliding faster.

1905-1909
Passing trains on parallel tracks

Perhaps to plug holes in the club's bank account, Forest embarked on a successful summer tour to South America. Following Southampton's trip there a year earlier, the Argentine Football Association contacted the club about going over and playing a few games in the summer of 1905. The Reds promptly did so and won all eight fixtures, scoring 56 goals and conceding only three, with Billy Shearman continuing his good form by playing in each one and scoring in seven, racking up an impressive 13 goals. Club secretary Harry Hallam kept the Nottingham public abreast of the tour in a letter published in the *Nottingham Evening Post*, 'A feature of the games was the bowling of young Holmes, the outside-left, and also the smart fielding of our players, which very much pleased onlookers.' Surprisingly, this is not a report of a football match against Rosarinos of Rosario, Argentina, but a description of the team passing the time on board the *Danube* en route to Argentina. As a side note, although they didn't play Independiente, it is believed that so impressed were their fans by seeing this dashing team tear the opposition apart, they adopted the Garibaldi red shirts as their own colours.

The success of the tour was short-lived though as Forest made a sluggish start to the season, while Derby got off to a flyer, winning their opening five games. The Boxing Day clash at the Baseball Ground ended 2-2, with Morris bagging a brace for the Reds and Thomas Fletcher and Freddie Wheatcroft netting for the Rams. Curiously, both sides played the day before, on Christmas Day, with Forest losing to Notts County and Derby to Manchester City.

March 1906 was a seismic month in Derby as Rolls-Royce Limited was registered as a car manufacturer. In need of a site to start mass production of cars and after considering but rejecting Manchester, Coventry, Bradford and Leicester, they took up the offer from Derby's council of cheap electricity on a site of 12.7 acres on the southern edge of the town. Less cause for celebration was Middlesbrough swooping to prise the great Steve Bloomer from Derby County for the sum of £750. It was a curious move as Middlesbrough themselves were struggling at the wrong end of the table. The sale of Bloomer arguably meant the end of a successful era for Derby.

The First Division expanded to 20 clubs for this season and relegation was stalking Forest as the campaign reached its climax. With three league games remaining, Derby were the visitors to Nottingham and the home side came into the game after a promising tussle against fourth-placed The Wednesday, which offered hope after a battling 4-3 defeat. With both the Reds and Rams having played the previous day, the game was somewhat scrappy on a dull and chilly bank holiday. Both teams improved in the second half, culminating in Douglas Hardcastle thinking he'd scored for Derby, but it was disallowed, apparently for handling. Morris and Jack Craggs went close for Forest, but a 0-0 draw was decreed to be a fair result.

With Wolves rock bottom, Forest had two games to save themselves. They needed to beat Birmingham in the next match – which they did, 2-1 – to give themselves a chance of catching Bloomer's new club, Middlesbrough. Bury, Notts County and even Derby were still in the mix, but Forest's final game was a tough one, away at FA Cup holders Everton, who only a week earlier had beaten Newcastle United in the final at Crystal Palace. The *London Evening Standard* talked up their chances of avoiding relegation among those grasping for survival on a hectic final day of the season, 'Notts Forest are the most favourably situated, for should they manage to share the points with the cup holders, who by the way make their first match and last appearance at Goodison Park since their Crystal Palace success, they will be safe from the danger which threatens them.' The *Nottingham Journal* put it rather more bluntly, 'The task that lies before Forest at Goodison Park today is so plain that no words can emphasise the magnitude of it or detract from the unenviable character. They must win!'

Forest lost 4-1 and were relegated into the Second Division for the first time in their history.

Middlesbrough required a point at Blackburn to avoid relegation and managed it thanks to a 1-1 draw, with Bloomer getting the goal. All of which meant that they stayed up by the slightest of margins with a goal average of 0.789 to Forest's 0.734. On top of the three hat-tricks he scored against Forest, he also played a huge role in relegating them despite not even playing for Derby anymore. It's little wonder that Steve Bloomer's statue sits watching on at Pride Park these days.

As for Forest, perhaps the pre-season tour of Argentina took its toll, or just as likely, the club had been drifting for the previous three years and it had finally caught up with them. The *Nottingham Journal* cautioned against the rising quality on offer in the Second Division and issued a rallying cry to supporters to stick with them on the grounds that smaller gates would mean smaller receipts and, in the current climate, no club could be run without great expenditure. Somehow, Forest's situation in 1906 seems so very modern.

If Derby supporters were wallowing in their rivals' relegation, it would be very short-lived. They started the 1906/07 season sluggishly, winning only one game from the opening six before a disastrous run of five straight defeats as Christmas loomed and Florence Nightingale, whose family hailed from Matlock, Derbyshire, became the first woman to receive an OBE. Their poor form continued and culminated in their relegation, along with Stoke City, come the end of the season under the leadership of club stalwart Jimmy Methven.

Replacing Bloomer was always going to be an impossible task, but the *Sheffield Daily Telegraph* cited a lack of goals

End of a century; end of an era: 1899–1915

as a major factor in their downfall, 'The management has recently busied itself in securing the aid of certain young and promising amateurs ... [money] was not invested in two first-class forwards.' The *Derbyshire Advertiser and Journal* Friday played the bad luck card, 'They have to a large extent been the victims of bad luck, which seems to have their footsteps to the very end of the season, for even on Saturday, when their fate hung in the balance, they were deprived of the services of their regular goalkeeper and had to play a substitute.' That might have been so, but the club had, like Forest, been drifting towards the lower reaches of the First Division for a while. So, like their rivals, they swiftly followed suit and took the plunge into the Second Division for the first time in their history.

As for Forest, they prepared for life outside the top division by signing Enoch West from Hucknall Constitution to supplement Morris's goals. They started slowly, without a win in their opening three games, but rallied and with Morris banging in 21 league goals and West weighing in with 14, made light work of the Second Division and claimed the title and promotion. Like Helen Watts, who was inspired to dedicate herself to the suffragette cause after hearing Christabel Pankhurst speak at the Nottingham Mechanics Institute in December 1907, Forest sparked into life. From 19 January, they went 17 games undefeated and won 15, leading the *Nottingham Journal* to claim, 'The Reds soon found their feet and for months have been astonishing the football world by their extraordinary consistency of form.'

Like passing trains on parallel tracks, Forest and Derby waved to each other between the junctions of the First and Second Division.

1909-1914
They came in droves

Derby, like Forest initially did, struggled to acclimatise to their new environs. Crowds dwindled to 7,000 and in December 1908 the club reported that it was £2,000 in debt and losing £50 a week. They finished a respectable sixth in the Second Division – a position they would hang around in for the next three seasons after, finishing fifth, fourth and sixth again in 1910/11. The Bloomer era appeared to be well and truly over and, although they repeated their trick of a good FA Cup run in 1908/09, they also repeated their regular trick of losing at the semi-final stage, this time to Bristol City.

On the way to that semi-final, Derby enjoyed a comprehensive and rather surprising 3-0 victory over Forest at the Baseball Ground in the FA Cup on 6 March 1909. The *Bolton Evening News* singled out the fourth-round tie as one to watch, 'But no match of the series would be marked by more keenness than this one at Derby, for the County team and Nottingham Forest are old and bitter opponents whose rivalry will be accentuated by the fact that they are meeting in a cup tie.' A sizeable crowd of 16,000 turned up in expectation of a game that never actually happened as owing to a blinding snowstorm, the game was called off before the gates even opened. A week later it did go ahead on 13 March and conditions were very different as spring-like weather prevailed. As expected with the teams not playing each other regularly and this being a cup tie, anticipation was keen. *Football News* set the scene, 'They came in droves, starting early, and making the streets resound with their boisterous greetings and good-humoured repartee when the opposing factions clashed.' With rail the primary means of transport, the scene at the station was one to behold, 'Even the characteristic phlegm of the railway porter was disturbed, and the station officials bustled about giving and taking instructions in a state of excitement as train after train laden with hilarious enthusiasts from Nottingham, Ilkeston, Long Eaton and the surrounding districts steamed fussily in. Numbers of street hawkers crowded the outskirts of the station, their various-toned cries mingling raucously together, as they vied with one another for the custom of the club's supporters as the stations belched them forth in an apparently never-ending stream.'

Alfred Bentley invoked the spirit of Bloomer and scored a hat-trick to dump Forest out of the cup. Just for good measure, West was sent off for a foul on Tommy Barbour in front of an estimated attendance of 22,000, the second-highest gate of the day, beaten only by that at Chelsea where 30,000 watched a 1-1 draw with reigning cup-holders Manchester United in the First Division.

Forest's debut season back in the First Division went well as they finished in a respectable ninth place, with West doing a Bloomer and topping the division's scoring charts around the time that Nottingham's first public telephone box was installed in Theatre Square. They followed this up with a 14th-placed finish in the 1908/09 season, while Derby came close but never close enough in the Second Division. In April of that season, Forest chalked up their record 12-0 victory against a wretched Leicester Fosse. Forest went into this game with the threat of relegation hanging over both them and Leicester, so few expected the result to turn out as it did. The lop-sided nature of the result prompted an inquiry, held at Leicester on 6 May 1909. It transpired that two days before the game, the Leicester players had attended the wedding of their team-mate Bob Turner, and that the celebrations had continued until the early hours of the morning of the game. Three players scored a hat-trick that day: Bill Hooper, Spouncer and West. Complaints were made and objections raised, but a Commission of Enquiry set up by the Football League concluded that everything was above board, and the Forest team were simply remarkably good.

The season after was much like the previous as Forest again finished 14th, while Derby again missed out on promotion back to the First Division. Both clubs were in danger of treading water: Forest headed towards the bottom and Derby towards the top, but neither was close enough to be relegated or promoted. It seemed that Derby needed that something extra to get them over the line. Cue the return of Steve Bloomer in September 1910. The Rams had only one win in five at the start of the season until Bloomer took the field at the age of 35 in the game against Lincoln City. He picked up exactly where he left off by scoring two goals in a 5-0 win. His return was not enough for promotion, though, and Derby finished in their customary sixth place. Yet the following season was decisive as Bloomer powered Derby to the title and promotion by scoring 18 goals along the way in the 1911/12 season.

Forest's 1910/11 campaign could not have been more different as a disastrous run of form in the new year meant they lost 11 in 13 games, sending them spiralling to the bottom of the table and relegation, to be reunited with Derby in the Second Division. Perhaps Forest were still suffering from failing to replace their England international goalkeeper Harry Linacre (nephew of the Formans and winner of two England caps in 1905) who moved on in 1909, alongside the absence of Grenville Morris who was injured while playing for Wales against England right in the middle of Forest's horrendous run of form. Forest's committee came under pressure from their members in a crisis meeting when it was revealed that the club were in debt to the tune of £2,388. Wherever the recrimination lay, Forest were back down in the Second Division just when Derby were getting good, with Bloomer once again up front and scoring goals. While Bloomer did as he always did under Jimmy Methven, it was Forest's turn to stagnate, and they could only post a 15th-placed finish in the second tier while Derby claimed the title.

The two clubs met on Boxing Day 1911 and, unsurprisingly, Derby beat their old rivals at the City Ground 3-1. Henry Leonard and James Bauchop scored one each for Derby and there are no prizes for guessing who scored their third. All of this in front of a new Forest record attendance of 35,000.

Derby did experience a serious blip in February, losing four consecutive games, but after that they were unstoppable on their run to the title, winning nine of their remaining 12. Towards the end of that run was a vital victory against Forest at the Baseball Ground, which would prove to be the clubs' final meeting for a while as Forest were to labour without much reward in the Second Division. The only surprise in the 1-0 win for Derby is that it was Leonard who scored a late winner and not Bloomer. The fixture also doubled as a testimonial for James Bagshaw whose service to Derby during the past five or six years earned him such recognition. He wasn't entitled to the whole of the gate money but a substantial sum and a collection at the ground took place in acknowledgement of his record. The *Derby Daily Telegraph* described how, 'The goal aroused an enthusiasm which betokened the immense satisfaction of the Derby supporters. The strong wind hampered both sides but the victory is too gratifying to admit of fault finding.'

Derby were now in second position, locked in a battle with Burnley and Chelsea. Burnley led the way with 50 points and two games remaining. Derby had 47 points but had four matches left. Chelsea were in third with 46 points and also four to play. The Rams pipped Chelsea on goal average by beating Barnsley 2-0 at Oakwell to claim the title barely a week after the *Titanic* sunk.

While Forest struggled in the Second Division, posting a worrying 17th-placed finish in their first season back there in 1912/13, Derby enjoyed an impressive return to the First Division and finished a very respectable seventh, with Bloomer still banging them in – 14 goals in total – while Sunderland won the title and Aston Villa the FA Cup.

The great blizzard of January 1913, which played havoc with various sporting fixtures and daily life in general, was perhaps a portent of the storm brewing, not just at Derby but of the conflict to come in Europe. Derby's resurrection was short-lived, and they came back to earth with a bang, finishing bottom of the pile in 1913/14. Not even Bloomer could help them as he was reduced to only six appearances and the wheels fell off spectacularly. There were no wry smiles down the road though as Forest went from bad to worse and emulated Derby's 20th-placed finish in the First Division by doing exactly that in the Second Division.

Between the tail end of the previous season and the start of this one, Forest contrived to lose 14 consecutive matches, yet somehow they were re-elected and would renew their rivalry with Derby in the 1914/15 season in the Second Division. While the suffragettes set fire to the Nottingham Boat Club just by the City Ground to protest at it being a men-only organisation amid wild disorder following a Suffragist meeting in the Market Place, East Midlands football was at a low ebb.

1914/15
Burst ball

On 28 June 1914, Archduke Franz Ferdinand was assassinated. A month later, Steve Bloomer took up an offer to coach in Berlin at Britannia Berlin 92. His timing could not have been worse. After only three months, the ripples from the assassination were truly felt as war broke out and he was interned as a civilian prisoner of war. He ended up in Ruhleben Camp in the Spandau district of Berlin along with 353 other men. He grew popular with his fellow prisoners and organised football matches for entertainment, boosting morale and as a way of keeping fit.

Despite the outbreak of war, the 1914/15 season not only started but finished too. The first fixture between the two sides was on Christmas Day and ended 2-2 after Forest threw away a two-goal lead. In tribute to Forest's steady decline since 1907, the ball burst after 35 minutes. The day after they played again, this time with Derby winning by a single goal at the Baseball Ground, propelling the Rams upwards and ultimately on to promotion. By this time, Forest were themselves one again undergoing a financial crisis in their jubilee year and were forced to advise the Football League that they were struggling to pay their bills. They received a grant of £50 plus £10 per week until the end of the season to pay the players, who took a 25 per cent pay cut.

On the very same day, the *Derbyshire Advertiser and Journal* published an advert targeted towards employers in which it asked them four questions, 'As an employer have you seen that every fit man under your control has been given every opportunity of enlisting? Have you encouraged your men to enlist by offering to keep their positions open? Have you offered to help them in any other way if they will serve their country? Have you any men still in your employ who ought to enlist?' It concluded, 'Our present prosperity is largely due to the men already in the field, but to maintain it and to end the war we must have more men. Your country will appreciate the help you give.'

A notice elsewhere in the paper centred on a Derby widow's bereavement, 'Mrs Murphy, of 49, Jackson-street, Derby, has lost a second son in the war. She has received an intimation that her son, Private James Murphy, of the 1st Battalion Sherwood Foresters (regimental number 9979), has been killed in action in Flanders, and by strange coincidence he was buried on the same day her other son, Lance-sergt. Murphy, whose funeral took place at Derby, the body being brought from the Cambridge Hospital at Aldershot.'

Yet football, despite the public's dwindling appetite to watch young men running around a field for sports, continued. Seemingly, the authorities would much rather see them running across no-man's land. *Punch* magazine published a cartoon directed towards the footballer, stating, 'No doubt you can make money in this field [indicating a football field], my friend, but there's only one field today where you can get honour.'

Derby claimed the Second Division title while Forest languished in 17th, establishing a pattern that would define the clubs and their orbits around footballing success: fleeting moments of cup glory intertwined with repeated stumbling at the final hurdle, while in terms of league positions, similar flashes of glory closely followed by hard falls, with both clubs all the while following and emulating each other's trajectory. But football and local rivalries and bragging rights all suddenly seemed rather trivial and unimportant.

4

Between the wars: 1919–1939

FOREST LOST their last five competitive fixtures in 1915 before the cessation of league football, culminating in a miserable away 7-0 away defeat at The Arsenal. When football resumed on 30 August 1919, they picked up right where they left off with an away defeat at league debutants Rotherham County. It was to be another season of struggle as the Reds chalked up only three wins in their opening 17 games in the Second Division. It was the same story the season after as Forest again finished in 18th place.

In contrast, Derby – having gained promotion as champions in 1915 to the top division – were itching to get started and duly went unbeaten in their opening five games before their form tailed off and they finished 18th under Jimmy Methven. If some thought this was a season of consolidation, they were wrong as they unravelled in the following campaign, resulting in relegation to the Second Division. If there was any consolation in this, it meant they would once again meet their old rivals who were barely treading water down in the deep end.

While the 1920s were roaring in the States, Derby and Nottingham were clearing up their slums. The population in Derby in 1921 had grown to 142,824, while Nottingham's was recorded as 269,000. Although the rate of increase had slowed since the exponential rise through the previous century, it was still up by 20 per cent on 1901. So slum clearances started with the aim of reducing Derby's density of population as families were moved out to the suburbs on to new council estates and the building of private housing gathered pace. It was a similar tale in Nottingham, too, in terms of overpopulation and the clearing of slums, despite the rate of population increase finally slowing. Raleigh was now the largest cycle works in the world, producing approximately 100,000 cycles a year, and Helen Watts's protesting was bringing about small but positive change as the Nottingham city police force recruited its first female constable, following in the footsteps of Edith Smith who became the first warranted female police officer in 1915 with Grantham Borough Police.

The literary world was reeling from the commercial publication of *Women in Love* by Eastwood-born D.H. Lawrence. Although now perceived to be a sharp response to the huge changes in society brought about by the Industrial Revolution, it was dismissed by many as simply disgusting. His earlier work, *Strike Pay*, told the tale of miners walking nine miles from Eastwood, through Kimberley, Nuttall and Bulwell into Nottingham to watch Notts play Aston Villa, while enjoying a few pubs along the way. The protagonist, Ephraim, witnesses a navvy's death near the ground, having fallen into drainage. Lawrence wrote, 'The crust had broken, the man had gone under the horse, and it was some time before the people realised he had vanished. When they found his feet sticking out, and hauled him forth, he was dead, stifled dead in the mud. The horse was at length hauled out, after having its neck nearly pulled from the socket.'

With Eastwood being close to the county border, Lawrence's stories of men working in the pits, drinking hard, speaking in broad dialect and going to the football, captured the life of the working man. But more than that, they document a period when 'it was still possible for a man both to have direct access to the age-old springs of peasant life and also to acquire a good education for himself,' wrote Anthony Beal in his introduction to *Sons and Lovers*. 'A generation or so earlier, the education would have been denied him: a generation or so later, the old natural way of life would have succumbed to mechanisation.' A crowd at the City Ground or the Baseball Ground would have consisted of this type of man. As Forest and Derby renewed acquaintances in September 1921 for the first time since December 1915, the first amusement park in England, Wicksteed Park in Kettering, opened.

Bruised from their brief flirtation with the First Division, Derby welcomed Forest to the Baseball Ground in decent form, having won three of their previous four games, suggesting they were well equipped to make their stay in the Second Division a fleeting pit-stop. Forest, on the other hand, had made an impressive start to the 1921/22 season, putting their opening-day defeat at Crystal Palace behind them to post five successive victories. The two games provided a clear sign as to where the two teams were heading. The Baseball Ground turnstiles closed ten minutes before kick-off on 24 September for the first meeting with

22,803 fans inside, including 4,000 Forest supporters who had travelled to Derby on special trains.

Jack Spaven flashed the ball into the net to give Forest the lead and doubled it when he steadied himself and drove a low shot home. William Patterson pulled one back before half-time for the hosts. In the second half, James Barnes of Derby missed practically an open goal and the game deteriorated into 'rush and scramble', according to the *Derby Evening Telegraph*. It was agreed that the better side won, with the difference being the quality of the teams' respective forwards as Spaven was singled out for praise. 'The Reds proved the faster side and were always more accurate in their shooting,' and boasted the more 'clever forwards and a great marksman in Spaven'. The *Nottingham Journal* was cautious in getting too carried away though with the return fixture back in Nottingham the very next Saturday, 'The value of this win away from home will be best realised next Saturday, when in the return at the City Ground, the ability of the Rams will be more readily understood.'

Under a bright and warm sun, an expectant crowd of around 25,000 turned out the following Saturday at the City Ground, including 'an enthusiastic gathering of supporters of the visiting team', reported the *Nottingham Journal*. Such conditions might well have favoured the Australian cricket team who had played a stone's throw away at Trent Bridge that preceding summer and won the first Test by ten wickets in May, which meant that they had won eight in succession. This was an unequalled sequence in Ashes Tests, following the 5-0 drubbing they had administered to England in the 1920/21 season in Australia. Once again, the Australians took the Ashes back home.

Derby looked the better side to start with until Walter Tinsley opened the scoring for Forest by nodding in at the back post. The usual bruises and battles of such a fixture were in evidence as a collision between Derby's Harold Whiteman, an ex-Forest man, and Fred Parker resulted in a cut over the eye for the visitors' centre-half. After half-time, Derby again did most of the running until Spaven blasted in from close range and a minute from full time, Bobby Parker made it three, thus making clear the value of the previous week's win at Derby.

Forest were on the rise after two deeply mediocre seasons which frustrated their fans, something which the *Nottingham Journal* was all too keenly aware of, 'To the credit of the football enthusiasts of the district, they turned out in their thousands to show their appreciation of the efforts of their players and were forced to admit they had their money's worth. Saturday, it is to be hoped, set the seal upon the good feelings between the public and the club, which have so far this season been steadily reviving, and the former will surely now keep its bargain to support a clever and winning team.'

They did indeed and gained promotion as champions after an absence from the top division of, owing to the war, 11 years, with Bob Masters at the helm and Spaven top-scoring with 22 goals in cup and league. As for Derby, they 'proved beyond a shadow of a doubt that they are a thorough set of sportsmen, both players and officials alike'. Which is all well and good but little consolation when your rivals go up as champions while you finish in mid-table, resulting in the end of an era as club legend Jimmy Methven stepped down as manager.

1922-1939
Human freight from Derby

In terms of derbies, there would be no more for another two seasons as Forest emulated the Rams' brief and underwhelming stint in the First Division by posting consecutive 20th-placed finishes before sliding through the trap door without grace in 1925. Meanwhile, Derby endured another disappointing 1922/23 campaign in the Second Division, as they ambled to 14th. They did derive some joy from a run to the semi-finals of the FA Cup where they lost 5-2 to West Ham at Stamford Bridge before getting themselves together and chalking up consecutive third-placed finishes under Cecil Potter. The first of these was heartbreakingly unfortunate as they missed out on promotion by 0.015 of a goal, before their and Forest's worlds collided again in the 1925/26 season.

With both teams going into the season under new management – John Baynes at Forest and George Jobey at Derby – there was a sense of expectation at both clubs: Derby of finally getting over the line and achieving promotion and Forest of an immediate bounce back. Indeed, Derby signalled their intent by purchasing their stadium outright on 9 March 1925 for £10,400 and immediately began improvements in the form of rebuilding all four stands over the next decade. Jobey himself was a renowned name having previously managed Northampton Town and Wolverhampton Wanderers, where he presided over their promotion from the Third Division North to the Second Division. The Geordie had retired to run a hotel in 1924 after winning the Third Division North with Wolves, but was tempted back into football by the Rams. He had been the first Woolwich Arsenal player to score at Highbury in 1913 after Leicester's Tommy Benfield scored the first goal at the stadium.

After seven games of the season, Forest were still seeking their first win. As for Derby, they enjoyed an encouraging start by losing only one of their opening six matches. As usual in these fixtures, a strong contingent made the way across the county border to comprise a crowd of 20,000 on 26 September 1925 at the City Ground. In keeping with this fixture's history and future, the game featured a player who had represented both clubs. Harry Bedford made his debut for Derby, having signed the day beforehand from Blackpool. Derbyshire-born Bedford started his career at Forest and made 18 appearances between 1919 and 1921 before being sold to Blackpool, where he proceeded to make a name for himself before Derby claimed his signature.

He was straight into the thick of the action, too, as he played a role in a spot of farcical comedy. In the first half, Forest keeper Leonard Langford and Bedford collided, resulting in the striker's stud becoming entangled in Langford's jersey. Seeing the ball roll towards the net, Bedford desperately tried to free his boot despite being able to stand only on one leg. The ball trundled safely out of play before the referee disentangled them.

Noah Burton – previously of Derby – opened the scoring for Forest before Harry Thoms and then Lionel Murphy swung the game Derby's way. Thoms shot through a crowd of players after Langford had punched clear to equalise, and then Bedford did more than just get his boot stuck in a goalkeeper's jersey. It was he who laid on the pass for

Murphy to hit home. 'Up to then the man who just two days before had set the football world agog was just one ordinary player among 21 others. Derby had paid £3,000 for Bedford. A fortune! Spent in the one hope he would help to win matches,' scoffed the *Nottingham Journal*. It was money well spent as he would go on to score 28 times that season.

Despite losing, Forest played well and, ironically, it was apparently their insistence on close passing that contributed to the defeat. They could at least take solace from being involved in a thoroughly entertaining game. 'Considering the measure of responsibility each man felt and the typical "derby" atmosphere that permeated the game, the fight was as clean as it was fierce,' wrote the *Journal*. The *Derby Daily Telegraph* agreed, up to a point, and stated that Forest would not have been unlucky if they had scored three or four, with Burton especially standing out, 'Burton was keen on making it known he had not left the Baseball Ground a damp squib.' Yet Bedford had already done enough to convince spectators that he would propel Derby forward. There was a sense that when they clicked, they would start racking up goals and, naturally, points.

Such optimism proved entirely justified. Following this hard-earned away win at their rivals, Derby embarked on a 19-game run during which they lost only twice. The very next match saw them beat Swansea 5-0, with Bedford claiming a hat-trick. Two games further down the line, they beat The Wednesday 4-1 (Bedford got two) and they followed that by beating Stoke 7-3 (Bedford claimed another hat-trick). By the time the two teams faced each other again on 6 February 1926, Derby were flying while Forest were stumbling. Since defeat at home to Derby, Forest had steadied a little by posting a scattering of wins, but they went in with two successive defeats under their belts. In contrast, Derby had lost just one in ten league games, but to offer Forest some hope, they had just been defeated by Southend of the Third Division South 4-1 in the fourth round of the FA Cup. So Forest weren't entirely without hope, especially with Bedford absent owing to a leg injury. Then again, Derby were league leaders.

Pouring rain accompanied Derby kicking off towards the Osmaston End and, having started his career at Derby before switching to the Reds, Randolph Galloway of Forest was cheered by home fans – a gesture that would dumbfound many modern supporters of either club. Lionel Murphy's first-half drive left Langford floundering on 20 minutes to give Derby the lead before John Leslie Hart made it two early in the second half. That's how the game ended. The consensus was that the main difference between the two teams was a quality centre-forward able to find the net. Derby had Bedford and Murphy, while Forest's top scorer that season was Sidney Gibson with an underwhelming 11 goals. 'Our Nottingham neighbours are a team abounding in energy, much of which is misdirected in absence of skill and a good deal dangerous to wind and limb,' opined the *Derby Daily Telegraph*.

Owing to a run of five consecutive wins towards the end of the season and propelled by Bedford's goals – 28 for the campaign – Derby achieved promotion just behind The Wednesday and would challenge the mighty Huddersfield Town, themselves making light of Herbert Chapman's defection to Arsenal, in the top division the following season. This was the first of five years in which Bedford would be Derby's top scorer, thus ensuring a stable period for the club as they finished outside the top seven only twice between then and the Second World War.

As for Forest, a much-needed run of five consecutive wins towards the end of the season – mirroring Derby's – steered them clear of any relegation threat and a period of mid-to-lower-table finishes in the Second Division beckoned. There would be no league meetings between the clubs until well after the Second World War – 1954 to be precise – as Derby established themselves as a force in the First Division, while Forest garnered an unwanted reputation as second-tier strugglers.

Despite Derby's joy at promotion, both counties, being reliant on the coal mines for employment, were hugely impacted by the General Strike between 4 and 12 May 1926. Called by the General Council of the Trades Union Congress, the aim of the strike was to force the Conservative government into action to prevent wage reductions and worsening conditions for 1.2 million coal miners. Riots in Nottingham were reported, yet by October hardship forced men back to the mines and by November most were back at work. Also in May, Wollaton Park was opened to the public, a future setting for Wayne Manor in the *Batman* film of 2012 and of numerous and arduous pre-season training runs for Nottingham Forest players at the behest of their future manager, Brian Clough.

However, the FA Cup pitted the clubs against each other in 1928 and, given the clubs' contrasting trajectories and lack of regular meetings, the ties were as eagerly anticipated as D.H. Lawrence's *Lady Chatterley's Lover*, which was published privately the same year. So shocking was the abundance of sex and swearing in the book that it would not be openly published in the UK until 1960.

Come 28 January and the fourth round of the FA Cup, Derby were enjoying an excellent season in the top flight. Bedford was scoring freely and his side enjoyed a nine-game unbeaten streak from December to mid-January, the only fly in the ointment being a 4-0 reverse against Leicester the week before they would meet Forest at the Baseball Ground in the cup. In fairness, Leicester, too, were going well and would end up in third place. Forest's form was inconsistent and although they were perfectly capable of scoring goals – they had scored at least four times in six games already that season – they were also a bit leaky at the back.

Despite the fanfare and excitement, torrential rain fell from 10am on the day of the tie, resulting in two special trains from Nottingham being cancelled. Pools of water formed an hour before kick-off and the main stand at the Baseball Ground was waterlogged. Volunteers swept the rainfall off the pitch in order to make the surface playable, but it was a losing battle. In farcical conditions, the game ended goalless.

So, it was back to the City Ground on the following Wednesday for a replay which turned out to be rather eventful. The excitement started early on in the day as the desire among the Forest-supporting public to see this game remained strong. The Taylor Bros. iron foundry at Sandiacre had acquiesced to its workers' request to start at 4am, so they could have the afternoon off and see the game. It seemed that many other factories closed early too, if the throng making its way down Carrington and Arkwright Street was anything to go by. The number of overloaded cars and motorcycles seemed like scenes out of the great American migration from the dust bowl to California, so weighed down by their human cargo were the various forms of transport.

Derby fans too had gorged on a huge slice of FA Cup cake. 'Matters began to liven up as the special excursion trains carrying their human freight from Derby and the surrounding district arrived,' reported the *Nottingham Evening Post*, 'and there were animated scenes at the Victoria and Midland stations as the hordes of enthusiasts poured through the barriers en route for the City Ground. Favours of black and white, the Derby colours, were in evidence varying from the common or garden rosette to the coloured umbrellas sported by a few of the more riotous spirits, and the row that their wearers made would not have disgraced a cup final.'

Before the game could kick off, flood water was pumped away from the foot of the terraces by the fire brigade, so heavy was the rainfall during the day, just like it had been the previous Saturday. The attendance swelled to 35,625, generating receipts of £2,719, a new record for the City Ground, surpassing the game against Sheffield United in 1899. Not unusually for such a fixture, the gates closed before kick-off, locking hundreds outside. At some stage a mob forced the gates open, resulting in hundreds of people gaining entry, meaning that the touchline was ringed with fans standing around the edge of the pitch, watched carefully by mounted police.

Given the frenzied atmosphere, the game was a pulsating affair with chances at both tends, yet it remained goalless after 90 minutes. Extra time beckoned. Forest broke the deadlock a minute into the additional period when Harold Wadsworth crossed and the ball dropped at the feet of Gibson who lashed into the roof of the net from close range.

Cyril Stocks, joint top scorer alongside Burton that season, added another just to make sure as Forest claimed their first win over Derby for seven years. They progressed past Cardiff City – the cup-holders – in round five before being comfortably beaten 3-0 by Sheffield United. Blackburn Rovers beat Huddersfield in the final that year, while Dixie Dean scored an incredible 60 goals for Everton as they took the league title.

For Forest, an unexpected victory against Derby – although no doubt sweet – was only a brief glimmer of escape from a period of predominantly lower-half Second Division finishes until war once again intervened. A month later, the author Alan Sillitoe was born in Nottingham. He would go on to capture working-class life in Nottingham evocatively in his writing, most notably in his depiction of Raleigh factory worker Arthur Seaton in *Saturday Night and Sunday Morning*. In April, the last execution in Nottingham took place at the New County Gaol (Bagthorpe Prison). George Frederick Hayward was hanged for the murder of Derbyshire woman Amy Collinson at the New Inn pub in Little Hayfield in the Peak District.

Stan Hardy's reign as manager was short-lived as he could lift Forest no higher than mid-table between 1929 and 1931. After Hardy, it was Noel Watson's turn to see if he could light a Forest fire and, although an encouraging fifth-placed finish was achieved in 1932/33, the story remained the same as the club loitered around the lower reaches of the Second Division.

As for Derby, they shook off the cup upset and maintained their upwards trajectory by finishing only twice below seventh place in the top division until 1939, including two second-placed finishes in 1929/30 and 1935/36 and, slightly depressingly, yet another FA Cup semi-final defeat in 1933, this time to Manchester City at Huddersfield's Leeds Road stadium. In between these successful campaigns, Jack Bowers established himself as an elite scorer of goals by breaking the great Steve Bloomer's single-season club record with 39 in 1930/31. He would beat that two seasons later by scoring 43 goals in all games – a record that still stands today. Not to be outdone in the record-setting department, the following season Jack Nicholas played in what would be the first in a run of 328 out of 331 league games up to the end of 1938/39. In among this purple patch for Derby, Sally Clough gave birth to a baby boy at 11 Valley Road in Grove Hill, Middlesbrough on Thursday, 21 March 1935. She and husband Joe decided to call the child Brian.

Games between Forest and Derby remained a distant possibility unless they were drawn together in the cup, which they serendipitously were for the fourth round in 1936, just a week after the death of King George V on 25 January. His passing meant Edward VIII ascended to the throne, but sat for less than a year as on 11 December 1936, he explained his decision to abdicate in a radio broadcast and departed for Austria the following day.

As always, and just like in 1928, a cup tie stimulated a frenzied atmosphere, especially as it had been eight years since the two clubs last met. The Baseball Ground gates closed at 2.15pm, leaving thousands turned away. Prior to kick-off, both sets of supporters sang 'Abide with Me', while the two teams solemnly stood facing each other in honour of King George V.

Forest were without their captain, Tom Graham, owing to a pulled thigh muscle in the defeat at Swansea the previous week, and although Derby's form was stuttering after a blistering start to the season they were the clear favourites as they were eyeing up another top-seven finish, while Forest were in their default position for this period – languishing towards the bottom of the Second Division. It came as little surprise when David Halford put Derby ahead after 17 minutes in front of 37,830 – at the time a record attendance at the Baseball Ground – and Bowers made the tie safe in the second half.

Derby reached the quarter-finals before crashing out to Fulham, but their finest achievement was coming second to Sunderland in the top division, matching their second-placed finish in 1930, their highest position between the wars, perhaps aided by Steve Bloomer returning as a general assistant around the club. As successful as Derby were, Forest were drowning in mediocrity as they slipped to five consecutive bottom-five finishes from then until football ceased again for war. Not even a visit to Nottingham's University College by Professor Albert Einstein in June 1930 could inspire the team. Fitting with Forest's fortunes, Einstein was delayed by an hour and a half after insisting on visiting Isaac Newton's house and birthplace at Woolsthorpe before calmly and serenely delivering a lecture on relativity, using a blackboard and chalk to aid his explanations.

Events were moving fast, illustrated by Derby goalkeeper Jack Kirby refusing to give the Nazi salute during an end-of-season tour to Germany in May 1934, after the British Foreign Office had advised against any political controversy. Yet for the time being, life and Derby's status as railway central rumbled on and, in 1936, a steam locomotive named Derby County was built and ran passenger services down the east coast into London.

On 1 September 1939, Germany invaded Poland, so two days later France and Britain declared war. The Racecourse, having staged its final race meeting in August, was taken over for military use by the Royal Artillery and anti-aircraft guns were positioned there (after the war, the town council confirmed that racing would not be resumed in Derby, as it would 'bring the wrong sort of people into the town'). Council workers at the Guildhall in Derby Market Place moved the town's municipal archives deep underground and Derby-born artist Ernest Townsend was commissioned to create a design for the roof of the Rolls-Royce factory, so it would appear to be like an ordinary village rather than the centre for aircraft engines. The rumours of war were reality. Even so, despite tensions, the Stuttgart Police Boxing Club visited Nottingham in October, an occasion marked by a Union Jack and a Nazi swastika being flown from the now demolished County Hotel, which may be the only time the two flags have flown together in Britain.

The 1938/39 season would be the final one until hostilities ceased. When football resumed in 1919 after the First World War, Derby were in the First Division, while Forest were in the lower reaches of the Second Division. With war once again looming, the only difference was that Derby were established as a serial top-seven club, rather than making up the numbers. As for Forest, Harold Wightman's three-year reign was going nowhere fast. A change was needed if they were to improve upon a meagre three seasons in the top division since the war, in which they couldn't muster up anything better than third from bottom. Perhaps the appointment of Billy Walker as manager in March 1939 could have been the catalyst for a change in fortunes, but it was far too early to say. Perhaps also the opening of Nottingham Ice Centre on 10 April might have one day inspired a couple of youngsters to take up ice skating and put Nottingham on the global sporting map, but again, it was far too early to tell at this stage.

And once more, football ground to a halt as the sounds of leather on leather, balls hitting nets and cheering crowds were drowned out by the ominous rolls of distant thunder.

The town, as Derby was then, was spared much of the horrendous bombing that affected many large cities, such as London, Coventry, Swansea and Portsmouth, yet it did suffer particularly badly on the night of 15 January 1941. Air raids took the lives of 75 people across the county and injured 300 others, while in Derby alone the death toll was 45 and between 3,000 and 4,000 homes were destroyed or damaged. The Midland Station was badly damaged and the Baseball Ground, specifically the Osmaston End, took a battering too. Nottingham's only major air raid in World War Two took place on 8 May 1941 as 159 people were recorded as killed with 274 injured, while many serious fires resulted in a number of damaged and destroyed buildings. Once again, football became an irrelevance.

5

The see-saw years: 1945–1973

FOOTBALL ALWAYS finds a way and had continued in some form during the war. Given the regional nature of the war leagues, Forest and Derby were able to maintain their rivalry on the pitch. Games were patchy affairs, though, with teams fielded mostly according to who was available, leading to some odd results. But such fixtures served to provide some much-needed escapism. Perhaps the most notable came in August 1944, especially for Derby-born Fred Tapping, who scored a hat-trick against Forest in a 5-0 win at the Baseball Ground.

To commemorate the formal acceptance by the Allies of Germany's unconditional surrender of its armed forces in World War Two, Victory in Europe Day, Forest visited Derby for a celebration friendly fixture at 3pm on 8 May 1945. It was a sporting double header of sorts as, in the evening, the City Ground would host the Notts Amateur League Division Two championship decider between Newton and Gedling Colliery.

The *Derby Daily Telegraph* reported that the 'opportunity may be taken to try out some new players. Among these are B. Mozley (Shelton United).' The game ended 1-1 and Bert

Mozley went on to make 297 appearances for the Rams over the next ten years.

On the same day, the press reported on how the forthcoming season would be organised. After much debate, competitive football resumed, with the 44 clubs in the top two divisions of 1938/39 maintained and split into a north and south league, without relegation and promotion from the previous peacetime season. Forest and Derby found themselves in the same league – the Football League South, despite Derby being in the First Division and Forest in the second tier before war broke out.

Anticipation was high for the first meeting between the two clubs, at the City Ground on 6 October in 1945, since the outstanding Derby team of 1935/36 dumped Forest out of the FA Cup on their way to the quarter-finals. A bumper crowd was expected, including the usual large away contingent, not just because of the nature of the occasion but also in expectation of and excitement at, seeing Derby's guest from Manchester City, the Irish international striker Peter Doherty, play. He had played in the VE Day game at the Baseball Ground back in May. This was the first time the City Ground had housed a 30,000 crowd since an evening game against Aston Villa on 2 September 1936.

Those keen to see Doherty play were not disappointed as he opened the scoring in the 18th minute, yet it was Forest who were the better side, at least in the first half. Their efforts were rewarded just before half-time when Thomas North equalised. Derby were much the better team in the second half but couldn't find a way past the Forest defence. The match more than lived up to the hype and excitement that preceded it, the *Derby Daily Telegraph* calling it 'a spectacular game to watch with rarely a dull moment', while the *Nottingham Evening Post* declared, 'The game certainly kept the crowd of 30,130 on tiptoes of expectation throughout.'

It would be deeply insensitive to suggest that the horrors of war could be wiped away by a game of football. After all, this fixture took place just two months after the United States detonated two nuclear weapons over the Japanese cities of Hiroshima and Nagasaki, thus bringing about the end of World War Two, and at this game a collection was made within the ground for the Notts. Comforts Fund, a charity set up to provide Christmas relief for Nottinghamshire soldiers or POWs serving abroad, raising £61.

Yet football has a habit of reasserting a sense of normality – it is a reassuring presence in the lives of so many and offers a sea of calm amid an often confusing world. The *Nottingham Journal* called the game 'as exciting and thrilling as meetings between these old rivals usually are' and with an East Midlands derby under everyone's belts, it was seen that life would go on. As Derby player, manager and legend Tim Ward later explained, 'The war had just finished, you must realise, and we were glad to be back alive. We were going to enjoy life to the full and we did that. And of course, football reflected this. People went out to enjoy themselves. They went out to watch football or they played football. Saturday couldn't come around quick enough for us.'

The prediction that 'on current form, few sides will take more than a point from Forest at home' proved to be mere wishful thinking on the part of the *Nottingham Journal* as the Reds would win only six more games at home that season and finish a lowly 15th.

The two teams met again a week later, this time at the Baseball Ground, for the return fixture. A crowd of 22,000 turned up to see Billy Price, guesting for Derby while registered with Huddersfield Town, score a hat-trick as Doherty and Douglas 'Dally' Duncan caused the Forest defence problems all afternoon. It would have been more but for Lawrence Platts in the Forest goal. Price completed his scoring midway through the second half, at which point Forest rallied, but despite Thomas Johnston's two goals they couldn't overhaul the deficit and lost 3-2.

Derby went on to post an impressive fourth-placed finish yet, much more significantly they finally won the FA Cup that season, burying the ghosts of numerous semi-final losses, and heavy cup final scorelines including that record 6-0 against Bury, and the 1898 defeat to Forest.

While players guesting for other clubs as normality fully returned was standard for league games, clubs were not allowed to use guests for the final, so Ted Magner, successor to George Jobey throughout the war campaigns, had to move quickly in making the signatures of Doherty and Raich Carter permanent. It was a slice of good fortune that both happened to be stationed at nearby Loughborough during the war. Carter had enjoyed a superb career with Sunderland, captaining them to the league title in 1936, but in 1945 he found himself transfer-listed by his boyhood club after they failed to see eye to eye on his request for a ten-year contract. Derby made his signing permanent for £6,000 minutes before the FA Cup transfer deadline on 2 December 1945.

All ties were played over two legs for the 1945/46 competition, apart from the semi-final and final, and with

Derby having eased their way past Luton Town 9-0 on aggregate in the third round, Magner left to take the reins at Metz in France, allowing Stuart McMillan to take charge. Forest lost to Third Division Watford in the first round in a replay after the sides couldn't be separated over the two legs. West Bromwich Albion and Brighton and Hove Albion were comfortably dispatched by Derby before a dramatic 5-4 aggregate win against Aston Villa at the quarter-final stage, the first leg played out in front of 76,500 people at Villa Park which Derby won 4-3. Birmingham City held the Rams to a 1-1 draw in the semi-final, but in the replay at Maine Road, Derby romped to a 4-0 win in front of a typically enormous postwar crowd of 80,407.

Finding themselves in their third FA Cup Final, alongside their seven unsuccessful semi-finals and still without their name on the silver pot, drastic action was required. The legend of the gypsy curse, allegedly placed on the club by a gypsy community that was forcibly evicted to make way for the Baseball Ground, raised its head and it was decided that no chances would be taken. Club captain Jack Nicholas crossed a gypsy's palm with silver, albeit for the benefit of the press, in the hope of breaking the curse.

With the hoodoo apparently dispelled, all that stood between Derby and their first cup success was Charlton Athletic. In front of a huge crowd of 98,000 at Wembley Stadium, it seemed like extra time would be required until the 85th minute and a dramatic intervention. Dally Duncan's shot was deflected into his own net by Charlton defender Bert Turner, and it seemed like an own goal would decide the game. Yet bizarrely, a minute later, Turner hammered a free kick goalwards and his shot was deflected into the net for a most improbable equaliser. There was still time for more drama before extra time. Derby's Jack Stamps, wounded at Dunkirk and told he would never play football again, unleashed a shot that seemed bound for the net until, incredibly, the ball burst. With rubber being a rare commodity and an increasing amount of cheaper imports being used, this wasn't such an unusual occurrence, but then again this was a much-anticipated FA Cup Final. In extra time, Derby romped home with goals from Doherty and two from Stamps to make it 4-1. *Children's Hour* was delayed on the BBC in order to cover extra time.

One wonders what the reaction might be today among rival supporters should either club be fortunate enough to reach a final, let alone lift a much-coveted trophy. It is reasonable to suspect that the reaction would not be as magnanimous as that of the *Nottingham Journal*, which declared, 'All lovers of sport will congratulate Derby County most heartily on winning the FA Cup after their fourth appearance in the final. It was a real Derby day, in truth a more genuine people's festival than that which takes place at Epsom. The better side won on the day's play in a game fought in the most genuine spirit of effort and rivalry without any untoward incident. In every respect it was a day in a great tradition and Derby County is a club with as fine a tradition and a record as the best. A club that produced Steve Bloomer has a right to figure in the classic chronicle of Cup winners.'

Having passed away on 16 April 1938, Bloomer didn't get to see his beloved club lift the cup, but he remains today, in the words of the official club anthem, 'Steve Bloomer's watching, helping the fight, guiding our heroes, in the black and white.' The FA Cup was paraded around the streets of

Derby by the players on the back of a lorry underneath a banner proclaiming, 'Bravo Boys!'

Playing for Charlton that day was Bert 'Sailor' Brown, who impressed Billy Walker so much that a month later, the Forest manager signed the 30-year-old as he set about building a team. It would get worse before it got better for Forest under Walker, but with time and patience he would steer Forest on an upwards curve from 1955 to 1959. For Derby, cup success was not quite the long-term spur to greater things that they hoped it might be. Yet the immediate future was one of Forest decline and Derby success, at least until the see-saw flipped.

1947-1950
Fossil fuels replace steam

Attendances continued to surge as the appetite for football and normality after the war remained huge. For the visit of Forest to Newcastle, a crowd of 56,827 turned up at St James' Park for the Second Division fixture. That figure was topped when Forest travelled to Manchester United for an FA Cup fourth-round tie when 58,641 clicked through the turnstiles. Surprisingly, Forest beat their hosts, managed by Matt Busby, 2-0. The confidence of their FA Cup win encouraged Derby to break the British transfer record for Scottish winger Billy Steel, who signed from Morton for £15,000. Since Doherty was seen to be an unsettling influence in the dressing room, he was moved on to Huddersfield Town after only 15 appearances. It was anticipated that Scotsman Steel would replace him.

In 1947, the first mainline diesel locomotives, numbers 10000 and 10001, were built by LMS Derby Works.

Stoking a fire to produce steam to power an engine seemed increasingly of another time and inefficient in the face of new technology. The era of steam was coming to an end as fossil fuels would now be king. If this was some kind of portent for the end of an era in Derby, nobody bothered to tell the football club, at least not yet anyway, as they finished fourth in the First Division, and the signing of Steel was looking like money very well spent. They also reached the semi-final stage of the FA Cup but lost out to Manchester United at Hillsborough. Maybe the gypsy curse wasn't quite fully erased.

In stark contrast, Forest were relegated to the Third Division South. A run of eight games without a win in February and March did more damage than five wins in seven to finish the campaign and they would slug it out with Notts County the following season in the third tier for the first time in their history. Yet two key signings were made around this time: Wally Ardron joined from Rotherham United, who would go on to become Forest's top scorer for the next four seasons (and remains the club's third highest top scorer to this day), and a year earlier, Jack Burkitt, who would become club captain and talisman under Billy Walker, was signed from Darlington.

Over at Derby, the departure of Raich Carter was softened by the signing of Johnny Morris from Manchester United, the second time in quick succession that the Rams had broken the British transfer record. He helped Derby to go one better than the previous season in the top tier as they finished third, below United on goal average and five points adrift of champions Portsmouth. Forest were finding their feet and finished fourth, a promising first season in the Third Division South but an achievement somewhat belittled by city rivals Notts County winning the title.

By the end of the 1949/50 season, and at the second time of asking, Forest were back in the second tier as they followed in Notts County's slipstream and won the title. Ardron scored a record 36 goals to propel the Reds to promotion, while strike partner Thomas Capel bagged 24 for himself. Derby were still secure and comfortable in the First Division despite finishing mid-table after two successive top-four finishes. However, the love-in with Steel turned a little sour as he was often accused of earning a little money on the side by writing columns for newspapers and only really turning it on for high-profile fixtures, especially those in the capital. Such antics and his apparently flashy lifestyle led him to being hung on a peg in his own dressing room. He was sold to Dundee, who he helped to claim successive league titles. From then on Derby struggled, heading only one way, and it wasn't back to the higher echelons of the First Division, or cup glory. Yet neither club endured anything as traumatic as that suffered by the all-conquering Torino side when their plane, carrying the entire team, crashed into a retaining wall of the Basilica of Superga on 4 May 1949, killing all 31 people on board.

1950-1955

No reason to wreck the Forest

As the 1940s evaporated and the 1950s jumped into existence, England participated in their first World Cup in Brazil, perhaps surprising given that the competition had been up and running since 1930. England's non-participation was down to the FA declining invitations to join, perhaps borne of pragmatism in wanting to maintain the British Home Championship but also out of arrogance, as if playing fancy foreign countries at football was beneath them; after all, what could the inventors of the beautiful game possibly learn from these Johnny-come-latelies?

As it turned out, quite a lot. Having beaten Chile 2-0 in their first group game of the 1950 finals, England then faced the United States, a fixture considered so easy that the England players were laughing and joking as they made their way to the Mineirão stadium in Belo Horizonte on the day of the game. The selectors stuck with the same team that beat Chile, meaning no place for Stanley Matthews, who sat and watched from the stands. A first-half goal from Joseph Edouard Gaetjens (a Haitian who also played in a World Cup qualifier for the country of his birth) was the difference as the States inflicted a humiliating defeat on England. Matthews shared the nation's shock. 'I sat with bowed head until the players had left the field. I never thought I would live to see this,' he wrote in his autobiography, *The Stanley Matthews Story*. 'As I raised my head to look around me, I felt a pain in most of my fingers. I looked down at my hands and saw specks of blood on the palms. I had been so tense in the closing minutes of the match that I had dug my fingernails into my flesh without at the time feeling a thing.'

England lost to Spain in the final group game, and Brazil later lifted the trophy after defeating Uruguay in the final. Walter Winterbottom's men traipsed home with their tails very firmly between their legs. Unsurprisingly, no Forest players were selected to represent the national team, but Derby's inside-forward Johnny Morris could consider himself a little unlucky not to be involved after scoring on his England debut on 18 May 1949 in a 4-1 win against Norway and then adding two more in his second game four days later against France.

The post-World Cup season saw Derby maintain their resolutely solid mid-table positioning in the First Division, while for Forest Ardron and Capel continued to score freely in the Second Division after the club had wrestled free of the Third Division South following two seasons down there. Things were getting better under Walker – very slowly, but very surely. They would go on to consolidate in the Second Division, while Derby's slip was becoming a worrying slide.

By the end of the 1952/53 season, Derby found themselves relegated and the two clubs' fortunes criss-crossed as Derby entered a downward spiral, emulating that of Forest as they too were not content with one relegation and nosedived into the third tier. Forest, on the other hand, were very much on an upwards trajectory, a pattern reflected in the four games between the two sides in the two seasons they would spend together in the Second Division between 1953 and 1955, before Derby tumbled into the Third Division North.

On 7 November 1953, the two sides met at the City Ground and, just like in 1945, interest in the game was sky-high as 31,347 Forest fans squeezed in to see their team face their old rivals for the first 'proper' league meeting in 28 years (the 1945/46 season was still regionalised on resumption after the war and, as such, could be perceived as not officially a league season as we know it). Despite their troubles, Derby had started the season well, having lost only once in the opening nine games. However, the week before their visit to Nottingham, they had relinquished their unbeaten home record when losing 4-2 to Birmingham City, prompting Nottingham's *Football Post* to publish a cartoon depicting a man stuffing dynamite into the letterbox of a house marked up as N. Forest and a policeman bearing down on him with the caption, 'Ere You! Just becos your home record's been blown up there's no reason why you should want to wreck Forest's.'

In difficult conditions owing to a strong wind blowing towards the Bridgford End, Alan Moore opened the scoring for Forest in the 13th minute after a fine move down the right wing led to some pinball in the box, with the ball rebounding off both defender Keith Savin and Ray Middleton in Derby's goal before Moore struck home. That was how it remained until half-time. In the 65th minute, Thomas Capel carefully picked his place and slotted past Middleton to make it 2-0. Arthur Lemon smashed into the roof of the net to make it three before Hugh McLaren reduced the arrears and swept home for Derby, maintaining his excellent scoring record with his ninth in eight games. With two minutes remaining, Capel scored his second goal of the game and Forest's fourth, before Ray Wilkins – a namesake, not the England international of the 1970s and '80s and later a highly regarded coach and manager – gave the result a sheen of respectability by heading a second for Derby right on the final whistle.

Derby's season unravelled and, when 1954 dawned, they went 13 games without a win before the return fixture at the Baseball Ground on 10 April. This was Forest's first trip to the Baseball Ground since their 3-2 win in 1945. Prior to that, their last visit had resulted in defeat in 1936 in the FA Cup when Derby were riding high and challenging for the First Division title, while Forest moped around at the foot of the Second Division. Things were quite different this time around, significantly so for Derby. While Forest arrived looking to sustain their promotion challenge, Derby needed the points for quite different reasons as relegation to the third tier was a real threat.

Jack Burkitt's run of 103 consecutive appearances for Forest came to an end as he was ruled out with damaged ribs, while Derby would have to make do without their inspirational captain, Bert Mozley, as an injured leg did for him.

As usual in such games, thousands of away supporters made the short journey to support their team. In the opening stages, the Rams looked precisely what they were – a struggling team, reflected in Forest taking a deserved lead after 12 minutes as Ardron nodded into the corner of the net. Against the run of play and despite Forest going close, on numerous occasions to doubling their lead Derby somehow conjured an equaliser on 34 minutes when Tommy Powell guided a corner home with a well-placed header. The home side rallied and, although Forest were still the better team, they were no longer having it all their own way. However, it took the away side barely a minute into the second half to reassert their superiority as Alan Moore restored Forest's lead by neatly flicking in after hesitancy in the Derby defence. From then on, the Rams found the going tough and their frustration was evident when Colin Bell (not to be confused with the England international of the 1970s, known mainly for his career with Manchester City) raised his fist to Ardron and an ugly scene unfolded before the referee intervened and dished out a couple of cautions. There was just enough time for Ardron to commit a hefty foul and narrowly escape being sent off before the final whistle blew in front of 21,961 fans, leaving most still apprehensive about relegation yet some excited about a possible promotion.

Forest played well and were guilty only of not putting the game to bed earlier; the *Football Post* succinctly writing, 'It must be a long time since [George] Walker [in goal] had such an easy 45 minutes but yet had a goal recorded against him.'

Come the end of the season, promotion was beyond the Reds and Derby survived for another year, while Leicester City took the Second Division title. During the season, Derby installed floodlights at the Baseball Ground and trialled them in a series of friendlies, one being against East Fife on Wednesday, 24 March. Even that didn't go so well, though, as the Scottish side raced into a 3-0 lead within 25 minutes and won the game 3-1 in front of a crowd of 5,527. Derby could have used some of the pace exhibited by Roger Bannister as he ran the first sub-four-minute mile at the Iffley Road race track in Oxford on 6 May, with Derbyshire-born Tom Hulatt far exceeding expectations and coming in in third place with a time of four minute and 16 seconds.

While industry was booming in the town – Rolls-Royce had recently showcased its new engine, the Avon RA28 gas turbine, which would power a new generation of aircraft – and unemployment stood at 0.4 per cent while industrial estates were springing up everywhere, the state of the football club did not reflect this prosperous state of affairs. Derby were relegated from the Second Division in 1955 for the first time in their history. Only six years previously, they had finished in third place in the First Division. The fall was hard and fast.

The teams met at the City Ground in pouring rain on 13 November 1954. Walker was present for the first time in a while after a long absence forced upon him by illness. The inclement conditions meant that only around 10,000 spectators were there for kick-off, but this swelled to around 14,000 once the game got going. Forest were largely in command, but it took a penalty for their dominance to be translated into goals. Noel Kelly's shot was blocked by Mozley with his hand on the goal line and the Dubliner fired home the resulting penalty. Just before half-time, Kelly scored his second with a quite remarkable goal as his corner flew straight into the net, despite Thomas Wilson loitering to apply a finishing touch that remained unwarranted. Incredibly, Kelly almost claimed a quickfire hat-trick moments later, but his shot was cleared off the line. The points were sealed in the 73rd minute when a clever throw-in by Burkett put Thomas Martin clean through and he squared for Ronald Blackman to fire home and claim his first goal for the Reds. By now a crowd of 16,386 had turned up to see Forest win 3-0, just as they had the previous Saturday away at Doncaster Rovers.

By the time the two teams met again on 2 April, Derby had managed only two wins in 20 games and lay at the foot of the table. Forest hadn't fared much better but came into this game on the back of three consecutive wins. One more and they could probably count themselves out of the relegation scramble. Derby started well enough, but their enthusiasm and confidence fizzled away once Forest got their noses in front after 11 minutes in front of 18,722 at the Baseball Ground. James Barrett fired home with a right-footed shot from the edge of the area and they doubled their lead on 23 minutes when Hugh McLaren fired home after whisking the ball away from Geoff Barrowcliffe, who tried to dribble his way to safety in his own area. After half-time, Derby huffed and puffed but without much success. They did pull a goal back in the 75th minute as the rain poured down when Ray Young headed home from Ken Harrison's corner. Yet Forest weathered not only the rain but a short-lived difficult spell and finished the game on top again and were unfortunate not to add to their goal tally. On the wrong end of a 2-1 defeat, Derby looked doomed.

Having lost the previous Saturday at Ipswich Town, and now again at home to their fierce rivals, Derby found themselves in a tailspin from which they wouldn't recover as they then lost their next five games, meaning a run of seven consecutive defeats. A final-day win at home against Hull City was not enough to save them from relegation.

1955-1958
Handbag

With Derby at their lowest ebb in the Third Division North, Forest signed winger Stewart Imlach from their rivals; he had spent having spent only a year with the Rams and played against the Reds on both occasions the previous season. Derby were looking to economise and the club started to save money wherever they could, in doing so putting various players' noses out of joint, most notably the long-serving and Derby-born captain Bert Mozley, by refusing to pay him his full entitled benefit of £750 on his retirement. Newly married Imlach and his wife were expecting a house of their own in Derby as arranged by the club – this having been the case with his previous club, Bury – but they were offered only a bedroom in a shared house with team-mate Ken Oliver and his young family. This was far from ideal. When a house did become available, Derby gave it to the latest signing, Jock Buchanan, which was the last straw for Imlach's wife who then attacked the manager Jack Barker with her handbag. A transfer request was promptly slapped in, and Billy Walker brought the pacy winger to the City Ground.

On the same day that Derby drew 2-2 with Scunthorpe in the Third Division North and Forest hammered Doncaster Rovers 5-0 in the Second Division, a striker by the name of Brian Clough made his debut as a player on 17 September 1955 for Middlesbrough against Barnsley in the Second Division in a 1-1 draw. He scored his first goal in a 4-2 win against Leicester City on 8 October and, by the end of his debut season, he had notched a very respectable three goals from nine appearances.

Just when Derby felt that things couldn't get much worse, they endured a particularly low point when they lost 6-1 at home to Boston United in the second round of the FA Cup on 10 December 1955. Boston were managed by former Derby goalkeeper Ray Middleton, and his team featured six ex-Rams players. The 6-1 scoreline is still a record for a non-league club against a Football League club on their own ground. Middleton was in jubilant mood afterwards, telling the *Sunday Mirror*, 'This was no fluke. I had a hunch that Geoff Hazledine would come off against Derby's shaky defence – and his three goals proved I was right.' The other five former Derby players on the winning side were Geoff and Don Hazledine, Ray Wilkins, Dave Miller and Reg Harrison, boasting at least 400 appearances for the Rams between them. To compound the town's misery, just four months later, a fire tore through the Derby Playhouse, leaving the venue reduced to a smouldering rubble of ashes.

The next season, 1956/57, saw things get better for Derby as they won the Third Division North title, having spent just two seasons down there. The Rams would find their level in the Second Division as they finished no higher than seventh and no lower than 18th for the next 11 years. Not to be outdone in the promotion stakes, Forest deservedly went up too, from the Second Division to the First Division. They were back in the top division for the first time since 1924/25 when they tumbled back down after only three unremarkable seasons at that level. Under Walker's steady stewardship, Forest were on the verge of a very successful and memorable period in their history.

Despite Forest achieving promotion by finishing runners-up in the Second Division, a fly in the ointment came on 10 November 1956 when they lost 4-0 at home to Middlesbrough. The Boro side, managed by Bob Dennison, featured a goalkeeper by the name of Peter Taylor, while their precocious and cocksure striker Brian Clough scored his first league hat-trick.

On the morning of 10 September 1957, the Carriage and Wagon works, next to the Midland Station in Derby and one of the country's most important railway manufacturers, was wrecked by a fire. Fortunately, nobody was injured in the blaze and the *Derby Evening Telegraph* sought to reassure readers that jobs were safe, but the era of the steam engine was under serious threat due to the rise of diesel and fossil fuels.

While Derby were struggling to adapt back to life in the Second Division, Forest were having a grand old time in the First Division and going toe to toe with the very best, most notably Matt Busby's defending champions Manchester United. Imlach in particular was finding life in Nottingham much more suited to his tastes than at Derby and scored against United in a 2-1 defeat at the City Ground on 12 October in front of 47,634, on the day the new End Stand was opened. The game was a cracking one, thoroughly enjoyed by both managers. 'I'll have to cast my mind back some way to recall a game as good,' offered Busby, while Walker said, 'Give me such matches and I might forget we didn't get the points.' Five days earlier, on 7 October, Betty Torvill gave birth to daughter Jayne in Clifton, Nottingham. Betty worked as a machinist in the Lace Market area, while father George worked at the world-famous Raleigh bicycles factory. Jayne could barely be more Nottingham if she tried.

On 22 February 1958, Forest were the opposition at Old Trafford for United's first league game after the Munich air disaster. Bill Foulkes played for United, as he had done for the game at the City Ground. He was the only United player to appear in both league matches against Forest that season. Harry Gregg played in goal for the Red Devils, weeks after pulling his team-mates and friends from the burning wreckage of a plane on a freezing runway in Munich. In the programme for the game, United chairman Harold Hardman wrote, 'It is the sad duty of we who serve United to offer the bereaved our heartfelt sympathy and condolences. Here is a tragedy which will sadden us for years to come, but in this we are not alone. An unprecedented blow to British football has touched the hearts of millions and we express our deep gratitude to the many who have sent messages of sympathy and floral tributes. Wherever football is played United is mourned, but we rejoice that many of our party have been spared and wish them a speedy and complete recovery.' The game ended 1-1, with Alex Dawson scoring for the hosts and Imlach for Forest. United would indeed rise again as they won the FA Cup five years later, the league title in 1965 and the European Cup at Wembley a decade after Munich.

Derby fared reasonably well by placing 16th in their first season back in the Second Division, not a spectacular return to the league but certainly preferable to being in the third tier.

1958-1960
Elton John

The summer of 1958 saw the World Cup being contested in Sweden. Imlach, despite not being fully fit, played in Scotland's opening group game against Yugoslavia, but a kick to his knee aggravated his pre-existing injury and he spent most of the time hobbling around on the wing, this being before substitutes were allowed. The Scots finished bottom of the group, while Wales made it through to the quarter-final stage before being beaten by Brazil, thanks to a single goal from some young upstart called Pelé, whose team went on to beat the host nation 5-2 in the final. Two days before that final, on 27 July, Mavis Dean gave birth to baby Christopher in Calverton, Nottingham. Christopher's father worked as a miner. Nobody knew it yet, but the city boasted two ice-skating prodigies and an ice rink on which to practise. All that was required now was time, patience and a chance meeting.

The postwar period of prosperity was grinding to a halt by the mid-50s, meaning fewer jobs, especially for the 2,500 West Indians and 600 Asians absorbed into the community, all searching for the same thing, work. Violence erupted in the St Ann's area of Nottingham on 23 August, comprising fighting between black and white male communities. The *Manchester Evening News* reported, 'Two hundred coloured and white men fought a 90-minute battle in the streets using knives and hatchets and eight people were taken to hospital.' And the *Nottingham Evening Post* wrote, 'The whole place was like a slaughterhouse.'

It remains unclear precisely what sparked the riots, a precursor to the mass violence that followed a week later in Notting Hill, as accounts vary, with one being that a mixed-race couple were turned away from a pub on St Ann's Well Road, igniting tensions within the community. Magistrate Eric Irons played a part in addressing such issues and also played an instrumental role in getting Nottingham City Council to lift a ban on hiring black bus and transport workers. There was suspicion that this was the case in Derby, too, amid talk of black school leavers finding it difficult to get work, prompting a columnist in the *Evening Telegraph* to write, 'No firm will admit publicly ... that the colour of an apprentice's skin could affect his chances of securing an apprenticeship.'

Two months later, Alan Sillitoe released his novel, *Saturday Night and Sunday Morning*, fictionalising the drudgery of working-class life in Nottingham through the protagonist, Arthur Seaton, a worker at Raleigh, just like Jayne Torvill's father, and two years later to be portrayed on screen by Albert Finney.

Seven days later, the Carriage and Wagon works in Derby suffered another fire, while the *Evening Telegraph* reported that convictions for drunkenness were at their highest since the war. Despite the tribulations in the town, Derby County improved and rose to seventh in the table in 1958/59 and, while consolidation is never to be dismissed lightly, it was dwarfed by Forest winning the FA Cup on an eventful day at Wembley on 2 May.

The run to the final wasn't a smooth one for Forest, with the most difficult obstacle – and also the most surprising – being the one presented to them in the third round, away at amateur club Tooting and Mitcham United. Walker took one look at the frozen pitch covered with snow and told his team that the game would not go ahead, so made plans for a spot of lunch before the train back to Nottingham. However, the match was very much on and Forest found themselves 2-0 down at half-time. A huge slice of fortune in the shape of a frozen rut diverting a back-pass into the Tooting net and an odd refereeing decision to award a penalty, converted by William Gray, earned Forest a replay, which they made much lighter work of and eased through 3-0. Grimsby Town were dispatched 4-0 before the deadlock against cup-holders Birmingham City was finally broken in the second replay as Forest hit five at Leicester's Filbert Street. The Reds squeezed past Bolton in the quarter-final, meaning they would face Aston Villa at Hillsborough for a place in the final. A single goal from John Quigley meant Forest reached their first FA Cup Final at Wembley where they would face fellow First Division team Luton Town. It was a tough game to call as Forest finished in 13th, while Luton were 17th.

Cup finals were a profitable business back then. A year earlier, the maximum wage had gone up to £20 a week, although not year-round as had been hoped and expected by the players. A chance to earn a little extra money was a rare and welcome opportunity for the Forest players, who formed a pool with the intention of making the most of any commercial opportunities that came their way in the build-up to the final. This was noted by the public and lampooned in the *Daily Express* in the form of a cartoon that depicted Walker and his team in a bowler hat with a speech bubble emerging from the manager's mouth with the words, 'I'm confident my team of businessmen will remember enough to WIN', while his players stood behind him with signs draped around the rim of the hat, 'PSST TICKETS?', 'PERSONAL EXPERIENCES' and 'AUTOGRAPHS ~~GIVEN~~ SOLD'. The main accusation levelled at the players was that they were selling their allocation of tickets for outrageous profit.

After the team were presented to the Duke of Edinburgh, newly arrived back in the country after his three-month Commonwealth tour, Forest got down to the business of football under a sweltering sun as Britain was about to enjoy a scorching summer. After ten minutes, Imlach cleverly picked out the on-rushing Roy Dwight who found the net to put Forest ahead. Five minutes later, the lead was doubled when Billy Gray floated over a delightful cross for Tommy Wilson to deftly head back across the goal and into the net. Forest were flowing and confident until Dwight remained prone on the turf after an innocuous-looking challenge, and having received attention on the field he departed on a stretcher. Only half an hour gone, and Forest would have to play the rest of the final with ten men. If the name seems familiar, it's probably because Roy's father Edwin had a brother called Stanley, who had a son called Reg Dwight, better known as Elton John.

Midway through the second half, Dave Pacey pulled a goal back for Luton who naturally enough dominated play against the ten men. Despite four minutes of added time, Forest hung on to claim their first silverware since the 1898 FA Cup. Ever the organiser, Walker had made his men practise walking up the steps to collect the trophy for a week before the game. However, meeting the Queen in person was still quite the deal, so much so that Imlach collected his medal without his teeth, having removed them for the game and forgotten to collect them from the big red handkerchief in which he and his team-mates had left them for safekeeping. Stanley Matthews named Imlach man of the match.

Years later, under the ownership of Fawaz Al-Hasawi, a replica trophy was commissioned for the club to commemorate the achievement of 1959. Yet when his tenure came to an acrimonious end in May 2017, the trophy disappeared with him too. 'If this is an issue, I will bring the cup tomorrow to the club. I will give it to them for free,' he told The Athletic. 'I bought this with my own money. I am the one who put the money in the club. And I am the one who gave the authority to bring the cup. I will bring them the cup tomorrow. The cup is not an issue. It is only £23,000. I am the one who ordered it.' The cup is yet to be returned.

Derby improved on their previous season's placing in the Second Division by finishing seventh, but this would be as good as it would get for them in the league until a young manager would sweep through the Baseball Ground doors and finally elevate them back to the First Division. In what might be interpreted as a symbolic gesture reflecting Forest and Derby's contrasting fortunes, the steam locomotive called the Derby County, built in 1936 for running passenger services down the East Coast into London, was scrapped.

1960-1967
Mud, blood, and Bury

As the Swinging Sixties dawned, both clubs remained resolutely stationary as they slummed around towards the bottom end of their respective divisions. Derby, like Forest before them, suffered the indignity of a 7-1 home loss to a Middlesbrough side featuring Peter Taylor in goal and Brian Clough up front. Surprisingly, the name Clough didn't trouble the score sheet that day.

As progress at Forest under Billy Walker stalled, he stepped aside yet remained on the committee, replaced by Andy Beattie, who presided over a rather undistinguished and short-lived reign as he couldn't rouse the team from their lower-table slumber.

While Eric Irons was appointed as the United Kingdom's first black magistrate in May 1962, the year was substantially less successful for Clough. On Boxing Day, his Sunderland team faced Bury at Roker Park, with both teams in the hunt for promotion. In the 26th minute, Clough collided with Bury goalkeeper Chris Harker on a muddy and frozen pitch, and was carried off on a stretcher. Bury centre-half Bob Stokoe urged Clough to get up and told the referee that he was feigning injury. The official wasn't convinced. With blood streaming down his face and in excruciating pain, Clough was laid on a plinth in the dressing room as the blood seeped through the white sheet. The cruciate ligament was badly torn. Bury beat their hosts 1-0 but it was the sickening collision that would ultimately cause Clough's playing career irreparable damage, just two weeks after scoring his 250th career goal against Huddersfield Town at Leeds Road, the fastest player to achieve this target.

Although Forest didn't play on Boxing Day, they were enduring a seven-game losing streak and had earlier that season suffered the indignity of a 9-2 home defeat at the hands of Tottenham Hotspur, who would finish runners-up, on a day when Jimmy Greaves helped himself to four goals. It could have been more, too, were it not for the heroics of Peter Grummitt in the Forest goal. 'In the last 15 minutes,' Jimmy Greaves wrote in *Greavsie; The Autobiography*, 'only some terrific goalkeeping from Peter Grummitt prevented us reaching double figures. In that final period Peter twice denied me and made a spectacular one-handed save from a stinging shot from Ron Henry.'

It was a chastening experience indeed for this Forest team. Nonetheless, the Beatles brought some cheer to Nottingham by playing at the Elizabeth Ballroom at the top of the Co-op House on Upper Parliament Street on Thursday, 7 March 1963 and, just two months later, Muhammad Ali (at the time, Cassius Clay) was in town to watch the British middleweight title bout between champion George Aldridge and Michael Leahy at the Ice Stadium on 28 May. Leahy landed a knockout blow in under two minutes, prompting Clay, Randy Turpin and Sugar Ray Robinson to enter the ring and celebrate with the new champion.

Derby were lumbering around in 18th spot in the Second Division, going nowhere fast, not dissimilar to its railway industry as Richard Beeching's report, The Reshaping of British Railways, was published, in which he identified 2,363 stations and 5,000 miles of railway line for closure, 55 per cent of stations and 30 per cent of route miles, with a view to reducing large losses and stimulating a period of competition from road transport. Within a year, Derby Friargate Station would close to passengers, meaning redundancies and an increasingly uncertain future for workers and families who depended on the railways for a living. As if to compound Derby's concerns and misery, the Assembly Rooms suffered severe fire damage in February, as did the Drill Hall in Becket Street a few months later.

At the close of the 1962/63 season, Johnny Carey replaced Andy Beattie and Ken Smales took charge of the committee at Forest. Money was spent on Terry Hennessey, Alan Hinton, Joe Baker and in came Ian Storey-Moore. The foundations were in place for an exciting team to flourish.

And at only 27 years old, Clough was forced to retire from playing the sport at which he excelled. Nonetheless, that desire to succeed burned just as fiercely within him as it ever had. He would just have to channel his energy into doing something different to scoring goals at a ridiculous rate. His time would come.

The mid-1960s truly were a time of change. It didn't take long for Clough to find something to pour his boundless energy into as he took charge at Hartlepools United in October 1965 and brought along Peter Taylor to assist him (it would be another two years before the 's' and United were dropped from the name, although United eventually returned). Clough got the town onboard and garnered their support by visiting pubs and clubs to raise funds for the club and lay the foundations for one of the most successful eras in Pools' history. Six months later, on 19 March 1966, his wife Barbara gave birth to a young son called Nigel.

A couple of months down the line, on 16 May, Bob Dylan swung by Nottingham on his way from Leicester to Sheffield on his notorious 'traitor' tour, in which he performed the first half of each show alone and acoustically before picking up his electric guitar and rocking out, or according to some, selling out his folk credentials. He swung by the castle and posed for a photograph outside a bookies on Castle Boulevard. On 21 May, the final day of the season, John McGovern made his league debut for Hartlepools in a 1-1 draw against Bradford City, at the age of 16 years and 205 days – a club record.

The last through service from Nottingham to London passed by Nottingham's Victoria Station on 3 September 1966. A year later, the station was demolished and all that remains now is the clock tower, which is surrounded by a shopping centre. Steam was well and truly extinct, overtaken in the name of progress. Despite that, Forest were tearing it up and coming as close to a league title as they ever had in their history. In the 1966/67 season, the Reds finished runners-up by just four points, second only to Manchester United who boasted Bobby Charlton, George Best, Denis Law and Nobby Stiles. They also reached the semi-finals of the FA Cup, but lost out to Tottenham. It was the glory days of Ian Storey-Moore, Joe Baker, John Barnwell and Frank Wignall in their pomp, with Storey-Moore being a particular favourite of a young Scot by the name of John Robertson.

While Forest were riding high, Derby endured some underwhelming seasons in the Second Division and chairman Sam Longson dispensed with the services of manager Tim Ward. His attention was caught by the achievements of Clough as Hartlepools finished eighth in the Fourth Division, an improvement on 18th the previous season.

Like in Nottingham after the closure of its Victoria Station, another nail in the glorious era of rail transport was hammered home as Derby's trolley bus system, running since 1932, was closed, replaced by diesel-powered buses. The 1960s well and truly landed in Derby when concern was expressed in the *Evening Telegraph* about drug-related crime. Mention of Indian hemp and reefers came from a columnist with the moniker Albert Street, who asked, 'What is the truth about drug-taking in Derby and Derbyshire?' If the youth of Derby were indeed looking to experience a giddy high, they needn't wait too much longer as Brian Clough was coming to town. He was appointed in May 1967 and Derby County would never be the same again.

6

The pendulum swings this way: 1967–1973

DERBY COUNTY'S appointment of Brian Clough and his assistant Peter Taylor was a gamble. Hartlepools had hardly set the world alight. Yet in typical, brash Clough fashion, he removed the pictures of the 1946 FA Cup win from the walls and sacked Sammy Crooks as chief scout, allowing Taylor to apply his expertise. Ian Buxton was sold to Luton Town as his desire to keep playing cricket for Derbyshire in the summer and into the start of the football season clashed with Clough's ideas about being a professional footballer and the dedication required. In came John O'Hare, Roy McFarland, Alan Hinton and, later on, Willie Carlin, John McGovern and Terry Hennessey. The trade routes between Forest and Derby widened in this period as Hinton and Hennessey were signed from the City Ground, while O'Hare and McGovern would eventually follow Clough to the east. Also, Dave Mackay somehow found himself being the manager of first Forest, then Derby, paving the way for Clough, Billy Davies and Steve McClaren. Clough's arrival was more like a whirlwind of transformation than a gentle wind of change.

The pendulum swings this way: 1967–1973

An improved crowd of 19,412 saw Derby beat their 1946 FA Cup Final rivals Charlton Athletic 3-2 on the opening day of the 1967/68 season. However, that initial whirlwind reduced to a slow-moving gust as Derby finished an underwhelming 18th in the league, a position lower than the previous season. They did, though, make it through to the semi-finals of the League Cup, losing to Don Revie's Leeds United 4-2 over two legs, something that particularly rankled with Clough as, eerily, both were born just a short walk away from one another, in the shadow of Middlesbrough's Ayresome Park.

The following season, just like at Hartlepools, Clough not only energised the town but the whole area too. He espoused the virtues of starting from the bottom and learning the trade. 'I used to go round the working men's clubs and the pubs virtually begging,' he wrote in the *Sun Soccer Annual* in 1972. 'We had to appeal for cash to keep the club going. And we succeeded. I spent one afternoon unloading corrugated metal from a lorry and helping put a new roof on the stand.' Clough's knack for revitalising everyone around him by rolling his sleeves up and getting busy rubbed off as Derby romped to the title seven points clear and lost only five games. The season was crowned in front of 31,000 fans at the Baseball Ground with a 5-0 win against Bristol City. While Rolls-Royce won the contract to produce RB211 engines for aeroplane manufacturer Lockheed for its 1011 Tri-jet airliners, generating around £98m of business, Derby had lift-off under Brian Clough.

Over at Forest, the First Division party was slowly drawing to a close. On the opening day of the season, 24 August, while Derby were kicking off their title-winning campaign, a fire broke out in the main stand just before half-time. The teams were heading off towards the tunnel with the game at 1-1, in front of a 30,000 crowd, when smoke began to pour from the stand and people evacuated their seats. *Football Post* reported, 'Terry Hennessey, the Forest captain, battered down a door to make an escape route.' Low water pressure hampered the fire brigade's hoses in tackling the blaze, not helped either by the large crowds leaving the ground and restricting the efforts to get enough lines going. It is a minor miracle that no lives were lost that day. Important records were destroyed in the fire and Forest then played six games at Meadow Lane, failing to win any of them, before returning to the City Ground. Johnny Carey lost his job in December and Matt Gillies was appointed as his replacement but couldn't halt a slide towards 18th place, just two seasons after giving champions Manchester United a real run for their money.

While Forest and Derby prepared to resume their bickering on the pitch for the first time in 15 years, there was a brief moment of unity among some supporters. On 2 May 1969, Enoch Powell appeared at the Gold Mine bingo hall in Chaddesden, Derby. A year earlier, he had delivered his 'Rivers of Blood' speech in Birmingham, a criticism of mass immigration, especially Commonwealth immigration, to the United Kingdom. His appearance in Chaddesden was met with hostile demonstrations as members of the Indian Workers' Association from Derby and Nottingham were joined 'by Communist Party members,' according to the *Evening Telegraph*.

As the Swinging Sixties drew to a close and Neil Armstrong and Buzz Aldrin walked on the Moon, the only game between the two clubs in this memorable decade took place. Forest were struggling and without a win in 12, while Derby had enjoyed a terrific start to their first season back in the First Division since 1953 after their title win and promotion. They were undefeated in their opening 13 matches, including a run of eight straight wins, the most notable being a 5-0 hammering of a glittering Tottenham Hotspur side in front of a Baseball Ground record crowd of 41,826. In his book, *From Bo'Ness to the Bernabeu*, John McGovern recalled how his 'first reaction at the final whistle was to run over and shake hands with Jimmy Greaves. Jimmy has been one of my boyhood heroes, and I kept a scrapbook of him, which I still have today, so after shaking his hand I refused to wash mine in the bath afterwards. I went out for a celebration drink that night with the dirtiest hand in Derby.' Derby and McGovern were clearly living the dream.

Yet November brought a patchy period, and they went into the 29 November home meeting with Forest in barely much better form than their rivals after two straight defeats. In the matchday programme for Forest's last home game before the trip to Derby, it was noted, 'Here, at last, is the opportunity for the two clubs to meet again in the First Division; an event that hasn't happened for many a long year.' Indeed, the last occasion that the two clubs met in the top tier was in April 1906, with the last First Division fixture at the Baseball Ground being on Boxing Day 1905. *Forest Review* warned that around 8,000 Reds would be travelling to Derby for the all-ticket game.

The lead column in the Derby programme was penned by George Edwards, sports editor at the *Derby Evening Telegraph*, who was excited about the two teams meeting again, 'Some games need building up into something special – others don't. And today's game certainly falls into the latter category, for the mere announcement "Derby County meet Nottingham Forest in a First Division game" is sufficient to pack the Baseball Ground.' He was also conscious that the return of the fixture might mean the return of violence. 'Unless the match is drawn then some fans will have to be disappointed and one only hopes that they keep their heads. Trouble afterwards will not do the reputation of either club much good,' he wrote. 'Some say that rough play on the pitch incites fans to violence, in which case one also hopes things do not get too violent out there on the grass. Yet nothing is more certain that than there will be plenty of needle in today's game.'

There was indeed. With Derby in sixth and Forest seventh from bottom, it was a typically frenetic and sometimes ill-tempered game which featured most incidents one would expect from this derby. The home crowd called for Ronnie Rees to be sent off after he laid a clumsy challenge on O'Hare by the corner flag, Sammy Chapman required treatment as he crashed into a perimeter fence, wrapped tightly around the pitch, and McFarland was warned for kicking Ian Storey-Moore – and all this in the first quarter of the game. On 27 minutes, Storey-Moore headed home direct from a corner into the Osmaston End goal, eliciting pockets of celebrations from visitors in among the home crowd. Tempers continued to simmer as Henry Newton brought down McGovern, sparking a melee as both captains tried to calm their players down.

This was McGovern's first experience of an East Midlands derby. 'In those days the game was more physical,' he explained. 'If somebody passes you the ball, you'd better know where it's going before it comes to you, or you found yourself on your backside.' Motivating the players was not a problem when it came to such games. 'It's the only week of the season where a manager needs to take the week off,' said McGovern.

Midway through the second half, Storey-Moore's shot from the edge of the area was blocked at source, but it fell kindly for Barry Lyons to pounce and make it 2-0. In the Popular Side, Forest fans waved their scarves and chanted 'easy, easy' and although it wasn't quite *that* easy, Forest were well worth the win. 'REDS TAME THE CLOUGH BOYS!' roared the *Football Post* headline. Perhaps more remarkable was that it was Forest's first away win in a campaign in which they won only twice away from home, the other being on their very next trip, to Southampton. Hennessey and Storey-Moore excelled for Forest and it was reputed that Clough coveted the Welshman for his own team. He would eventually get his man and also very nearly got Storey-Moore too.

New handling arrangements were brought in to accommodate the thousands of Forest fans who travelled to the game in the shape of local volunteers, or 'sheriffs', who helped them settle into their places. Despite this, four arrests were made before the game and five fans were stretchered away by the St John Ambulance team. *Football Post* reported, 'The St John's men were so busy that a red-and-white scarfed Forest supporter had to take the stretcher ends when his fair-haired girlfriend was carried off with an ankle injury.'

That wasn't all. 'The scenes outside after the match were very ugly indeed,' wrote Chris Broughton in *Forest*

Ever Forest in 2020. 'Hundreds of rival supporters fought running battles with one another throughout the streets leading from the ground to the railway station. The sound of breaking glass, the roar of rampaging youths, and the wail of police sirens could be heard coming from every direction, as bottles, bricks and all manner of missiles were hurled from one side of the road to the other.' The vitriol from the stands was real. With the corner of the away end so close to the home section, little stood between the constant baiting, taunting and arrangements to meet outside after the game in one of the many narrow terraced streets and back alleys around the ground. One suspects that George Edwards would have been deeply disappointed.

This was a satisfying punch in the Derby gut from a Forest perspective before the pendulum well and truly swung away from them in the face of the Rams' meteoric rise under the motormouth that was Brian Clough. All they could do was lick their wounds and watch and wait until the Clough pendulum swung their way.

As the 1960s slipped away, Raleigh ensured its legacy by launching its famous Chopper bike, thus allowing a whole generation of teenagers to tear around the streets while perched upon its distinctive long seat.

The 1970s then sprang into life. Nottingham enjoyed the sparks of a design and fashion era as Paul Smith opened his first shop on Byard Lane. This mattered not to Derby, who in the same month flexed their hitherto dormant muscles in front of their rivals, foreshadowing a period of success and dominance.

For the return fixture, a crowd of 42,074 packed into the City Ground on a grey day in March, most hoping that their team could repeat their win against the old rivals back in November, while Clough sought revenge for that reverse. Terry Hennessey was now with Derby and seen as one day being a replacement for the veteran Dave Mackay, having signed in February for £100,000. Apart from Hennessey, it was the same side that earned promotion from the Second Division. Derby were in fourth and starting to find their form again after a run of four games without a win, while Forest were in the habit of drawing regularly in mid-table. As well as Hennessey, Alan Hinton and Frank Wignall were in the line-up to face their former club, while Mackay would manage Forest for a season in 1972/73 and O'Hare would later follow Clough to Forest.

The lead column in the *Forest Review* match programme, perhaps sensing Derby's pending superiority on the pitch, was decidedly bullish about Forest's own achievements. 'For those who feel that Forest have to "prove" themselves this afternoon by winning decisively over our visitors (as if, in doing so, demonstrating the win at Derby months ago was no "fluke") may we remind them of some facts.' The piece went on to remind readers of the club's rise in the 1950s and the FA Cup win and the high quality of the 1960s side. Furthermore it added, 'We have almost completely rebuilt and modernised our ground and our reputation, as it is today, was unquestioned. We are now regarded as a great club and an attractive footballing team. Naturally, victory today against Derby would be welcomed and boost morale but what matters most to us is that, as club, in the past few years we have gained a reputation as respected members of the world's best company … the First Division.' It was almost as if the club was re-asserting its value and reputation in the knowledge that its rivals were about to suddenly zoom past them in the outside lane.

Tackles flew in, including one particularly nasty challenge from Hennessey who swept right through Alexander Ingram. There seemed little danger when Willie Carlin floated a cross into the Forest penalty area, but Liam O'Kane stuck out a leg and the ball skidded off his foot and trundled over the line. Derby were on top and remained so while Hennessey expertly screened the defence, even if he continued to throw hand grenades of tackles willy-nilly around the pitch and, just before half-time, the better side scored again when O'Hare rose to nod home into the Trent End goal, despite David Hollins in goal getting a touch on the ball.

Tempers and tackles continued to simmer in the second half as Wignall left Forest captain Robert 'Sammy' Chapman requiring treatment. In the 58th minute, Forest pulled a goal back as Newton simply ran up and blasted a free kick home to spark his team into life. Yet Derby once again reasserted their authority and composure, culminating in Alan Durban firing through a crowd to make it 3-1 with three minutes remaining.

Rather surprisingly, given the size of the crowd, the nature of the game and the growing spectre of football hooliganism, it appeared to have played out reasonably peacefully in terms of the behaviour of each teams' supporters, with *Football Post* observing, 'As regards crowd behaviour, there seemed to be isolated incidents and a small number of fans were escorted from the ground.' Yet make no mistake, the game marked a distinct and real shift in power. 'Generally, Trentside had to bow to the superior craft and skill of a Derby side, emerging as a real soccer power and a candidate for Europe,' wrote David Lowes in *Football Post*, adding, 'So the balance of power swings back to the Baseball Ground after a match that lived up to its billing.'

The win, Derby's fourth in succession, contributed to Clough's Derby finishing in fourth place and they would remain unbeaten for the rest of the season, an excellent return for a first year after promotion. Forest would fail to win again until the very final day and finished 15th.

As if to underline the pendulum swing, this was Derby's first win over Forest since the days of the Football League South, immediately after the war. The 1970s looked like they would belong to Derby. There was, however, one fly in the ointment. They would not be allowed to compete in the Inter-Cities Fairs Cup the following season as a joint FA and Football League disciplinary panel found the club guilty of 'gross negligence' after an unexplained gap of £3,000 in season ticket income and payment of fees to Dave Mackay outside the terms of his contract. Europe would have to wait and lifting the Watney Cup provided only a small consolation.

1970/71
Pummelled

Further change was afoot in both Derby and Nottingham. Speedo made Nottingham its centre of European operations, while construction of the Queen's Medical Centre started in 1971. Change of a different kind was instigated by Clough at Derby as their black shorts were replaced by those of a navy blue colour. 'Now you look like England, go and play like them,' he told his players. Colin Todd and Archie Gemmill were added, yet it would be another year before the signings would settle and the team would indeed play like a successful England XI. Of more concern for the folk of Derby was the announcement on 4 February that Rolls-Royce had gone bust. The escalating cost of the RB211 engine and the high exchange rates surrounding the contract to supply engines for the American Lockhead Tri-Star Airbus had brought the Derby-based engineering firm to its knees. Of such deep concern was the news that prime minister Edward Heath called a cabinet meeting to discuss the situation, resulting in a £60m rescue operation.

After the giddy heights of fourth place the previous season, 1970/71 was more sober for Derby as they finished ninth, while Forest would continue to clumsily doggy-paddle towards the foot of the table and ended up in 16th. Joe Baker, John Barnwell and Peter Grummitt had followed in Hennessey's footsteps and left the City Ground. Only Ian Storey-Moore's goals kept them going, with the team seemingly stuck in an elongated transition between the outstanding team of 1967 and the next generation to come through, symbolised by a young Scot by the name of John Robertson making his league debut in October in the middle of a miserable run for the Reds in which they won only once between 15 September and January. One of these many defeats was 4-2 at home to Derby on 28 November, ahead of which the Forest programme was clearly mindful of the fixture's reputation for violence, 'Let it be said here and now that we at the City Ground do not want the fair name of either club marred by passions either on or off the field and before the kick-off we would appeal to supporters of both teams to concentrate on enjoying the game and not to become involved in dispute. We all know that the kind of scenes which occur from time to time on all football grounds are inspired only by a minority. Let the good sense of the majority prevail!'

Despite going a goal up after only eight minutes as Chapman rifled one in from close range, Derby equalised when Gemmill scored his first goal for the Rams at the Trent End, in front of a crowd of 30,539. In truth, it was an untidy and scrappy goal as the ball seemed to canon off various legs, including Gemmill's own, before lazily rolling into the net. Just before half-time, Storey-Moore restored the home team's lead with a clever header back across goal after a lofted cross from the right. They were good value for their advantage too, yet Derby always looked dangerous going forward and it seemed as if neither team had finished scoring.

The Rams came out with even more purpose in the second half and again equalised when O'Hare finished off after excellent work down the right by Gemmill, who cut into the penalty area and fired across goal at the Bridgford End. Judging by the reaction of the fans in the Bridgford End, pockets of both Forest and Derby supporters were mixed in together on the same terrace. Five minutes later, Derby were ahead after more penalty area pinball was halted when Wignall blasted home. Just as Forest seemed to be getting back in the game, McGovern finished them off with a superb drive from the edge of the area which found the top corner.

'Frank Wignall told me off,' McGovern reflected. 'The ball got knocked into him and as a supporting midfield player and after I had put it in the top corner, he said, "How long does it take you to get with me? I've got the centre-half kicking me and it took you ten minutes to get up with me and I've laid on the perfect ball for you to score." So, I got a telling off for not getting to him quicker and was only forgiven when I put it in the top corner.'

There was even time for Storey-Moore to fire wide from the penalty spot after Peter Cormack was fouled, an action that prompted a mass exit by home supporters.

Although it might have been 4-3 if the late penalty had been converted, the gap between the sides seemed wider. 'RAMS ROAR BACK TO ROUT REDS' was the headline in *Football Post*, while Clough claimed, correctly, 'I don't think many people would disagree with me when I say that we deserved to beat Forest.' Derby had now scored seven goals in their last two visits to Nottingham and been victorious on both occasions. While something wasn't quite right in the woods, the Rams were enjoying the freedom of the fields. Perhaps McGovern put it best, 'We pummelled them that day.'

When the sides met again on Wednesday, 17 March, Forest showed that though they were down, they weren't quite fully out – they would not go quietly into the night. Derby were winless in four games and on the back of two successive away losses at Liverpool and Newcastle United. For once, Forest were heading in the right direction and had won their previous two matches, thanks largely to the form and goals of Storey-Moore. They weren't quite safe from relegation though, fourth from bottom and six points from the perforated line. They could certainly use the points, perhaps more so than Derby who had slipped to 14th, a fact underlined by Clough in his column in the programme. 'Should WE lose to Forest this evening our Nottingham neighbours will be only one point below US, which, considering the high spirits and optimism that came with our victory over Arsenal just a month ago, is a trifle off-putting to say the least,' he wrote.

Paul Richardson was at the centre of events as he was carried off to receive treatment by the touchline after a collision with Colin Todd. Four minutes later, he started and ended the move that put Forest ahead. It was a vital goal if Forest were to get any much-needed points from the game. The home side came back strong and had numerous chances, but were unable to convert any of them as the match grew scrappier. This suited Forest who sealed the points with just nine minutes remaining when Storey-Moore converted to make it 2-0. With only seconds remaining, Derby got a goal back when Hector's harmless-looking shot somehow ended up in the net after bouncing off keeper Jimmy Barron's body. So Forest landed one last punch to their rivals' gut before their jig became well and truly up. Derby, though, were just getting started and finished the season unbeaten, in doing so climbing to ninth. They were on their way to great things.

1971/72

Cheated out of a signature

With Dave Mackay leaving Derby to take up the role of player-manager at Swindon Town, Les Green going to South Africa and John Richardson sold to Notts County, Clough's squad was thinner than it had been for the coming new season. By the time Derby travelled to Nottingham on 30 October, they had lost only one league game, away to current league leaders Manchester United, and sat third in the table. Forest were the inverse reflection and sat third from bottom with a measly nine points from 15 games, and only two wins to their name. It seemed like there would be only one winner.

Looking ahead to the fixture, Clough said, 'Local derbies have their own particular problems. They defy normal predictions, preparation and form. There are added tensions and the players on both sides put in that bit more effort.' In the Forest programme, the lead column focused on the curious nature of a derby, 'What is it one wonders that gives such matches that special mystique? For there's no denying that there is a certain "something" in the air that is not present when other matches in the footballing calendar are played.' The column then zoomed in on the East Midlands derby, 'Rivalry between today's contestants has never been so high as in recent years, particularly so since County gained promotion to the First Division.' It noted that the previous four meetings saw the visitors take the points on each occasion.

A low autumn sun beamed into the eyes of the 37,170 crowd as Forest started brightly and McFarland had to be in the right place at the right time to head a speculative shot from Lyons off the line, but some beautiful interplay between Hector and O'Hare resulted in the latter stabbing the ball just wide of the Trent End goal. The move illustrated the quality Derby had in their side and, at the same time, the lack of quality in the Forest defence. Storey-Moore, pretty much Forest's only goal threat throughout the season, forced goalkeeper Colin Boulton into a fine save as he tipped a header over the bar.

Youngster John Robertson was growing into the game and he was involved in releasing Duncan McKenzie to have a run at the Derby defence. He slalomed into the box, forcing Todd into committing a hasty challenge that left him sprawling on the turf. The referee had no hesitation in awarding a penalty to Forest after only 12 minutes. With nine league goals to his name already, including three successfully converted penalties, the smart money was on Storey-Moore putting Forest ahead. But his shot was tame and too close to Boulton, who easily saved. This is how things go when you are down towards the bottom and up against your high-flying rivals.

It took until the 58th minute for Derby's quality to shine though. McGovern made his way to the byline before sending over a deep, swirling cross, which Hinton headed back over goalkeeper Eric Hulme, making one of his only five appearances, and towards the net. Rather than watch the ball plop over the line, Chapman couldn't stop himself volleying it off the line, but with his hand. From the very same spot that Storey-Moore had shot so meekly, Hinton, white boots gleaming, made no mistake as he found the very bottom corner of Hulme's net to put his side 1-0 up. Once again, the Bridgford End was packed full of supporters of both sides as small pockets of groups cheered while most remained resolutely silent.

Forest weren't quite done yet, or at least long-serving defender Pater Hindley wasn't, as he stormed forwards on a powerful run and unleashed a shot that Boulton needed to stretch for. Moments later, full-back John Robson picked up the ball deep in his own half and ran – and kept running unchallenged – until he reached the edge of the penalty area and let fly with a belting shot, which nestled beautifully in the corner of the net. It was a fitting goal to seal the points and Derby's third consecutive win at the City Ground, maintaining the curious run of away teams prevailing in recent derby games between these two.

The win lifted Derby up to second while Forest laboured on with a young team, struggling to pick up points and going into the reverse fixture on 19 February without a win in seven games. They had lost their last four games and scored only two goals in the process, Storey-Moore being responsible for those, ultimately his last ones in a Forest shirt. As if it couldn't get any worse, Forest were rock bottom, four points from safety. Derby had hit a slight bump in the road as they had lost 2-0 at Arsenal but were adamant it was just a blip as they were in third, just three points behind leaders Manchester City, and unbeaten at home. They were starting to believe in Clough's words spoken in August, 'We aim for the top two this season. There is no point in just surviving in the First Division. You must feel capable of winning something and I sincerely believe that we have the qualities to do just that.'

Starting on 9 January 1972, the miners' strike was rumbling along heavily in the background as muzak to Derby's rise and Forest's demise. The reduced production and transportation of coal led to power shortages and as the weather turned exceptionally cold, a state of emergency was declared by Heath's government on 9 February. Clough offered to picket with the striking miners. 'I am a member of the Labour Party as everyone knows. There is no doubt that this strike was forced on the miners by the Government's attitude right through,' he told *The Ram*, Derby's matchday newspaper. 'I am only trying to do my little bit to help out – to make my gesture.'

On a typical Baseball Ground gluepot of a pitch, Forest's much-changed side from the previous meeting was game, but a post match for their opponents. The usual late and occasionally violent tackles went flying in, as they tend to do in such fixtures, yet Derby knew all too well how to play on the sticky wicket while Forest got bogged down in the mud. Derby took the lead when Hinton's centre caught James Barron off his line and dropped teasingly just under the bar. Tempers flared when John Winfield smashed into Ron Webster and the Derby players surrounded the long-serving Forest defender.

Derby's second goal was not long in coming and the notorious mud could claim an assist as it refused to yield a clearance by Richardson, allowing McGovern to take possession and slide the ball through to O'Hare – these future Forest players seemed to love scoring against the team they would ultimately play for. Forest were now in self-preservation mode and, after the break, Hinton curled in a delightful free kick before Hector completed the rout in the 74th minute in front a crowd of 31,801. It was all far too easy for Derby and Forest looked doomed, while the home side dared to dream. The two teams would have to wait six years until they would meet again, and Derby would have to endure ten years until their next victory over their old rivals, but all that was in the future. For now, Derby had a title to win – and they embarked on a run of eight games unbeaten, winning seven of them – while Forest had a relegation to claim.

But not before one of the more bizarre episodes between these two clubs – some achievement given the sheer number of them. Ian Storey-Moore was increasingly unhappy with his lot and summed up the deteriorating situation at the City Ground perfectly, as he later told the Forest fanzine *Bandy and Shinty*, 'They just seemed to be happy going along and if they stayed in that division they were happy.' Clough was a known admirer, but Manchester United also liked the look of him, leading to the bizarre sight of Storey-Moore being paraded before the Derby fans at the Baseball Ground before a game with Wolverhampton Wanderers, despite him never actually signing for the club.

With both United and Derby vying for his signature, Forest were keen to make sure that he didn't follow the likes of Hennessey and Hinton to their major rivals. Storey-Moore said, 'They called me in on the Friday morning and Gillies said that two clubs were prepared to pay the fee, well I knew actually because I had been tapped up, Manchester United and Derby. He said they wanted me to speak to Manchester United first, so I met Frank O'Farrell and there was Matt Gillies, the assistant manager Bill Anderson and Ken Smales, the secretary, there with me. I went into a private room and we couldn't agree terms, so I came out, told Gillies and he says, "OK, I'll get you Brian Clough on the phone," and he rang the number, so I've got Clough saying, "Where are you then?" so I told him and he said, "We'll be there in half an hour." I came out of the phone box, which is all you had then, and said Clough and Taylor are on their way and all three of them just left me on my own to negotiate a transfer with those two.'

It would have taken either a foolish or strong player to turn down Clough and Taylor as their side was challenging for the title, so Storey-Moore signed for them. Taylor took him to the Midland Hotel, while Clough headed to the City Ground to tie up the deal. Around 7pm, Clough returned as Storey-Moore was having dinner with the other players ahead of the Wolves game. He was told he was a Derby player and, as far as he was concerned, that was that. 'Well, I believed him, but of course they hadn't signed anything,' continued Storey-Moore. 'Then I was on the pitch, I was really embarrassed afterwards.'

Derby beat Wolves 2-0, but the deal was far from done and dusted. Forest chairman Tony Wood was far from happy at losing his best player to their rivals and blocked the move. 'The chairman had said there's no way you're going to Derby County,' said Storey-Moore. Nothing was signed, or at least, the clubs hadn't signed off the deal. The following Monday, Busby, now a director at United, and manager Frank O'Farrell visited Storey-Moore's house and agreed a deal. The incident was, according to Taylor in his book, *With Clough, by Taylor*, a significant one for relations between the two clubs who had traded players freely up to that point, 'In my opinion, Forest cheated us out of his signature and their actions soured relationships between the clubs for years.' The spirit of the acrimonious transfer of the Forman brothers lived on and few players would move between clubs without a degree of acrimony in years to come.

As for Storey-Moore, the next time he stepped out on to a football pitch, it would be in the red of Manchester United. Derby received a fine for their conduct and the tension between Clough and his chairman, Sam Longson, grew. With Derby's burgeoning reputation, Clough increasingly resented, at least as he saw it, Longon's attempts to hog the limelight and milk the acclaim. In truth, both had inflated egos and the working relationship was always precarious.

Storey-Moore eventually left Nottingham just five days before Paul McCartney's Wings played their first gig, in the Portland Ballroom at Nottingham University on Wednesday, 9 February, while Derby went marching on. They finished their season with a 1-0 win at home to Liverpool and, having qualified for the UEFA Cup, took a break in Mallorca to unwind, sit back and reflect on a job well done, regardless of whether Liverpool or Leeds, each with one match left to play, would overtake their points haul as they sat at the top of the pile. Leeds, in search of a First Division and FA Cup double, having beaten Arsenal at Wembley, lost at Wolves, while Liverpool could only draw at Arsenal. Derby County were champions of England for the first time in their history.

A day later, Nottingham Forest were relegated to the Second Division, their 15-year residency in the First Division at an end. In those years, they had won the FA Cup and finished runners-up to a worthy Manchester United team, while their rivals were bobbling along without much intent in the Second Division. The boot was now very firmly on the other foot.

1972/73

Wavy lines and resignations

Matt Gillies remained in charge at Forest but only until October, by which time he was replaced by Dave Mackay as the wheels fell off after a reasonable start to life in the Second Division. Under Gillies, Forest finished in a very underwhelming 14th place, made all the more difficult to swallow as their rivals down the road were enjoying famous European nights under the lights at the Baseball Ground, beating, among others, Benfica 3-0 and making their way to the semi-finals of the European Cup, where they faced the mighty Juventus.

In the first leg at Juve's Stadio Comunale, Derby went into the break with the score at 1-1 after Kevin Hector's goal, the first scored by an English club in a European Cup match in Italy. Yet that was only a small part of the story as both Gemmill and McFarland were booked for trivial offences, meaning they would miss the second leg, a detail made all the more suspicious by the sight of the German referee, Gerhard Schulenberg, deep in conversation with the Juventus player Helmut Haller at half-time. Juventus won their home match 3-1 and, back at the Baseball Ground, Derby's frustration grew after Hinton missed a penalty in the second half, culminating in new signing Roger Davies getting himself sent off for reacting to provocation. Clough's ire for Juventus remained undimmed, labelling them 'cheating bastards'. A 0-0 draw was not enough to turn the tie around and Juventus progressed to the final where they lost to Ajax, who claimed their third successive European Cup.

Back in Nottingham, while Derby were gallivanting around Europe, the opening of the Victoria Shopping Centre – the first enclosed one to be built in the UK and boasting what was thought to be the largest car park in the world at the time and the now-famous elaborate and unusual Emett Clock – was, at best, diverting in comparison to Derby's forays to the quarter-final of the FA Cup, a seventh-placed finish and a journey deep into the European Cup. Yet change was afoot.

The *Nottingham Evening Post* launched a competition to invite designs for a new badge for Nottingham Forest to replace the city's coat of arms. The winner would receive £25. It was specified that the proposed design should not be more than six inches in depth and be adaptable for reproduction. Although not explicitly stated, if the badge could be doodled on pencil cases by bored kids in a maths class, even better. The winning idea was submitted by the specified deadline, 31 March 1973, by graphic design lecturer David Lewis of Trent Polytechnic – a slightly awkward situation given that one of the five judges was his own head of department. Nonetheless, to keep everything above board, Lewis submitted his entry of a tree hovering above some wavy lines under his mother's maiden name, Lago, to maintain anonymity and impartiality.

Lewis's design was one of 855 submissions from around the world, one of which came from Wally Ardron who incorporated Nottingham lace and a Raleigh bicycle into his design. 'I wanted to retain some of the history of what had gone before,' Lewis told The Athletic. 'The tree had been part of the previous crest, from the Nottingham coat of arms, and I wanted to retain it. Then I wanted to take into account the fact the City Ground was on the banks of the River Trent. I know the Trent isn't the sea, but waves represent water.' The lettering underneath the tree is distinctive too. The capital R curls underneath the lower-case e, negating the official appearance of the design and making it unique. The opening game of the 1973/74 season saw the first airing of the design as Forest beat Luton Town 4-0.

The iconic badge was also sported during Forest's infamous FA Cup quarter-final game against Newcastle

United at St James' Park, in which home fans invaded the pitch with their team 3-1 down and reduced to ten men. When the game eventually restarted, Newcastle stormed back to win 4-3. Forest lodged complaints on the basis that fans around the pitch interfered with the match and it was replayed. Despite this, Newcastle progressed to the final where they lost 3-0 to Liverpool. Yet all the while, time was ticking on the Clough and Taylor era at Derby.

There was, and always had been, tension behind the scenes between Clough, Taylor and Longson, culminating on 13 October 1973. After a win at Old Trafford lifted Derby to third place, Clough appeared to stick two fingers up in the general direction of the Derby board. Already smarting from Manchester United not providing seats in the visiting directors' box for the wives of the Derby players and management staff, Clough was in a belligerent mood as he left the pitch. Although the situation regarding tickets was resolved by the time the game played out, it probably didn't help matters that his wife Barbara was never that keen on going to watch matches but made a rare exception for this one, only to be messed about by the United hospitality system. On top of that, he was not a huge admirer of Matt Busby after the fall-out from the Ian Storey-Moore incident a year previous.

In addition, his relationship with Longson was on the brink of irreparable damage as the chairman objected to Clough's increasing number of appearances as a pundit on television. Clough would claim he was waving at Barbara, but the damage was done and there seemed no way to rebuild bridges as Longson demanded that Clough cut down his number of TV appearances. Never one to bend to a chairman's will, Clough went one better and put his resignation in writing, in a gesture akin to, 'I never wanted to work with you anyway.' The Derby board met and squabbled, but ultimately accepted Clough and Taylor's resignations, but that wasn't quite the end of the matter.

'He [Brian] wanted us to go on strike,' said John McGovern. Yet after the PFA pointed out that to do so would be a breach of contract and, in sporting terms, illegal, the players backed down. 'I'm glad the players decided not to go on strike. To be honest with you, and although I was one of the younger players, I've always been pretty strong-minded when I have sized up a situation and made my decision, then I wouldn't have done it anyway,' McGovern added. Clough was indeed stirring the pot. 'And I have to confess, for the first time, that I was behind much of it,' the manager wrote in his autobiography. 'I was involved in the meetings where the players plotted and planned their moves that brought a state of siege to the Baseball Ground.' In Setúbal, Portugal, perhaps a ten-year-old lad by the name of José Mourinho was watching and taking notes. Years later, Mourinho would take a trip to Nottingham to see the City Ground for himself in an effort to comprehend the scale of Clough's achievements in leading a provincial team to European glory.

Stunned and saddened by events, the Derby players managed to focus just enough to beat Leicester City the following Saturday, but the sight of Longson in one stand and Clough in an adjoining one as the game played out was pure theatre. Longson lapped up the applause, mistakenly thinking it was for him, while Clough's long-time trainer, Jimmy Gordon, took care of matters on the pitch. In between all of this, Clough somehow found time to appear as a pundit on television for England's crucial World Cup qualifier against Poland, in which he infamously dismissed the Polish keeper, Jan Tomaszewski, as a 'clown' on a night when England could only draw 1-1 and watch their qualification hopes for the 1974 finals in West Germany go up in smoke.

After the Leicester game, Roy McFarland handed the board a letter demanding the reinstatement of Clough and Taylor, yet the board were already in negotiations with a replacement and, just to give the whole drama a touch of East Midlands comedy, that man was Dave Mackay, manager of Forest. Not content with a letter, the players took their demands to the Baseball Ground and insisted they speak with the board, prompting the directors to repurpose an ice bucket as a urinal. 'We players were livid,' explained Alan Hinton in *Triumph and Tragedy: The Alan Hinton Story*, 'and pieced together a hand-written note to the chairman and board of directors. Once each player's signature was added, captain Roy McFarland led the team to the Baseball Ground to deliver it in person to the chairman. That letter, in my handwriting, sold at auction a few years ago for £4,000.'

McFarland managed to speak to Mackay and suggested it would be unwise to take the job given the current strength of feeling, yet the Scot had a huge and hefty contract dangled before him. He pacified the restless players by explaining that he wanted the job and would have been sick to the stomach should someone else have been given it. He also reminded them of the hurtful truth: Clough and Taylor resigned. 'Mackay came in the dressing room,' McGovern explained, 'and put a sheet of paper out and said, "Whoever wants to back me as a manger, I want you to sign it, so I know where I stand." I was the first player that got up and signed it. Then I got a rollocking from Roy McFarland, "What do you think you're doing?" I explained, "That's the manager. That's why I've signed it. Brian Clough's not coming back, so what is the point in not signing it?" And funnily enough, John O'Hare was the next one to sign it.'

After more meetings, letters and countless phone calls, Clough and Taylor met the players at the Midland Hotel and informed them that the situation had reached an impasse – like a lover determined to leave, they told the players that it was time to move on, find someone else and let go. 'Sometimes I wish that 1973 had been wiped off the calendar,' Taylor later wrote. 'It was a year of troubles for us and the shemozzles in Turin were far from the worst of them. The climax, of course, came in the autumn with uproar over our resignations from Derby County.' Clough shared Taylor's regret over the way it all came to a grinding halt, 'Some of my fondest and dearest memories are from my time at Derby – despite even greater achievements at Nottingham Forest.' The players could keep the memories and the cups and the titles, but Clough and Taylor could not go back. It was some ride while it lasted but it was over – really, and properly, over.

7

The pendulum swings that way: 1973–1980

BRIGHTON & Hove Albion did not seem like a logical place for Brian Clough and Peter Taylor to pitch up at next in an attempt to reproduce the magical resurrection of a provincial club. Or maybe, on the surface, it was the perfect destination to replicate their achievements at Derby. Or perhaps they fancied a bit of sun and a change of scenery after the drama of the previous month. Either way, with the fall-out of their elongated exit from Derby still settling, Clough and Taylor took charge of Brighton on 1 November 1973. Albion were newly relegated from the Second Division, severely strapped for cash and playing in front of around 5,000 fans at home. Yet somehow chairman Mike Bamber lured them to the south coast, while that Christmas, arguably the finest *Robin Hood* film – the animated Disney one with the incredibly catchy whistling tune – was released in the UK.

The Brighton adventure turned out to be a brief British holiday romance, or more accurately, a best forgotten fling for their partnership. It was a mixed bag when it came to results. Under the pair, Brighton won just one game in their first ten, including a famous 4-0 home defeat in the FA Cup to Walton & Hersham of the Isthmian League on 28 November. Moreover, this wasn't a fluke as the two teams had met four days earlier and played out a 0-0 draw at Stompond Lane, followed four days later by an 8-2 home defeat to Bristol Rovers, who would earn promotion that season. Things did take a turn for the better in the new year when Brighton strung together four straight wins from 23 February to 10 March, but from then on, inconsistency ruled with a curious run of three straight defeats, followed by three straight wins, bookended by another three straight defeats. By April 1974 Clough, to borrow Muhammed Ali's words, had had enough and left Taylor to it, where he seemed happy and set about building a promising side.

In the First Division, Leeds won the title in Don Revie's final season as manager, while Manchester United were relegated from the top tier just six years after winning the European Cup. Revie left to take charge of England, a job Clough himself had coveted. All the while, back in the East Midlands, Derby barely missed a beat under Dave Mackay and worked through the trauma of October to claim a very respectable third place, while Forest still laboured in the Second Division. Brighton finished 19th and Clough later admitted, 'The spell was a disaster.'

Even with Revie settling into Lancaster Gate wearing an England blazer and Clough out of work, the notion of the outspoken former Derby man replacing his old rival at Elland Road still didn't seem a logical fit, mostly as a result of Clough taking a verbal swipe at Revie's Leeds team and the way they went about their business at every available opportunity, and given how much he was on television in those days that amounted to a fair number of oratory punches. Regardless, with a point to prove that he could be just as successful as Revie but with more class, Clough was appointed manager of Leeds on 22 July.

Things didn't work out despite Clough bringing along his old allies, John McGovern and John O'Hare. After 44 days and extraordinary scenes in the Charity Shield game between Leeds and Liverpool, in which Kevin Keegan was sent off for the heinous crime of being punched by Johnny Giles and Leeds captain, Billy Bremner, received his marching orders too, Clough was sacked. He walked away with a cheque for £92,000 in compensation yet without McGovern and O'Hare, who would have to bide their time until they got the call from Clough to join him again at some stage in the future.

In Nottingham, Forest chairman Brian Appleby watched and wondered and pondered. Could he? Would he? Calls were made, negotiations took place and on 6 January 1975, Brian Clough was appointed manager of Nottingham Forest. The club didn't know it at the time, but their world and Nottingham's would be well and truly rocked over the course of the next 18 years.

This was more like it. This was closer in geography and in spirit to the Derby job he still, deep down, cherished. If he was going to do it all again, prove himself all over again, this was the perfect place. It would need a bit of time and some patience – in truth, it was a bit of a doer-upper, an end terrace with a decent back garden but a bit unloved and overlooked. Yet free from financial worries with his big cheque dangling from his back pocket, he would get to work for enjoyment.

Clough himself was under no illusions about the state of the club and the nature of the job ahead. 'It's a tragedy how they have gone downhill in the last seven years,' he told the *Birmingham Daily Post*. 'The chances of promotion this season must be very small.' Forest were in 13th place and had just lost at home to, of all clubs, Notts County. They were going nowhere fast and hadn't actually been anywhere in a hurry since 1967. They had settled into mid-table Second Division life like a beloved uncle settling into his favourite armchair at the end of a long working day.

'I want to prove to the Nottingham public that this club can do well,' Clough continued at his unveiling for the press. 'The situation is not unlike when I went to Derby. However, the quality of players I have at Forest is better and the ground is better equipped.' Clough's arrival, or second coming to the East Midlands as it were, certainly caught the imagination of the Nottingham public where support for the team had been dwindling. Two hours after his appointment, 30 season tickets were sold and office staff even received enquiries from the Derby area. Were they Derby fans simply wanting to watch a Brian Clough team? Probably not. More likely they were lapsed Forest fans in the Derby area letting their imagination run riot. Either way, Clough quipped, 'We must be the only club in the country selling season tickets in January.' The glint in his eyes remained.

As for the Forest fans, seeing their best players leave to play for Derby alongside a seething jealousy at their success meant that the rivalry was quickly re-established after years of lying dormant. It was difficult to find any antagonism towards Clough, though, and the overriding feeling was that with him at the helm, it was their turn to start winning things now.

What he would need to be successful was an understanding chairman. He needed to be given the keys and the security code and, in Brian Appleby, he found just that. 'I never had any problems with Brian,' Appleby later said. 'Every day I told him, "Do what you like." And he did.' This was in stark contrast to Sam Longson, whose micromanagement of Clough contributed to the irreparable schism. Sure, Clough perhaps needed reining in from time to time but with a friendly word and a drink, rather than a stick with keys to the locked drinks cabinet dangling from the end.

Taylor remained at Brighton, saying, 'I find it embarrassing to read unauthorised reports that I may be leaving when we are struggling.' For the time being anyway.

1975/76

Mammoth task

Like at Derby, there was no dynamite that blasted the club into orbit, but more of a slow-burning, sometimes disappointing Catherine Wheel. After Clough's first home game, a 2-2 draw with Leyton Orient, the size of the task ahead was clear. 'It was obvious at 4.45pm last Saturday that Brian Clough as, manager of Forest, has a mammoth task before him, if as he has suggested, Forest can be a force in the land again,' opined a writer in a letter to the *Evening Post*. 'The job will be made no easier by the disgruntled fans who, believing in miracles, attended the match doubling the gate only to go streaming across Trent Bridge well before the final whistle. The loyal supporters who have followed Forest all this dreadful season were eventually rewarded for putting up with 85 minutes' rubbish by a tremendous fightback and a point saved. Perhaps a "Clough Miracle".'

A Clough miracle? Or to be precise, *another* Clough miracle? Surely not. But hold that thought. Already at the club were Ian Bowyer, Viv Anderson, Martin O'Neill, Tony Woodcock and John Robertson. They didn't know it yet, but when Clough walked through the door and popped his coat on a peg in the dressing room, their lives would be changed and reshaped in ways they could scarcely imagine. McGovern and O'Hare finally escaped from Leeds in February to join Clough for the third time.

As if to cement the notion that something was stirring in the waters of Nottingham, at some stage in 1975 Jayne Torvill and Christopher Dean danced together on ice for the first time. To help the couple overcome their innate shyness and timidity, their newly appointed coach, Janet Sawbridge, asked them to stand in the middle of the rink in hold, face to face and pelvis to pelvis. Their awkwardness with each other was broken. 'It was where Jayne and Chris started to become Torvill and Dean,' said the couple in their autobiography, *Torvill and Dean*. The year sowed the seed of very big things to come for the city.

That was all in the future though as far as Derby were concerned. They had their own miracles to make. Dave Mackay set about gently tinkering with Clough's Derby team by bringing in Francis Lee and Bruce Rioch, whose goals kept them in contention at the top of the table. It was against his former club, Manchester City, that Lee scored a memorable goal at Maine Road, forever sound-tracked by Barry Davies's commentary, 'Interesting. Very interesting! Oh! Look at his face! Just look at his face!'

Derby beat City 2-1 on 28 December 1974, a result and goal which helped put an end to a losing streak and saw them embark on a five-game unbeaten run in both league and cup. February saw them wobble a little, whereupon they dropped to sixth. Yet with Kevin Hector and Roger Davies firing on all cylinders, an unbeaten run of nine games to end the season saw them clinch the title for the second time, ahead of Liverpool and Ipswich. They could even afford to draw their final two games without scoring a goal, including on the last day at home against a hapless Carlisle United. No matter, because as in 1972 they officially took the title while off the pitch – in a nightclub, as it happens, in midweek between their final two matches. On the evening of their awards ceremony in Bailey's, news filtered through of Ipswich's failure to beat Manchester City, meaning that Derby were once again champions.

Mackay's role often gets overlooked as it is assumed the title came courtesy of the squad that Clough and Taylor built. Yet that would be unfair as the players Mackay brought in complemented the likes of Gemmill, Boulton, McFarland and Todd wonderfully well. It was a squad built to stay competitive at the top too. The following season, the Rams finished fourth and reached the semi-finals of the FA Cup, losing 2-0 to Manchester United at Hillsborough. They also provided us with, alongside Barry Davies's commentary, another memorable image on 1 November 1975. Derby were hosting Leeds when, seven minutes into the second half, all hell broke loose as Norman Hunter and Francis Lee started trading punches off the ball, presumably out of frustration at Lee winning a penalty earlier in the game as a result of a Hunter tackle. Both were sent off, but that didn't stop them going at each other as they left the pitch. The sight of Lee's arms flailing around like windmill while Hunter raises his fists like a boxer is an iconic snapshot of English football in the 1970s.

Any thought of a miracle seemed very distant in Nottingham as Forest laboured in the Second Division, finishing eighth in 1975/76. However, suffering only two defeats in their final 16 games of the season hinted at better things to come. Down on the south coast, Taylor guided Brighton to fourth place, missing promotion by two points, before resigning on 16 July and once again joining up with his old mate in Nottingham, where they could get down to doing what they did best together: building a team through unearthing and making the very most of what they had at their disposal and bringing in the right players to complement them.

The East Midlands Clough-Taylor circle was now complete. For so long Clough and Taylor were synonymous with Derby County, yet were now at Nottingham Forest, and the situation was not dissimilar to when they walked through the doors at the Baseball Ground. Just for good measure, Taylor was home as he had been born in Nottingham. Once again, they found themselves at an East Midlands club wallowing in the Second Division, while their rivals were flying high towards the top of the First. Surely – *surely* – the wheel of fortune wouldn't turn in the same manner as it had last time?

1976/77
I'd have crawled to Derby

The 1976/77 season didn't start so well for Mackay and Derby as he was sacked after a poor run. By November, they found themselves out of the UEFA Cup after a second-round defeat to AEK Athens, while they were fourth from bottom in the First Division with only two league wins on the board, one of which was a bizarre 8-2 hammering of Tottenham at the Baseball Ground. Colin Murphy took the wheel after Mackay's exit, yet the situation was not much better by February 1977.

Where to turn next for Derby? Well, it was uncanny that a brilliant management team that had brought unprecedented success to the club just happened to be in the area. The lure of getting the old band back together was simply irresistible. So, incredibly, a call was made to the City Ground. The fact that Derby approached Clough and Taylor to return to the club is both wonderfully predictable yet utterly flabbergasting at the same time. Predictable as, on the surface, an approach made a lot of sense since Derby were in a much better state than when the managerial duo had first joined and with a little tweaking could be challenging for titles and European Cups again.

Yet the sheer brass neck of the approach is breathtaking, given that contracts were in place with Forest and the pair were, in relative terms, fairly newly installed – they were just getting their feet under the table and warming to their theme. Then again, in the context of the frequency with which players headed up and down the A52, which would in later years be matched only by the rate at which managers did the same, perhaps it's less surprising once the initial shock subsides.

'CLOUGH AND TAYLOR SET FOR DERBY,' screamed the *Coventry Evening Telegraph* headline. Derby were given permission to speak to Clough and Taylor and Derby's vice-chairman George Hardy was confident, 'We have had a long chat and a very good meeting and I think I was able to provide the right answers to the many questions which were raised. Now they have gone away to deliberate, but I am hopeful of getting their reply within 24 hours. All sorts of things were discussed, and it is natural they should want to consider every aspect of the matter. I'm hopeful it will produce the right result and that Derby will soon have, once again, the best management team in the business.'

This was actually happening and, what's more, it seemed that everyone was quite pleased about it. Even Sam Longson, who was still at Derby, albeit no longer chairman. 'Colin Murphy has been informed and he knows of the approach to Clough,' Hardy opined to the *Birmingham Daily Post*. 'It is my personal hope that he will stay on the payroll if and when our offer is accepted. The fact that Clough is meeting with us is a good indication that there is a chance of his return and we are hoping for a prompt decision.' It wasn't only Hardy going public about getting their men either as Derby secretary Stuart Webb, according to the *Birmingham Daily Post*, 'had reason to believe that the meeting with Clough and Taylor would not be fruitless'. Taylor was keen on a return and felt the time was right, but Clough was reticent as his wife Barbara's words rang in his ears, 'Never go back while Sam Longson and Stuart Webb are still at the club.'

Their efforts came to nought. Clough told David Moore of the *Daily Mirror*, 'The relief at having finally made what was an agonising decision is unbelievable.' He was staying put. 'It would be impossible to build a better team than the one Peter and I left at Derby.' Clough went on to explain his decision at length, 'I have still to sense the same intensity from the Nottingham football public as one gets at Derby. Perhaps that feeling will grow at Forest; perhaps all the work, love and care I intend to put in here will eventually be reciprocated. Forest fans should get one thing clear – I have paid them the biggest compliment I can by turning down Derby's offer.'

Clough seemed keen to get his thought process out to the public as he also told David Davies at the *Birmingham Daily Post*, 'I have always wanted to come back to Derby every hour of every single day I have been away. I wanted to come back for three and a half years so badly it was unbelievable.' Clearly, his fondness for Derby and his time there was not diminished by the way it all unravelled. Yet at the same time, Clough felt a sense of gratitude and loyalty to Forest and especially the vice-chairman Stuart Dryden, summed up when he said, 'Derby has always held this bond but I didn't turn them down under any compulsion. There was no pressure from me. I made a free decision to stay with Forest and I did it because I've been happy with them in the 25 months I've been at the City Ground. When I was out of work one man came for me. That was Forest vice-chairman Stuart Dryden, and that has meant something to me this week. If I'd have been out of work I'd have crawled to Derby, but I'm Forest's manager and the supporters don't have to worry about my commitment to the club. I'm totally happy. Derby's offer aroused a lot of sentimental and emotional things for me, but I made my decision and that is it as far as I am concerned.'

It is difficult to know what to make of Clough's comments here. He clearly spoke from the heart regarding his time at Derby yet seemed conflicted regarding his thought process in turning them down. On the one hand, he said it was a straightforward decision to turn them down owing to his loyalty towards Forest and Dryden, yet on the other, he called it an 'agonising' decision to make. Of course, Clough was adept at managing the press and specifically, individual reporters and one gets the feeling that perhaps he was doing Moore a favour by giving him a headline or soundbite. Yet his comments regarding the difference between Derby and Nottingham were interesting and the feeling has never quite been shaken off that he perceived Derby to be more of a football place than Nottingham.

Naturally, he was speaking here in the infancy of his tenure at Forest where league titles and European Cups were still a fantasy. Furthermore, perhaps he remained unsatisfied with what he achieved at Derby, especially in Europe after the Juventus experience. His nemesis, Longson, was no longer chairman, allowing Clough to wonder just how good things could be at Derby if he wasn't being told to keep in line or being carefully watched over; he could have free run of the place. Besides, at this moment, his Forest side were sixth in the Second Division and by no means guaranteed promotion and, while Derby were four places from the bottom of the table, they would rally to 15th come the end of the season. Regardless, it seems fair to say that his heart still belonged in Derby. It was where he first enjoyed real success and that never left him. He would later say, 'I wish

I'd never left. It was the best job I ever had ... Some of my heart, wherever I have wandered, was in Derby. It's like your first girlfriend. You don't forget, do you?' Of course, none of this prevents fans of either club claiming him as theirs. That's the beauty of it all.

The dust eventually settled and football, as it is wont to do, went on. Once again, a team managed by Clough finished their campaign before others and sat in third place and, as things stood, were promoted. The problem was that Bolton, just four points behind, had three games in hand. Bolton beat Cardiff City in the first of those three, meaning they were just two points adrift, albeit with a vastly inferior goal difference. So Clough flew everyone out to Mallorca for a holiday. After all, the situation was out of their hands and no amount of pacing, pondering or worrying would change anything. While airborne, the pilot informed the plane that Bolton had lost at home to table-toppers Wolves – Forest were promoted no matter how Bolton got on in their final game away at Bristol Rovers.

The goal that set Forest off on their journey is worth a moment, given not only its importance but its uniqueness. Wolves were awarded a free kick around 30 yards from goal, slightly to the right of centre. Kenny Hibbitt and Willie Carr stood over the ball conspiratorially. Carr had form for invention when it came to free kicks as it was he who flicked the ball from between his legs for Ernie Hunt to fire home on the volley for Coventry City against Everton in 1970. Clearly, these two were planning something.

Hibbitt ran up to the stationary ball as if to kick it, yet continued past it and on towards goal. The crowd groaned and laughed as it looked like an ill-conceived fancy-pants free kick gone horribly wrong. Yet he had ever so slightly flicked the ball as he ran over it and, while everyone was distracted, he had made his way to the penalty area without stopping to look back at the chaos behind him, especially Carr who looked flustered and frustrated. Yet he was anything but as he suddenly sprang out of his supposed stupor and lofted a perfect ball forward on to the left foot of the unmarked Hibbitt to volley goalwards. His shot was partly blocked by Seamus McDonagh in the Bolton goal but not enough to prevent it from trickling over the line.

Wolves secured the title and Forest were promoted as well as lifting the Anglo-Scottish Cup after beating Orient in a two-legged final. Derby, labouring under Colin Murphy, finished in 15th. As the Queen celebrated her Jubilee, the Sex Pistols released 'God Save the Queen', the first episode of *Citizen Smith* (starring lifelong Derby fan Robert Lindsay) was aired and actress and director Samantha Morton was born in the Clifton area of Nottingham, the East Midlands derby was back on, and in the First Division.

Before that, though, there was a dress rehearsal of sorts. Just two days after Forest's season ended (Derby still had two games to play), Derby and Forest met at the Baseball Ground in a testimonial for Kevin Hector on Monday, 7 May. Clough was a huge admirer of Hector as a player and person. 'My first [memory] was seeing him play alongside Albert Broadbent for Bradford. I was at Hartlepool at the time and wanted to sign him,' he told *Football Post*. 'He probably caused me less trouble than any other professional footballer that I have known.'

Given the enmity between the clubs and their fans and the violence on the terraces, arranging such a fixture when the two rivals hadn't played against each other for five years was perhaps a surprising turn of events and, predictably, houses, cars and property were damaged around the ground and five police officers injured. The trouble came only hours after Forest's vice-chairman Stuart Dryden, commenting on violence at the City Ground the previous Saturday, had called for swift action to combat the thugs with Saturday courts.

All of which was a rather fierce baptism of fire for the 16-year-old Steve Sutton, who made his first appearance between the sticks in the second half for Forest. Born in Derbyshire and son of a Derby-supporting, season ticket-holding father, Sutton had spent time with the Rams on trial when Mackay was in charge and even trained with the first team but ended up at Forest. With his feet barely through the door, he received a phone call. 'I'd signed for Forest,' says Sutton, 'and Cloughie rang me on the Sunday night and asked, "What are you doing tomorrow night, Steve?"

'"I don't know, Mr Clough."

'"Well. There's a game at Derby, come along."

'I didn't even know there was a game, so I arrived with my boots and my gloves.'

Sutton came on for the second half to replace John Middleton in front of around 21,000 fans, with the game all square at 1-1. He said, 'There was fighting on the pitch. There was trouble at half-time. I was scared to death! We went on and ran to our right, which was the Osmaston End, I think. Sammy Chapman yelled at me, "Get back here, lad! Get back in! We're going back in."' Although a testimonial, this was, after all, Derby v Forest. 'I remember David Nish having a shot from just outside the box and I tipped it over, made a flying save to my right and kept a clean sheet. That was my first taste of first team football.' The game ended 1-1.

1977/78
No regrets

Despite the team's descent down the table, Derby did have something to cheer about as on 7 June the town was awarded city status by Queen Elizabeth II as part of her Silver Jubilee celebrations. She travelled there by train and, upon alighting at the station with the Duke of Edinburgh in tow, signed the visitors' book at the Council House and presented the charter scroll to mayor Jeffrey Tillet, before going on a walkabout in the Market Place to meet the gathered crowds. On the same day, they swung by Nottingham and officially opened the Queen's Medical Centre. It was a whistlestop tour as they also visited Ripley, Chesterfield and Mansfield before heading down to Dudley. Yet this was merely an appetiser for the football fans of each city as their teams renewed acquaintances on 27 August.

It was the third game of the season and Derby had lost on the opening day, 3-1 at Coventry City, then shared the spoils with Ipswich Town. They still had the nucleus of their glory team – McFarland, Todd, Gemmill and Hector – and perhaps under Murphy's steady hand, they could recover from the previous season's inauspicious performance. As for Forest, they had started the season in spectacular fashion by beating Everton 3-1 in their own backyard, despite going a goal down. A team talk delivered by Bill Shankly may well have helped turn things around. They followed that up with a home win against Bristol City.

Many had Forest down as mid-table at best, possibly even for a relegation scrap. After all, they had scrambled out of the Second Division by the merest of margins. Surely it was simply a matter of time before they would revert to the mean. But that time was not yet – not on derby day. Forest secretary Ken Smales took great delight in Forest surpassing expectations and used his programme column to reflect on the win at Everton, 'I was sitting in the directors' box up in the clouds, both literally and figuratively, when the teams appeared to face a posse of cameramen. Then they all dashed off in order not to miss the action behind the Forest goal – the fools!' Yet the spectre of violence remained. Forest had played Notts County a few weeks earlier in the County Cup at the City Ground, a game which witnessed a pitch invasion, prompting Smales to write, 'The violence that has already erupted up and down the country would seem to indicate that we are not "over the hill" with regard to hooliganism and I am praying that we, at the City Ground, are spared this torture.'

It was a cagey opening 30 minutes despite a cross from Robertson, after a typical jinking run down the left, causing panic in the Derby defence in front of 28,807. A minute later, Tony Woodcock's corner wasn't cleared, and Peter Withe took a touch from around ten yards before slamming into the top corner of the Trent End goal. Forest were starting to feel at home at this level and Withe had maintained his record of scoring in every game.

In the second half, Derby found themselves hanging on and perhaps fortunate to be only a goal down. Robertson sprayed a ball out to Woodcock to chase. He outpaced two defenders and bore down on goal but was halted by an excellent recovery tackle from Dave Langan before he gave the ball away to Martin O'Neill. He squared across the face of the goal, but it eluded everyone before Robertson appeared at the back post and squared for Withe to tap in and make it four goals in three games for him. Forest scored a scruffy third with 12 minutes remaining. O'Neill scampered down the right before crossing. The ball eventually found its way to the feet of Robertson, who, in turn, found the bottom corner of the net to make it a resounding 3-0. It was far too early to be drawing solid conclusions, but one thing was for sure: this Forest team was brimming with the confidence that many newly promoted teams carry. Naturally though, the naysayers said it was surely only a matter of time before the bubble would burst.

For Derby, it would get worse before it got better and on 17 September Colin Murphy was sacked. He lasted only another four matches in charge before being replaced by Tommy Docherty, recently fired from Manchester United following a well-publicised affair with Mary Brown, the wife of United's physiotherapist, and the pair later married. Murphy's sacking perhaps established the tradition of the unwritten law of the East Midlands derby which states that when managers lose heavily to the opposite team in such a game, they must be replaced. This law would reach its apex come the 2010s.

The appointment of Docherty created a happy byproduct for Clough and Taylor over at Forest as Gemmill wanted no part in a team managed by his old Scotland boss, who he blamed being 'bombed out' of the Scotland squad in 1972, meaning he would miss three years of international football. Gemmill signed for Forest for

£25,000 in September. Docherty's reign was a hectic one as players came and went through the Baseball Ground doors at a rate unmatched until Harry Redknapp would turn up at Portsmouth as manager many years later. Indeed, Peter Taylor used his column in *Football Post* to question Docherty's transfer dealings, 'There's just no pattern developing in his deals and I just wonder if he is nearer to getting his kind of team together than he was when he stepped into the job.'

As if in recognition of Docherty's rebuilding process, on 9 November 1977, the Assembly Rooms in Derby was officially opened by the Queen Mother. The original Assembly Rooms, built in 1755, suffered severe damage to the roof in 1963, leading to its demolition in 1971.

Forest's bubble remained very much intact by the time the return fixture came around in January. They had lost only twice all season and sat top of the table, five points clear of Everton and Liverpool. Things were getting real. Derby had steadied and sat in tenth, having won their previous three games, albeit one of those being an FA Cup win against Southend. The visit of Forest to the Baseball Ground on 14 January would be Clough and Taylor's first return since sitting in the stand adjacent to the one Sam Longson occupied that February day in October 1973. Moreover, they would have former Derby favourites Gemmill and McGovern in tow too.

Either genuinely, or simply to play down the fuss over their return, Clough focused on their title chances prior to the match. 'We are desperately keen to win the league and that is why I am treating this as just another game,' he told the *Aberdeen Press and Journal*. 'Obviously I am delighted to be going back but only as leaders of the First Division. My sole objective is to maintain our position. I am merely concerned with getting a point or two and keeping our run going. Our match at home to Arsenal next week is perhaps more important than this one.' Arsenal were in fourth place, six points behind Forest. When pressed on his rejection of a return to the Baseball Ground the previous February, Clough told the *Daily Mirror*, 'There is not the slightest tinge of regret. Peter Taylor and I are more convinced than ever that we did the right thing staying at Forest. We both realised there is no way anyone can turn back the clock and recapture old glories with a former club. We will turn up at Derby in charge of the First Division leaders instead. That is a nice feeling.'

Docherty was in bullish mood. 'The team are playing well and obviously we're hoping for a good result on Saturday,' he told the *Daily Mirror*. Derby striker Charlie George echoed his boss's confidence, 'There's not a team in the country you could back to beat us at the moment, and that includes Forest.' It promised to be a humdinger of a game with the usual fireworks.

In front of 36,500, the Baseball Ground's biggest crowd so far that season, the teams played out a 0-0 draw. 'Passion, power and pace ... they were all capsuled in an absorbing East Midlands battle of skills between Derby County and Nottingham Forest this afternoon,' reported John Lawson in *Football Post*. Peter Daniel received a booking for scything down Gemmill, who was free on goal, while Kenny Burns was troubled by a knock yet played on. The contest remained tight in the second half, despite it not quite being at the same frenetic pace as the first period. Robertson's effort from a corner was desperately scrambled away, while George's diving header was well saved by Peter Shilton in the Forest goal. It was a pulsating game with both sets of fans happy with their team's performance. Although it was McGovern's first visit back to the Baseball Ground, the fans were appreciative of his part in the club's glittering period of success, and he admitted, 'If the player had a successful record at their previous club, fans don't tend to antagonise them as much. I don't think there was any abuse.'

A week later, Forest would avenge their heavy defeat earlier in the season at Arsenal with a 2-0 home win in which Gemmill scored *that* goal. No – not that Scotland goal against Holland – but the one where he picked the ball up on the edge of his own area, travelled forward before laying it off to Withe on the wing and then powered ahead in anticipation of a return ball, which commentator David Coleman felt he would not receive, 'Withe hasn't seen him.' Until he did. 'He has now! 2-0!'

While Derby finished 12th, Forest's bubble remained resolutely intact. It didn't burst. The title was sewn up with three games to go as they finished seven points clear of Liverpool, having lost only twice all season and embarked on what was then a record unbeaten run, starting after defeat at Leeds on 19 November 1977 and ending 42 games and more than a year later on 9 December 1978 at Anfield. Just for good measure, they also lifted the League Cup after beating Liverpool in a replay at Old Trafford. Somehow, some way, Clough and Taylor had done it again. They had steered an ordinary Second Division team to the First Division title. That both teams happened to be just 16 miles apart from each other and shared an intense rivalry dating back to the transfer of the Forman brothers and the 1898 FA Cup Final was all the more remarkable. Derby and Forest fans would both now have to forever share the legacy of Brian Clough. As it is, the genius of the man is pretty much the only thing both sets of fans can find common ground on.

1978/79

One hundred tons of sand

Just like Derby before them, Forest would head into Europe under Clough. Well, kind of. The draw for the first round had not been what they wanted. No foreign adventures to crack eastern European teams or the traditional powerhouses of the continent for Forest as they came out of the hat alongside Liverpool. Still, if you are going to win the thing, you had to play the best at some stage and maybe it was better to play the reigning European champions early doors and get it out of the way. This they did and, over two legs in September, Forest dumped the holders out as their fire showed no sign of diminishing.

As for Derby, the better things got for Forest, the worse they got for the Rams. On 15 November, Docherty was suspended for seven days after he admitted that he lied under oath during a libel trial hearing, which he had brought against Willie Morgan and Granada TV when Morgan appeared on the football chat show *Kick Off* and claimed that Docherty was the worst manager there had ever been. Docherty was also a guest on the programme too. He sued for libel and the case ended up at the Old Bailey, but he eventually dropped it on its third day.

Meanwhile, on 29 November, Nottingham-born Viv Anderson became the first black player to play for England.

Forest also progressed to the quarter-finals of the European Cup, brushing aside an AEK Athens team managed by Ferenc Puskás to set up a March meeting with Grasshoppers of Zürich. Equally, their defence of the League Cup was intact, having reached the quarter-finals in that competition too. Meanwhile, Torvill and Dean competed in the European and World Championships for the first time and won the British Championships.

Perhaps feeling that the commute of players between Forest and Derby had slowed a little too much, Clough set about putting that right again by making a bid to take Charlie George off the Rams' hands on 6 December, with the striker himself apparently looking to move back down south. George was apparently keen on the move, but when he informed Docherty of his desire to switch to Forest rather than West Bromwich Albion or Southampton, George Hardy intervened and promptly announced that his board would not let the player make the switch directly to their nearest rivals.

George would eventually leave Derby but not to go south; he went to Minnesota Kicks in the North American Soccer League. Clough would later get his man for a loan spell in 1980 and, despite it being for a short period only, George would make a lasting impact at the City Ground. The attempted signing was to freshen things up a little as Clough knew all too well that his side were getting through an awful lot of games and would eventually come unstuck. And so it happened that on 9 December, Forest lost their 42-match unbeaten run as Liverpool gained revenge for their European Cup exit by beating them 2-0 at Anfield.

Forest and Derby had yet to meet in 1978/79, but the fixture computer had tantalisingly penned in Boxing Day for their first encounter at the City Ground. With Boney M taking the Christmas number one slot with 'Mary's Boy Child', many were no doubt keen to escape their homes to see this derby. Forest were, for all their lofty heights, in a slightly disappointing fifth, having chalked up lots of draws, especially at home, including four consecutive ones at the start of the season. Derby lay in 13th, largely as a result of their infuriating inconsistency. They were equally capable of stringing three wins together, as they did in November, during Docherty's suspension, yet also of racking up three consecutive defeats, like they did in early December. Docherty was seemingly in a continuous state of ringing the changes and had recently dropped the vastly experienced ex-Forest goalkeeper John Middleton for debutant David McKellar. Middleton moved between the two clubs as part of the deal to take Gemmill to the City Ground. Docherty said of his decision, 'He [Middleton] has made silly mistakes and unfortunately they have been punished. But this might shake him up a little and do him the world of good.' With comments like those, it is little wonder that there were more than a few noses out of joint at the Baseball Ground during his tenure.

The game kicked off at 11am and Forest should have gone ahead in the 19th minute when Gerry Daly and David Webb bundled over Archie Gemmill just inside the box. Forest were awarded a penalty, but John Robertson, usually so reliable from the spot, screwed his shot wide. Although Forest were in command for most of the game, Derby took the lead just before half-time. O'Neill was judged to have tripped Steve Carter just inside the area and Gerry Daly made no mistake from the spot, sending Shilton the wrong way. This was not in the script as far as Forest were concerned, yet it was just another example of the East Midlands derby caring little for the respective form and standings of the two clubs. Forest continued to make all the running in the second half and finally got their breakthrough in the 53rd minute following excellent work from Garry Birtles. He floated an inviting cross over to the far post where Woodcock was waiting to nod home and earn his team a fully deserved point.

This was Forest's 11th draw in 20 league games. In the *Daily Mirror,* David Moore wondered whether their cutting edge had gone for good. The Reds' defence remained as sturdy and miserly as the previous year, but after the sale of Peter Withe in August, goals were an increasingly rare commodity. Rookie Birtles was game and weighed in with 11 league and cup goals, including a crucial one against Liverpool in the first round of the European Cup, but Woodcock was perhaps missing the donkey work of Withe and had scored only four. *Football Post* was moved to ask in an opinion piece, 'Why has the Big Signing not materialised?'

It turned out to be just around the corner, and it was indeed a 'big signing'. The biggest, as it happened, as on 9 February Forest signed Trevor Francis in the first £1m deal. Eyebrows were raised, pearls were clutched, and the game was declared gone. Yet such a deal was merely a natural progression. After all, Derby had broken the British transfer record twice in two years in the late 1940s and again just seven years prior to this when Brian Clough signed David Nish from Leicester City. Francis's signing was admittedly a huge jump from the biggest previous record, which stood at £516,000, the fee paid by West Brom for Middlesbrough's David Mills just a month earlier. Yet Clough clearly thought Francis was worth it. History would confirm that he was.

By the time the return fixture rolled around in April, the gap between the two sides had widened. Forest had successfully defended the League Cup by beating Southampton 3-2 at Wembley; they were unbeaten in the league since the defeat at Liverpool in December, and had suffered only one defeat in all competitions, that being to Arsenal in the fifth round of the FA Cup at Highbury in February. They lay in fourth but with five games in hand on Everton in third. In second and three points ahead were West Brom, while Liverpool looked to have already sewn the title up. A slight wobble had occurred three days previously as Forest were held at home by Cologne in the semi-final first leg of the European Cup in what is considered by many to be the most dramatic game ever played at the City Ground. After going 2-0 down, Forest roared back to make it 3-2 before a last-minute howler from Shilton allowed the substitute Yasuhiko Okudera's shot to squirm under him and birthed the legendary headline 'JAPANESE SUB SINKS FOREST'. This meant the return leg in West Germany was now a daunting prospect, yet it was after this game that Brian Clough stared straight down the camera in his post-match interview and with a knowing smirk confidently proclaimed, 'I hope anybody's not stupid enough to write us off.'

By now, the Derby team was a shadow of the side that just four years before swept to the title and beat Real Madrid 4-1 in the European Cup when Charlie George scored a glorious hat-trick, before losing 5-1 at the Santiago Bernabéu Stadium in the second leg and crashing out. Yet Docherty's recruitment policy had decimated Derby to the extent that no survivors of that team took the field for this fixture. Without a win in six and with only one in their last 13, and sitting fifth from bottom, they desperately needed a victory.

The Baseball Ground pitch was not, for once, a pit of mud but instead dubbed the 'Baseball Beach', owing to 100 tons of sand that Chipmans, the contractors responsible for the maintenance of the stadium, had deposited on the playing surface. Chairman George Hardy absolved the club of blame. The sand, he said, was put on the ground 'under their instructions and under their supervision and I want no member of the staff or the board of directors blamed'. Steve Powell rattled the bar with a bullet header direct from an Andy Crawford corner and Shilton did well to save a follow-up shot from the rebound. At the other end, Francis went down in the box and legendary referee Roger Kirkpatrick awarded an indirect free kick to the right of the penalty area at a tight angle. Francis's shot was charged down. 'What a waste of money,' cried the home crowd. From the resulting throw, Woodcock shimmied down the left and crossed to the near post where Birtles glanced in to give Forest the lead on 27 minutes, his 24th goal of the season. Seven minutes later, the lead was doubled. Forest broke quickly and Birtles released Woodcock down the left who crossed to the far post, which was an invitation for O'Neill to launch himself, headfirst, towards the ball. He connected and his header struck the back of the net. Pockets of supporters cheered and celebrated in the Derby home end. Just before half-time, the Rams pulled one back. Fine work from Paul Emson forced a corner and, from it, Powell rattled the crossbar and Dave Webb was on hand to nod the ball in from close range to score his first goal for the hosts.

In the second half, Derby were unlucky not to equalise when a shot from Steve Wicks rattled the inside of the post and rolled along the line behind the bemused Shilton. Forest's goal was leading a charmed life. Yet at the other end, Woodcock was the source of all good things for Forest as his direct running and wriggling carved out numerous chances, including a particularly good one for Ian Bowyer who almost slotted in from a tight angle. Francis too jinked his through from the halfway line, but his low shot was well saved by David McKellar. Forest claimed the points with a 2-1 win.

'Derby County's endeavour and Nottingham Forest's sparkling skills whipped their big local derby match into an all-action thriller that could easily have swung either way,' was the opinion in the *Sports Argus*, and this neatly summed up the game. Even the Nottingham-based *Football Post* led with 'Out of Luck Derby'.

In the circumstances, a win at Derby on the back of the traumatic Cologne game was an excellent result and kept the pressure on Everton and West Brom for second, and owing to a particularly harsh winter and Forest's fixture pile-up they would face West Brom away on the final day of the season for what was shaping up to be a crucial encounter. The point for Derby kept rock-bottom Chelsea, Birmingham and QPR at bay, but it wouldn't prevent the club from unravelling under Docherty come the season's end.

Forest edged past Cologne 1-0 in the return leg, just like Clough thought they would, and they would then face Malmö in the Munich final. They also won their last three league games, including at West Brom, to clinch second place in addition to the League Cup and Charity Shield. Derby had their own drama to focus on, but theirs was substantially more farcical as, on 10 May, Docherty announced he was leaving to go and manage newly relegated QPR.

Just when it seemed Derby's woes and farcical scenes were over, they went up a notch when, on 17 May, police raided the Baseball Ground as part of an investigation into allegations of corrupt practice at boardroom level. Police sealed off the doors of an office in the administration block. Chairman George Hardy said in the *Daily Mirror*, 'I can confirm that police are carrying out investigations at Derby County Football Club – but I must stress that the investigations are not about the club. There is an important difference. There is no question of the club itself having done anything improper, but I have been advised by a senior police officer not to reveal anything further.'

Forest secured second spot the day after that revelation, and since 13 January they had lost only once in the league. They were in good shape as they prepared to face Malmö FF in the European Cup Final in Munich.

The Derby raid rumbled on with little closure. On 23 May, Stuart Webb told BBC Radio Derby, 'In view of the misinformed and scurrilous rumours circulating in the town, I wish to state that neither I personally, nor any company in which my wife or myself are concerned, have been involved in the transfer of any players to the United States or elsewhere.' Nothing came of the investigation, but regardless, none of what Derby achieved under Docherty that season was a good look when their rivals were preparing for a European Cup Final under their previous management team and with three key players who used to play for Derby. The Rams finished 19th, just above the dotted line – six points clear of QPR.

While the film *Alien* burst on to cinema screens in the States, featuring the memorable scene in which something terrible escapes from the stomach of Derbyshire-born John Hurt, not only did Trevor Francis justify his price tag but Nottingham Forest achieved what was previously thought unachievable, becoming champions of Europe in beating Malmö 1-0 as Francis stretched his neck muscles to head into the roof of the net from a delightful John Robertson cross before grazing his knees on a shot-put circle in Munich's Olympiastadion. The night went better for John McGovern than Archie Gemmill. McGovern, having followed Clough like a dutiful son throughout his career since he was 16 years old, and played for both East Midlands clubs, lifted the European Cup. In stark contrast, Gemmill wasn't picked to play in the final and stormed off and ultimately away from the club.

It was a truly remarkable achievement for Clough and Taylor. Being European champions eclipsed even the magnificent success of steering Derby to the title and then the semi-finals of the European Cup – something many thought impossible. Clough could have been forgiven for a degree of self-doubt after his bruising experiences at Leeds and Brighton. Yet this latest success must have made Leeds and Derby stop and wonder what might have been if they'd have given him the keys to the club, like Forest had. He had now taken two similar-sized provincial clubs to giddy heights from the Second Division. If Clough put Derby firmly on the British football map in the early 1970s, he had now put Forest on the world football map.

Their achievements mirrored a pattern around Europe. As David Goldblatt pointed out in *The Game of our Lives*, 'Before the 1990s football was one of the very few institutions in England that reversed the usual north-south polarities of power, wealth and influence.' London clubs, and indeed those from capital cities across Europe, tended to underperform in relation to larger, industrialised provincial cities. In *Why England Lose*, Simon Kuper and Stefan Szymanski opined that cities such as Milan, Amsterdam, Munich and Marseille were more industrialised than their older capitals, providing them with a larger working-class constituency from which to draw players and crowds. Arsenal, Tottenham and particularly Chelsea have grown since the formation of the Premier League to go some way towards gaining ground and trophies for London. While Nottingham and Derby certainly fit the description of being industrialised earlier than the capital and of having a substantial working-class demographic on which to draw, it still seems odd that teams from these cities rubbed shoulders with and surpassed those from places such as Milan, Marseille, Amsterdam, Munich, Porto and Glasgow. What Clough and Taylor achieved with Forest and Derby was truly exceptional for two provincial Midlands cities.

While Forest supporters lined the streets to welcome home their conquering European heroes, Colin Addison took charge of Derby in July to little fanfare.

1979/80

One last sucker punch

Could it get any better for Forest? What was left to achieve? Once you've climbed up the hill, taken a good look around and enjoyed the view, what next? If it seemed that the intertwining of the two clubs could not yin and yang any more furiously, they did just that as, a year later, Forest retained the European Cup while Derby were relegated to the Second Division.

A boxer may take delight in producing one last sucker punch to the guts as an opponent falls to the ground. At the start of the decade, Forest managed one in March 1971, just before Derby became champions and Forest were relegated. At the very end of the decade, Derby would do something eerily similar.

The writing was on the wall for Derby from the start. Still recovering from the ashes of Docherty's management style and recruitment policy, it took them five attempts to chalk up a league win, and that opening sequence of games to the season featured three consecutive defeats. A good victory against Arsenal was not the recovery springboard they hoped it would be as any win was invariably followed up with a loss. Another run of three successive defeats in October and a dreadful performance in November against a poor Ipswich side – who resided just one place below them – in November meant action had to be taken to help Colin Addison arrest the slide. In came four of their old guard, Willie Carlin and Henry Newton, to act as scouts, and Tim Ward and Frank Upton, in unspecified roles, to aid some sort of recovery in the week leading up to the clash against Forest at the Baseball Ground on 24 November 1979.

As for Forest, they seemed relatively unencumbered by the weight of their European crown. Gemmill had been sold to Birmingham after he fell out with Clough regarding his non-selection for the European Cup final against Malmö.

Francis was also missing until November owing to a curious agreement as part of his record-breaking transfer that he played out the season with Detroit Express in the North American Soccer League. In came Frank Gray at left-back after Frank Clark retired, and Asa Hartford lasted all of three games before Clough decided he had made a mistake and got rid of him – a characteristic of his that would become a recurring motif. In spite of all this, Forest won their opening four games and appeared to be making a good fist of maintaining their place at the pinnacle of English and European football as they had successfully navigated their way through to the quarter-final stage of the two trophies they were looking to retain: the League Cup and the European Cup. November brought a wobble, though, as they lost two consecutive league games for the first time since April 1977, back when they were a Second Division club. This was perhaps understandable given the sheer number of matches that came with the territory of being an incredibly successful cup team.

Yet Forest perhaps weren't in as great shape as appearances might have suggested. A week before the game, Tony Woodcock was sold to Cologne for around £600,000 and, after a disappointing home defeat to Brighton, Clough had set his targets on the 'uneducated' Nottingham public in defence of John McGovern, who had been criticised by some Forest fans. Clough lamented their 'lack of knowledge'. A win at Derby would ease the tension all round.

Passions inevitably ran high. 'Just before the start of the match fans spilled into the no-go area behind the Osmaston End goal as stewards battled to patrol Derby's biggest gate of this season,' reported *Football Post*. 'The start was delayed several minutes while police moved in to clear supporters from the touchline. Several young fans were carried away for treatment by ambulancemen.' Prior to the game, Derby secretary Michael Dunford was moved to justify a price hike of 20p for the visiting Forest fans in the matchday programme. Although the usual standing charge was £1.30, Dunford explained that the £1.50 fee for Forest fans to take their place in the Colombo End of the Popside was justified on account of extra printing and administrative expenses, in order to seal off the whole of this standing section for Forest fans. Reacting to press reports in both Nottingham and Derby that Forest fans had been exploited, he angrily denied this was the case. 'It is a pity that fuel has been put on the fire of the rivalry that exists between a handful of fans from each club, though in the past two years the behaviour of Forest fans here has been exemplary,' he wrote. 'Contrary to popular opinion, a good and understanding relationship exists between the Rams and Forest as clubs. It is a relationship which we hope will permeate among our supporters too. A close rivalry, yes, but always in the friendliest of fashions, as befits neighbours only a handful of miles from each other.' Dunford went on to remind readers that, after all, Forest charged Derby fans £1.50 to stand and, besides, admitted that they too would charge such a fee if they were European champions.

A goal for Derby after only 13 minutes went some way towards lightening the mood of the home crowd but did nothing to ease the crowded conditions. Gerry Daly tapped in after Shilton flapped at, then fumbled, a routine cross. The floodgates opened. It didn't just rain, it poured. In the next five minutes, Forest found themselves three down to a rampant Rams team. Some swift and neat passing freed Dave Langan down the right, and his cross – although partly parried by Shilton – fell invitingly for John Duncan to nod in. Almost immediately, two became three as Steve Emery capitalised on some hesitant defending and slotted home. Just two weeks previously, Forest found themselves beaten 4-1 at Southampton and earlier in the season they succumbed to a 3-1 defeat at Carrow Road. The defensive rock upon which the unprecedented success was built started to wobble. Only two minutes into the second half, Forest won a penalty when Gary Mills was tripped in the box. Robertson converted, but it counted for little as Duncan scored a fourth for Derby when he glanced a free kick beyond Shilton 13 minutes from the end.

Despite Forest sweeping all before them both domestically and in Europe, one might be forgiven for wondering whether a local derby would still get the competitive juices flowing when such an imbalance existed between the two competing teams. 'You still get the buzz,' said McGovern. 'It's irrelevant where the teams are in the league when it's a local derby. Even if a team is going to get relegated, if they win the derby match, it makes up for other failings and takes care of other feelings. It makes up for a lot if you can win the derby game. It forgives a multitude of sins if you can win your derby matches on a regular basis.'

Once again, the East Midlands derby gods had reinforced their power and reminded everyone that for any participant to think that the result of any such game is a foregone conclusion is the ultimate act of folly and hubris. Forest dropped a place while Derby climbed one. After the game, Clough struck a prickly note in his dealings with the press before flying out to Egypt for a match against a Cairo Select XI. When asked, 'Like a drink, Brian?' he retorted with, 'They don't call me Brian; they call me Clough ... just to let you know what mood I'm in.' Underlying his mood was a deep concern about his side's form. 'There are problems at Nottingham Forest because we're losing matches consistent with a side that's going to be relegated,' said Clough. 'We're having a nightmare by our standards and I don't think the management's working hard enough, I genuinely feel that.' This was one of many occasions in such periods when heavy defeat results in the losing manager partaking in some deep soul searching against the backdrop of a seemingly cataclysmic crisis. It was not the first time, and it definitely wouldn't be the last, when defeat in the derby made the losing club question everything and undergo a period of existential crisis.

The result certainly knocked Forest out of their stride as they drew against Arsenal, then lost their next two games. The League Cup was finally relinquished as a mix-up between David Needham and Shilton allowed Andy Gray to steal in and tap home for Wolves to finally prise the trophy from Forest's firm grip. Nonetheless, by the time of the second leg in April, they were one step away from another European Cup final after beating Ajax in the semi-final first leg 2-0 at the City Ground after a superb comeback in Berlin against Dynamo at the quarter-final stage. Just for good measure, the European Super Cup was now safely ensconced in the trophy cabinet after Forest beat Barcelona over two legs, the second coming in front of 80,000 at the Camp Nou, where Kenny Burns headed in to secure a 1-1 draw following a single Charlie George goal from the first leg on 5 February. Clough eventually got the former Derby man, but only for a brief loan period. The transfer treadmill between the two clubs remained as busy as ever.

Nottingham's sporting star continued to rise. In February, Torvill and Dean competed in their first Winter Olympics in Lake Placid and finished in a respectable fifth position. After years of combining work with ice skating, the time had come to commit full-time to their talents. They left their jobs and secured a grant from Nottingham City Council, which meant they could pursue ice skating with even more dedication.

Just like the previous campaign, the return derby was scheduled for August and given the timing, would be crucial in determining the overall state of the season. Forest sat tenth but just like the previous season, they had a backlog of games to get through. Derby were in the relegation zone, three points behind Everton despite having played two games more than the Merseysiders. With only three matches remaining, they simply had to win to give themselves a chance of survival. A victory the previous week against Brighton offered hope, but after Forest they faced title-chasing Manchester United, who were still in with a chance of snatching the crown from Liverpool. Clough was wary of the threat that Derby faced, 'You can be sure that they will take the field against us still believing that they have a chance of staying up and equally sure that their target is two points – not just one.'

The biggest home crowd of the season, 32,226 including a noisy contingent of Rams supporters, packed into the City Ground. The fact that the attendance bettered that for the

European Cup semi-final against Ajax tells you all you need to know about the rivalry between the two sets of supporters.

Just before half-time, Stan Bowles rolled a free kick to Gray who fired a thunderbolt shot through a gap in the wall and into the goal at the Bridgford End. It was a well-earned win for Forest whose home form had improved in recent months, while Derby seemed to revert to type after an encouraging run of five games unbeaten in March. Ultimately, despite that run, it was a case of too little, too late. 'This is the end of it,' lamented Colin Addison. 'We've had a couple of good months but now it's over.'

'You don't want your rivals to go down as you lose the derby matches for the next season,' said McGovern. 'Everybody wants to play in a brilliant atmosphere in front of a full house. The Baseball ground, with its high stands created, for the night matches with the floodlights, the best atmosphere I've ever played in. You could literally put a player into the stands with a tackle.' For the time being, such games were off the table as the teams headed in diametrically opposed directions.

All Derby needed now to compound their misery following relegation at the hands of their bitter rivals was to see Forest reach the European Cup Final and defend their trophy. The Reds did precisely this. A 1-0 reverse in Amsterdam was just enough to see them through to the final in Madrid at the Santiago Bernabéu Stadium, scene of a humbling and hurtful defeat for Derby in the 1976 European Cup. There, Forest faced a strong Hamburg side, spearheaded by Kevin Keegan. A single strike from John Robertson, provider of the cross that saw Francis score the deciding goal a year earlier in Munich, was just about enough to bring the big cup back to Nottingham once again.

All of which meant a complete reversal of both clubs' fortunes in the space of eight years. In 1972, Derby were champions of England under Clough, while Forest were relegated to the Second Division; yet just eight years later, Forest had not only claimed a league title of their own but were now double European Cup winners under Clough, while it was Derby who were on their way down. 'The beauty of it is that it was one manager that gave them the hopes and dreams that nobody else had got close to,' explained McGovern. It is little wonder that a statue of Clough stands both outside Pride Park in Derby and on Speaker's Corner on the middle of Nottingham's city centre today.

8

Empires crumble and walls come tumbling down: 1980–1993

AS THE 1980s dawned, two huge hangovers were being experienced in the East Midlands, but for very different reasons. One of the sore heads was reflecting on a long and boozy night spent hosting and beating Europe's most beautiful and talented hipsters, while the other emerged stumbling from the wreckage of a trashed terraced house, which slowly collapsed while inside everyone just stared into the distance, wishing they were somewhere else. Yet all parties, good, bad or indifferent, eventually end. If the immediate comedown for Forest seemed, at least at the time, underwhelming, Derby's hangover would be even harder and longer-lasting. As the decade unfolded, the black hole into which they were falling seemed bottomless.

While some Ipswich Town players spent the summer in Budapest with Michael Caine, Sylvester Stallone and Pelé filming *Escape to Victory*, the Forest squad might well have been entertaining thoughts of a third successive European Cup triumph. Yet the 1980/81 season was a frustrating one for the club after their stratospheric success of the previous three years, during which they scooped up everything apart from the FA Cup. A seventh-placed finish was reasonable, if disappointing, as was meekly surrendering their hold on the European Cup at the first hurdle to CSKA Sofia, who later succumbed to eventual winners, Liverpool, in the quarter-finals. Regret at not taking the World Club Championship in Tokyo against Nacional of Uruguay was expressed by John Robertson and losing out to Ipswich Town in the quarter-finals of the FA Cup signalled that Forest weren't quite their old selves, perhaps understandably given the intense rise from Second Division football just four years previously. Simply put, such success was unsustainable for a club the size of Forest when faced with the experience and wealth of Liverpool. Despite that, Forest did succeed in being a particularly irritating thorn in the side of that outstanding Liverpool side for a few years.

The team was ageing, and Brian Clough sought to rebuild after allowing Garry Birtles, Martin O'Neill, Ian Bowyer and Larry Lloyd to leave, with more of his stalwarts and names synonymous with the glory days also departing just a year later. Their return to solid mid-table was almost as swift as their rise from the Second Division. Besides, much-needed financial resource was diverted towards the funding of the Executive Stand, which opened for the first home game of the season. Forest would have to adapt to, among other factors on the horizon, the huge sense of expectation while trying to build a brand-new team.

But if Forest and their fans felt deflated, all they had to do was take a look down the A52 where a brief glance would offer some perspective and no doubt a smile. A promising start to the season at the Baseball Ground gave way to a steep drop in form after the turn of the year, despite the return of Kevin Hector in October 1980. The likes of Dave Swindlehurst and Alan Biley didn't hit the heights expected of them as the Rams struggled to replace the loss of Dave Langan, Gerry Daly, Aiden McCaffery and David McKellar. Roy McFarland, after his injury-troubled season, left to take the position of player-manager at Bradford City. Manager Colin Addison had quite a task on his hands. Finishing seventh was by no means disastrous for Derby, but the disappointment of not bouncing back and subsequently languishing in the Second Division was a depressing one, with just increasingly serious financial ramifications, none of them good.

Social unrest was in the air come the summer as, between 10 and 12 July 1981, riots broke out around the Hyson Green Flats complex in Nottingham, culminating in a battle between the police and the rioters. Just a few months earlier, serious riots had broken out in Brixton, Toxteth, Handsworth, Chapeltown and Moss Side, prompted in part by a mistrust of the police and authority and fuelled by racial tension and inner-city deprivation. The economy was in deep recession and unemployment was on the rise, from 5.4 per cent to 9.8 per cent in the space of just two years. Margaret Thatcher's Conservative government was struggling to cope with the rising anger, while 'Ghost Town' by The Specials hit the top of the charts and epitomised the despair and dark mood of the country. Attendances were falling and hooliganism was on the rise.

The following campaign wasn't any better for either Forest or Derby as the nationwide gloom persisted over the East Midlands. The 1981/82 season saw the introduction of three points for a win, the theory being that such a prize would prompt more attacking football. Perhaps word didn't quite get round to either end of the A52. With Derby rarely out of the bottom half of the table, inevitably Addison paid for this with his job midway through the season, but not before the obligatory headlines about him refusing to quit under pressure had surfaced in September. 'I'm not about to run away, and nor is my assistant John Newman,' the *Daily Mirror* reported him as saying.

Inevitably, any time a Derby manager was having a bad time of it, the spectre of Brian Clough's return loomed large, irrespective of Forest's position of strength compared to Derby's pending meltdown. 'These rumours concerning Clough have been floating around for so long, John and I decided to clear the air,' said Addison. Regardless, Derby's board saw things differently and, after he cleared his desk, Newman stepped in and took the helm. Charlie George returned towards the end of the season, swelling the gates a little and prompting an improvement, but they still required a result on the final day of the season to be mathematically safe from relegation, which they got, meaning they finished in 16th place. Just to make things that little bit more difficult, the club were also struggling financially and in January they launched a proposal to raise funds by selling 60,000 £10 shares. The following month, chairman Bill Stevenson admitted, 'We do owe about £100,000 in VAT and PAYE, but I am certain that this will not lead to the club's future being threatened.'

Things were not so rosy at the City Ground either. In September, John Robertson was made to play for Forest's third team against a side of Derby amateurs representing

British Rail. Peter Taylor was in the stands and saw the Scottish winger score twice in the first 25 minutes before being withdrawn. This was probably punishment for the previous weekend when Robertson was sent home before the game against Stoke City. Robertson himself played the incident down, explaining that he lost sight of the other players while he was signing autographs, 'After I had finished signing, I did not know which way they had gone and I headed in the wrong direction until I saw Peter Taylor coming towards me. There was no row or anything like that, but after the meal the boss come to me and said I would not be playing and to make arrangements to return to Nottingham.' This, coupled with the signing of the misfiring Justin Fashanu, all pointed towards a tetchy atmosphere in the Forest dressing room and was probably a symptom of the malaise the club found themselves in after scaling such heights.

In addition, and on the same day that Stevenson was trying to offer reassurance regarding the future of Derby County, Clough returned to work for the first time since being taken ill at Christmas. Even in among such testing circumstances for both Clough and Derby County, the rumours about a possible return to the Rams simply wouldn't go away. 'I said a couple of weeks ago while I was on holiday,' he told the *Aberdeen Press and Journal*, 'that I was not interested in the Derby job and the position hasn't changed. I've still got 15 months of my present contract with Forest to run and I hope I'll be here for a good deal longer than that. I mean it when I say I have no interest in managing any other club.' He was also forced to address rumours of a rift between him and Taylor. 'Our relationship now is exactly the same was it was ten years ago.' Be that as it may, Forest slipped to 12th in the table.

It also turned out not to be true and May 1982 saw the sudden resignation of Clough's long-time assistant and friend, Peter Taylor. Taylor felt physically and mentally drained, little wonder given that he had held the reins while Clough was ill and had seen his recommended signing, Fashanu, struggle so badly. Yet he denied talk of any falling-out. 'There has never been any rift between Brian and myself,' he told the *Daily Mirror*. 'Although I must admit we've had more ups and downs this year than most. I've never known a season before with Brian when we finished unable to win or lose anything, and the experience has left me exhausted.' Clough too toed the party line, 'I'm going to ring Peter in six months and get him out of retirement. Peter's decision didn't come as a surprise to me, because I know the stress and strain involved in top management. I won't be replacing him. That would be like trying to replace Lester Piggott or Geoff Boycott. But life will go on at Forest, just as it will after I have gone too.'

Despite the public platitudes towards each other, Taylor's book, *With Clough by Taylor*, had indeed been a source of tension between them. Clough resented Taylor signing a deal for it and writing it without letting him know and explained to Duncan Hamilton in *Provided You Don't Kiss Me: 20 Years with Brian Clough* that he felt Taylor was cashing in on his name. Perhaps most of all, he felt that the bond of trust had been broken by his old friend, and from that point on, there seemed little that could be done in the way of fixing old or building new bridges. As for Taylor, he clearly felt he was perfectly entitled to earn himself a little money, especially when he had stood by watched Clough write numerous columns and make countless television appearances. On publication of the book, the resentment grew from both sides, culminating in Taylor's paranoia as he acted as manager while Clough recovered from illness. He told Hamilton, 'I've been running this club for a few weeks now, and yet I keep reading – even in your paper – [he leant over, arm outstretched, and pointed at me] that soon he'll [he couldn't bring himself to call him Brian] be back in charge. That's the phrase. Back in charge. I don't like it. The suggestion is that I'm not in charge. Well, I am, and it's about time you knew it.'

It was a sad end not only to a legendary working partnership that elevated two middling clubs to the peak of their existence but also to a once deep and genuine friendship. Clough would have to rebuild his team alone.

The new campaign brought little grounds for optimism at Derby. They lost their opening game of the 1982/83 season 3-2 to Carlisle United in front of only 11,000 at the Baseball Ground. Both attendances and the quality of performances continued to fall, culminating in a crowd of 8,075 for the game against Chelsea in September. Something had to change. In November, Mike Watterson took on the role of chairman from Bill Stevenson. Times were hard, so hard in fact that one week Rotherham United chairman Anton Johnson paid the wages of the Derby staff. The services of John Newman, whose tenure seemed to have a whiff of impermanence about it from the start, were dispensed with. Yet few would have predicted the identity of his replacement as Peter Taylor made a surprisingly quick return from retirement.

Derby were bottom with only eight points from 13 games. Taylor set about doing the sensible thing in such a position and fell back on those he knew he could trust to perform. Back came Archie Gemmill as a player. Back came Roy McFarland as assistant manager, albeit at a cost as Bradford City successfully appealed for compensation after Derby prised him out of his successful managerial role at Valley Parade.

One can only imagine how Taylor's Lazarus-like return to management was received in Clough's office. And then, as if a stronger force was at work, Derby drew Forest in the fourth round of the FA Cup.

The depth of the narrative strands running through the fixture was frankly bewildering, even for these two closely intertwined clubs. Taylor selected Gemmill to stalk the midfield and youngster Gary Mills to shackle John Robertson. Mills, Forest's youngest-ever player, had played in the 1980 European Cup Final and was still technically contracted to the Reds, despite being loaned out to Seattle Sounders who in turn loaned him to Derby. As for Forest, double title-winning Derby legend Colin Todd was told minutes before the Forest team arrived at the Baseball Ground by Clough that he wouldn't be playing. 'I did not think Colin was ready for this particular game – and I am sure my decision came as a relief to him,' Clough rather enigmatically said after the game.

Just for good measure, Forest keeper Steve Sutton was born and raised in Derbyshire and would later play for the Rams and knew about the rivalry all too well. 'The under-18 games were big ones between Forest and Derby,' said Sutton, 'because there were a lot of players that had gone through school together and at county level together. There were one or two naughty games because those players went into the first team: Colin Walsh, Gary Mills, Steve Cherry [at Derby], Steve Blades. They were all roughly the same age and each team had half a dozen players that came from the Under-18s right through to senior level.' A further layer of plot complications was also percolating, if not yet fully realised, with the selection of Robertson.

The game was huge. Mills later explained how it was drilled into them ahead of the game that the league was the priority, with no mention of Forest until four days prior. 'So when we came back to training on Thursday, after four matches in eight days, it was all about Forest at last,' he told *The Ram*. The same publication sought score predictions from those who had represented both clubs. It was a long list: Colin Addison, Alan Hill, Frank Wignall, Jimmy Gordon, Colin Murphy, Charlie George, John Middleton and John McGovern all foresaw a tight game but favoured Forest to progress. Only Henry Newton and John O'Hare predicted the Rams would win.

Within ten seconds of kick-off, Nottingham-born Steve Hodge narrowly missed taking both Gemmill's legs from beneath him and Kevin Wilson barged Forest stalwart Ian Bowyer to the ground. Referee George Courtney blithely allowed play to go on and the tone was set. John Barton scythed through Robertson, who moments later was required to take a throw-in deep in enemy territory. A Derby fan returned the ball to him with the force of a Stuart Pearce free kick to the delight of the vociferous home crowd. He hugged the touchline, but with every ball played to him a flash of white hurtled in his direction, forcing him to take evasive action. All the while, the crowd, a metre behind him, lapped it up. Derby fancied this. 'Robbo took some stick,' confirmed Sutton. 'He was man-marked all game. We had nothing else. Derby were up for that game.'

Eventually, something resembling a football match almost broke out. Wilson latched on to a header and bore down on a loose ball in the Forest area, but Sutton dived to the floor and got there first. For his reward, he received an imprint of Wilson's studs in his chest. The ball was momentarily loose, a tiny white orb snatched at from all directions by snapping hungry hippos. All the while, Taylor calmly watched on, the collar of his tan jacket turned up, drawing attention to his Aquascutum scarf. Clough remained in the deepest shadows of the dugout in his green jumper. He was back at the Baseball Ground, but it was not the same. This wasn't how it was supposed to be. Not like this.

Forest couldn't get out of their own half, the mud weighing heavily on their shoulders. Gemmill was running the show, picking up the loose balls and calmly firing them back into positions the Forest defence didn't want it to be. Robertson was forced so far back that he was operating at left-back. Even when they did get out of their own half, the ball came straight back at them, turning the defence time and time again. A cross was flighted over and Mark Proctor's header forced an instinctive save from Steve Cherry in the Derby goal. It was the only time he was troubled in the first half as waves and waves of Derby attacks unrelentingly rolled into the Forest half. Gemmill glided across the Baseball Ground mud like it was 1975, not 1983. 'I sold Archie 12 months too early,' Clough said after the game. 'I have dropped a lot of clangers in my life, I dropped one when I sold him.' Clough knew. He had seen this all before. It wasn't going his way, for once. He didn't want to be there, not like this, with HIM sat yards away, back at the Baseball Ground, of all places. It was the football equivalent of watching your ex-lover, for whom you still pine, taking their new flame to where you used to lie down when you were together.

The second half continued just the same as the first. Derby won a free kick after Willie Young felled Wilson in desperation. Gemmill flighted the ball gently over the wall and into the bottom of the net. The place erupted. Chaos reigned and pandemonium ruled. Home supporters spilled on to the pitch, arms aloft, moving in concentric circles, a mass of iron filings zigging and zagging in isolation but also somehow in unison. The goalscorer wanted that and he wanted this, pumping his fist towards his team-mates, the message, 'We can do this. They might be First Division and European Cup winners and we might be struggling at the foot of the Second Division, but that doesn't matter right now, and neither is it important. They don't fancy it. We do.'

The memories are still vivid for Sutton. He recalled, 'Robbo was in the wall and he turned round and pointed, "He's going to put it that side." I've thought about why I didn't believe him. Maybe I was too headstrong. Perhaps I was convinced Archie was going to go the other side. I slipped and never got anywhere near it in the end. Had I set up differently, would he have put it in the other corner? You hedge your bets, but I was young and inexperienced.'

Forest got the game going again, but the white wave was relentless. Gemmill went down injured with a thigh strain. Robertson was substituted and hobbled off. It was tough out there and got tougher in that special shade of darkness that only Saturday evenings in January under the floodlights produce around 4.23pm. Gemmill was withdrawn, but his job was done. Chants pierced the dank air, 'Derby are back. Derby are back. Uh-oh. Uh-oh.'

Another brief Forest attack moored in the mud. Mike Brolly intervened and rescued the ball from the swamp. He skipped past an unrolled toilet roll and slipped in Andy Hill, who gently dinked the ball over Sutton. Game over. Forest were out of the FA Cup again, the only major trophy to elude Clough, and it was his old mate who ensured it continued to do so. At Derby. At the Baseball Ground. After he said he was going home for good, not sneaking out in the dead of night without him and going back to the old place.

Taylor stood for a moment then headed for the tunnel. He paused. Or did he simply get delayed by a body in front of him? When he did get moving again, a green jumper flashed away from him, ahead of him, into the bowels of the stand. They missed each other. No handshake. No acknowledgment. Lots of water but not under the bridge. If Taylor had emerged two seconds quicker, might they have? And if their paths had crossed, would an olive branch have been extended? Might it have been accepted? Maybe it was best they didn't. It could have been ugly. As it was, they each carved their own separate path into the night.

'Putting one over on Clough in the FA Cup third round at the start of 1983 was a considerable bonus,' wrote Archie Gemmill in his book, *Both Sides of the Border.* 'It felt good but strange at the same time. That 2-0 result was the shock of the round as the 22nd club in the Second Division beat the fourth in the First Division with the help of a rather fine free kick from yours truly. I curled the ball over and past Steve

Sutton. The atmosphere was terrific and Derby played far in excess of their capabilities on the day. Much of that was down to the superb job Gary Mills did on John Robertson, although I was named man of the match and recall getting a standing ovation as I reluctantly left the Baseball Ground mud-heap before the end with a hamstring injury.'

Clough sought out Gemmill to tell him what a superb game he had had. He didn't speak to Taylor. Both Steve Hodge and Stuart Pearce note how during their time playing under Clough at Forest, the games he was most revved up for were the East Midlands derby matches. 'He hated losing to them,' wrote Pearce. 'I can understand that in part – I don't like losing to clubs I used to play for. It was emphasised for him because of the bad feeling when he left the old Baseball Ground.' No doubt this game only added to that particularly bad feeling.

'He was so disappointed,' reflected Sutton. 'So disappointed. When we lost there wasn't normally a big show. There was very rarely anything after a game apart from "Go and have a nice meal with your wives ... I won't! You've ruined my weekend!" There was always a little barb tagged on at the end! But on that occasion, he was very quiet. It really hurt him, and it stayed with him for quite a while that game, I think.'

On the final whistle, the home fans invaded the pitch once more, some in delight, yet others spoiling for a fight as they ran towards the away supporters. For a moment, things turned nasty as the Derby fans tried to break the line of police that had hastily formed while the Forest fans tried to clamber over or through or simply to tear down the tall railings that were common around football grounds in the

1980s. It was a truly volatile atmosphere. 'I'm convinced, had it not been for the sheer scale of the police operation – not to mention the sturdiness of those fences – deaths would have occurred inside the Baseball Ground that day,' admitted Forest fan Chris Broughton. 'Without exception, I have never witnessed such hatred and loathing between rival supporters as was displayed on this occasion.'

One might imagine that, once the dust settled, heads were cracked together at the first Forest training session come Monday morning. But that wasn't the case. 'It wasn't until the Tuesday after the game that it came up,' Sutton explained. 'Cloughie never mentioned it after the game at all. I think we were doing free kicks or something down at the training ground and one went in the top corner. Robbo went, "Oh, don't suppose you knew where that was going either," or some sarky comment.

'Cloughie said, "Well, go on then Steve, tell me what happened."

'So I said, "Look, that's how I saw it. I slipped when I took off, to be fair, Robbo told me." There was a pause. "All right. Don't do it again."

'And that was it.'

After another resounding 3-0 defeat to Carlisle straight after this game, Derby embarked on a 15-match unbeaten run in the league. Yet two defeats towards the end of the season meant that they went into the final game against Fulham at the Baseball Ground not mathematically safe; somehow the Rams won 1-0 to seal survival for another year. Some pride was established, especially given their win over Forest yet behind the scenes they were still haemorrhaging money and, having had had enough of dealing with the trials and tribulations that came with running a struggling football club, Watterson resigned.

The FA Cup tie wasn't the end of the saga between these clubs though. Once the season was over, John Robertson joined Taylor at Derby. The rift was now an inseparable chasm.

'I suppose I have already gone down in history as the man responsible for the much-publicised split between Brian Clough and Peter Taylor,' is the opening sentence of a chapter titled, 'Parting of the Ways', from John Robertson's autobiography, *Super Tramp*. According to Robertson, the pair had been drifting apart for a while, prompted in part by Taylor's book. This apparently caused a major falling-out between them, during which words were spoken and the language used was 'a little bit on the blue side'. Their relationship deteriorated further when Taylor decided he was retiring in the summer of 1982, but what really irritated Clough was Taylor then surfacing as manager of Derby in November of that year. Of all the places to pop up again after apparently retiring.

Perhaps a part of Clough had stored away the happy memories of their time at Derby, to be opened once they were both old and grey as they sat together in a rose garden with blankets over their laps, enjoying a whiskey and a cigar. Yet Taylor going back – alone – sullied those happy memories for Clough. The thought of his old mate once again watching from the dugout at the Baseball Ground without him seemed too much to bear, a personal rejection, an erasing of their past and their principles. If they were ever going to go back, they would do it together, but for Clough that moment had come and gone.

Forest's European Cup-winning team was quickly and hastily dismantled, yet the players brought in were not of the same quality and performances suffered. By 1982, Robertson and Viv Anderson were the only players left at the City Ground who had a European Cup winners' medal in their pockets. Having turned 30 and recently suffered cartilage damage, Robertson felt vulnerable. Taylor was not backwards in telling him he could always start afresh with him at Derby. In his head, he had agreed to leave Forest; he just hadn't told anyone about it yet.

After Robertson had scored the last goal in a 4-3 win over Notts County in the final of the Nottinghamshire County Cup, Clough told him to see him the next day to discuss a new deal. He was offered a two-year contract, but that couldn't match the three-year one waiting for his signature over at the Baseball Ground. 'Looking back, it was the worst thing I could ever have done,' said Robertson. 'I am proud of what I achieved, but I do chastise myself when I think back to that day. I can also recall the telling-off I got from my Sally [his wife] when I told her I had gone against her wishes and not dwelt on the move. I had been a Forest player all my life and I hadn't taken into account what it meant for a player to jump ship and join the arch-enemy that Derby had always been. At the end of the day, I was committing professional suicide. I was leaving a team fifth in the First Division and looking forward to being back in Europe for one that was in the Second Division and struggling financially.'

His timing was poor too. While he and Taylor were discussing his move to Derby, Clough was participating in the Centurion Walk, a charity walk to raise money for an electric chair for a disabled girl in West Bridgford. It was his wife, Barbara, who told him that Robertson had signed for Taylor over at Derby halfway through the walk. No doubt the Yorkshire Dales air was turned blue once he put the phone down. He vowed never to speak to Taylor again, nor Robertson.

Shortly after Robertson finalised his move to Derby, his first child, Jessica, was born. Jessica was severely disabled. In Robertson's own words, 'It was the worst time of my life.'

Despite all of this tumult, Clough steered his side to fifth in the table. The return of Garry Birtles from his spectacularly unsuccessful spell with Manchester United and the signing of goalkeeper Hans van Breukelen, alongside the emergence of Steve Hodge and Peter Davenport, played key roles in this achievement.

As for Derby, a 13th-placed finish illustrated what a big part Taylor played in preventing his team's slide. If that final position seems comfortable, it tells only a portion of the tale of the last-day drama. To guarantee survival for sure, Derby needed a result against promotion-chasing Fulham. When Bobby Davison superbly put his team ahead with 14 minutes remaining, the jubilant home crowd invaded the pitch to celebrate. For some reason, huge numbers were never fully cleared from the perimeter and stood there for the remainder of the game, occasionally wandering on to congratulate their goalkeeper, Steve Cherry, for making a save and more sinisterly, aiming a kick at Fulham's Robert Wilson when he was down by the corner flag. At the sound of a whistle, the fans once again invaded the pitch to celebrate, yet in fact 78 seconds remained. The whistle they heard, from referee Ray Chadwick, was for offside. Clearing the pitch was now an impossibility and, although Fulham appealed to have the game replayed, there was nothing doing and Malcolm Macdonald's team, like Derby, remained in the Second Division for another year.

1983/84
Maxwell descends

The signs of a financial implosion at Derby were there for all to see in the 1983/84 season. Robertson's salary would not have been cheap and both wages and instalments for the transfers of the winger and Yugoslavian goalkeeper Yakka Banovic were overdue. Come January, things were getting serious as Derby were prevented from signing any more players as the holding company, Derby County Ltd, was staring down the barrel at bankruptcy. The abolishment of a percentage of league game receipts being given to away clubs after pressure from the bigger clubs with the bigger grounds to keep a larger percentage of the takings share meant that, especially for clubs the size of Forest and Derby, the capacity of your own home crowd was more crucial than ever in generating much-needed income. Forest's newly built Executive Stand, funded from the proceeds of their European success, meant – on the surface, at least – higher attendances and, thus, more income. However, the cost of building the stand rather scuppered mopping up all that perceived hypothetical revenue.

As for Derby, languishing in the Second Division while desperately spending in an effort to address that very problem pointed in only one direction. Whichever way you looked at it, the situation was growing desperate. Inland Revenue and Customs and Excise were banging on their door for around £1.5m, while the ground was now owned by

National Westminster Bank and their interest charges were significantly less than favourable. If there was one sliver of a silver lining to be found in among this mess, it was progress to the quarter-finals of the FA Cup, with both scenarios culminating in March. Yet such a run while the team were fighting relegation to the third tier was a classic case of deckchair rearrangement on a listing ship.

As if the situation wasn't desperate enough, Nottingham was enjoying European triumphs again when, in February 1984, Torvill and Dean become Olympic gold medallists in Sarajevo with a string of sixes to Ravel's Bolero, thus achieving perfection. Forest were also turning heads once again in Europe as they progressed impressively in the UEFA Cup. The spring of 1984 was seismic for their East Midlands rivals, but for very different reasons.

Despite seeing off non-league Telford United and First Division Norwich City, Derby stalled on paying their share of the gate receipts for those ties and thus briefly jeopardised their continued participation. Nonetheless, they faced Plymouth Argyle of the Third Division for a place in the last four on 10 March, just two days before a High Court date to address the claims for substantial unpaid VAT. This sparked a desperate scramble around for cash, mostly in the form of new directors turning up with fresh investment and present directors dipping even deeper into their pockets. There was also external interest in the shape of a millionaire publisher by the name of Robert Maxwell. Despite Maxwell's proposal of a bail-out, Mr Justice Mervyn Davies wasn't fully satisfied, and the case was adjourned.

Two days later, on 14 March, Derby faced Plymouth again after a goalless draw in Devon. Steve Cherry conceded a goal direct from a corner at the Baseball Ground to put Plymouth through to the semi-finals on the day that Maxwell withdrew his interest. With Derby third from bottom in the Second Division, this was not a good day in the history of a club quickly approaching their centenary year. Just ten years previously, they were on their way to the First Division title.

After numerous adjournments, court wrangling and meetings, the directors satisfied the claimants and Derby lived to see another day as the winding-up petition was withdrawn on 12 April, thanks in part to Maxwell's investment in the club. The days were bleak, though, as Taylor was sacked, and under McFarland's temporary stewardship, Derby were relegated to the third tier.

Meanwhile, in the same month, Forest progressed to the semi-finals of the UEFA Cup, having seen off Austria's Sturm Graz. All that stood between them and another European final was the highly rated Belgian side Anderlecht. A day before the withdrawal of Derby's winding-up order, Forest played the first leg at the City Ground where the smallest player on the pitch, Steve Hodge, scored two headed goals to give the Reds what seemed like an unassailable lead. The return leg in Brussels was never going to be easy, despite a two-goal advantage, and it quickly transpired that it would be nigh-on impossible since the Spanish referee, Emilio Guruceta Muro, was making some odd decisions. The fact that Anderlecht won the game 3-0 barely begins to tell the story.

With Anderlecht already one goal up on the night, thanks to an excellent strike by Enzo Scifo, Muro awarded the home side a penalty when a gust of wind upended an attacker in the penalty area. Kenneth Brylle converted to level the aggregate score. Clearly rattled now, Forest conceded again in the 88th minute when Erwin Vandenbergh danced through the defence and completed an outstanding turnaround. Yet a minute later, Forest forced a corner and Paul Hart headed in what looked like a perfectly legitimate goal, meaning that they would progress on away goals. It was not to be, though, as Muro somehow found a reason to disallow the goal. Anderlecht went through to the final where they would face Tottenham and lose in a penalty shoot-out.

Letting a two-goal lead slip doesn't reflect well on Forest, even if decisions went against them, and such a loss could easily be dismissed as the whining and moaning of a toddler that got what they wanted for their birthday but immediately dropped it, smashing it into a thousand pieces. Yet when documents came to light revealing that Anderlecht's former president, Constant Vanden Stock, had used a local gangster to pay the Spanish referee £18,000, the protests from the Forest camp look entirely justified. While Clough was initially angry, in the dressing room after the game, he was very subdued. 'Just really quiet,' Paul Hart told *The Guardian* in 2013. 'Unusually quiet.' Given his experiences as Derby manager in the semi-finals of the European Cup 11 years previously, perhaps he was resigned to such events. In a breathtaking exhibition of ostentation, Anderlecht's ground was called the Constant Vanden Stock Stadium up until 2019.

With Forest licking their wounds and Derby applying industrial amounts of sticking plaster to theirs, Maxwell's involvement in the Rams was under way, and it turned out to be quite the proverbial rollercoaster ride. Despite already owning Oxford United, Maxwell helped rescue Derby in September 1984, descending on the Baseball Ground in his own private helicopter. The fact that he left before the final whistle perhaps indicates where his interest in acquiring a football club really lay. In June 1987, he took over as chairman and started splashing the cash, propelling Derby to the top division and breathing much-needed life and glamour into the faded glory of the Baseball Ground, until it all came crashing down in a cascade of dust, ashes, smoke and mirrors.

Born in poverty in Eastern Europe and having lost his parents at Auschwitz, Maxwell enlisted in the British army and learned English by listening to Churchill on the radio. He was a ruthless soldier – once saying, 'I had a determination to kill Germans' – and highly regarded by superior officers and his men. After the war, he operated as a spy for British intelligence and along the way acquired a vast collection of scientific papers from Germany, which he began publishing, and in doing so was directly responsible for important advances in medicine and physics in the 1950s as his publishing gave academics a platform. His business grew to become the largest publishing business in the world of scientific papers at the height of the Cold War.

He dabbled in politics and was elected Labour MP for Buckingham in 1964, yet changed course and tried to get into newspaper publishing and ownership. In 1969, he tried to buy the *News of the World*, but Rupert Murdoch got there first and kept Maxwell at arm's length from the industry for a while, owing partly to anti-Semitism in the city. Not to be deterred and determined to muscle his way to Britain's top table somehow, he bought Oxford United and rescued the largest printing company in Europe, BPC, from bankruptcy and paid huge sums for publishers McMillan. In 1984, he eventually achieved his dream and bought the *Daily Mirror*, resulting in a long-running feud between his group and Murdoch and his papers, especially *The Sun*. It was at this stage that he rescued Derby County from severe financial strife. He organised the club's debts and bought the ground back from the bankers. He remained a distant owner, leaving the running of the club to son, Ian, who was installed as vice-chairman, and managing director Stuart Webb. Being the owner of a huge newspaper group, what he could do was use his influence in other ways. Most obviously, he could dangle huge sums in front of the eyes of prospective signings and, if that failed, he could have a word with the editor of his sports desk with a view to nudging opinion in whichever direction favoured him.

The extent of Maxwell's refusal to be told 'no' and his use of his media companies to curry support in his favour or otherwise is perfectly illustrated by the protracted transfer of Lee Chapman, caught in a tug-of-war between Derby and Forest in October 1988. When Chapman realised that his move to French club Niort was not quite what the brochure promised him, he got word that Forest were interested in taking him on and a fee was agreed. Derby, too, approached Chapman and were told that he had his sights set on Nottingham. Not content with this, Derby ramped up the pressure, with manager Arthur Cox and their new goalkeeper, Peter Shilton, attempting to talk Chapman into moving to the Baseball Ground. This culminated in Webb getting involved and Ian Maxwell saying that Derby had now done a deal for Chapman, who Niort were insisting could now only move to the Baseball Ground. Chapman apparently stood his ground and reiterated his desire to move to Forest.

At this stage, Robert intervened and offered Chapman whatever he or his actress wife needed. Despite the attractive offer, Chapman and Lesley Ash felt that, on balance, Forest was the better option. The ante kept being raised. 'In the Saturday edition of the Maxwell-owned *Daily Mirror*,' Chapman explained in his autobiography *More Than a Game*, 'the back-page lead proclaimed victory for Derby over Forest in the race for my signature. It also claimed that Brian Clough had "bungled" the move by sending his "office boy" Alan Hill to conduct talks instead of going himself.'

In fact, Chapman had been dealing with Hill from the start and Clough had already been on the phone to Ash aspect of his usual charm offensive regarding players' wives. As Chapman himself had already worked out, Hill did this so he could give the players hell knowing full well that their wives would find it hard to understand what the husbands were complaining about since, from their perspective, Clough was a charming and caring man. Maxwell was unccustomed to not getting what he wanted and, as Chapman told the story, tried to buy Niort, presumably as a lesson to any club that denied his wishes or to ensure the player would play for at least one of his clubs. Either way, relations between Clough and Maxwell, and by extension, Forest and Derby, were somewhat less than cordial, unsurprising given the two men's fundamental differences when it came to politics. Indeed, as Craig Bromfield described in his book, *Be Good, Love Brian*, 'Brian didn't like Maxwell, said he was "an enemy" and promised to "knock his team into the ground".'

His interest in the club was minimal and his time spent watching games dwindled from occasional to very rarely come the 1989/90 season. The chant of 'He's fat, he's round, he's never at the ground' from Derby fans, was quickly seized on by Forest fans and amended to 'He's fat, he's round, he's taking Derby down'. Indeed, if nothing else, Maxwell's tenure at Derby was a fertile ground for Forest fans to conjure up derisory songs about his running of the club. A particular favourite suggested that not only was Maxwell a bit of a clown and his ownership was taking Derby down, but also asserted (incorrectly, it should be stated) that Arthur Cox had somehow managed to contract smallpox, despite the WHO declaring that all cases had been eradicated in 1980. These were indeed curious times.

Yet the largesse and splashing of cash to bring quality to Derby was built on foundations about as solid as the famous Baseball Ground mud. Increasingly isolated and megalomaniacal, he morphed into a William Randolph Hearst figure, craving champagne, caviar and helicopters, as he bought the largest helicopter company in the UK. Yet still, like Hearst, he was missing something, with perhaps his Rosebud being closure to his tragic family background.

From 1988 to 1991, everything, including Maxwell, started falling apart, leading to him becoming paranoid to the point of bugging the offices of the *Daily Mirror*. With the Fraud Squad, Mirror Group pension owners and bankers all chasing him, he took to his yacht, the *Lady Ghislaine*, named after his favourite daughter, and sailed around the Canary Islands. He disappeared overboard in the early hours of 5 November 1991 and his body was found hours later in the Atlantic Ocean. Sons Kevin and Ian resigned from the board

Empires crumble and walls come tumbling down: 1980–1993

of Mirror Group Newspapers. Three weeks later, a colossal hole was found in the pension funds and the Maxwell empire plunged into bankruptcy, not helped by soaring interest rates and recession. The wealth was an illusion, funded by the banks, ignorant of his lack of solvency and blinded by Mirror Group pension funds. The timing couldn't have been worse with Sky on the horizon, fuelled of course by Maxwell's great nemesis, Murdoch, who would play a key role in the reformation of English football. Brian Fearn took over as chairman, then Lionel Pickering stepped in and picked up the broken pieces of Derby County and started the unenviable task of sticking them back together again.

Unsurprisingly, Clough was not a fan of Maxwell, given that they sat at opposing ends of the political and footballing spectrum. 'Arthur Cox has done as good a job as anybody in the last five years in management at Derby County,' Clough told his old friend Brian Moore in a TV interview. 'He's got a side from the third tier into the second, into the first. He's done it on low budgets. He's a bit lucky because when there's no money, he blames Maxwell. And to be fair, you blame Maxwell for anything. Him [Maxwell] and Murdoch have lowered the standard ... you'll never get this on, but we'll try ... because they own half the television, the two proprietors of our two national newspapers, the *Daily Mirror* and *The Sun*, are Murdoch and Maxwell. If I wanted to improve the standard of life in this country overnight, if somebody gave me a magic wand at Christmas, I would have them removed from this planet.'

In 1988, David Dein, then deputy chairman of Arsenal, and Greg Dyke, then both chief executive of London Weekend Television and chairman of ITV Sport, were looking to broker a deal to the rights to show the games of the so-called 'Big Five' clubs on television separately from the rest, thus effectively paving the way for a breakaway league. Discussions, and meetings occurred behind closed doors over the next two years or so until the FA announced plans for a new competition on 5 April 1991. Rupert Murdoch's BSkyB – eventually just Sky – was itching to get its hands all over the rights to show games from the new Premier League and blew ITV out of the water by offering £42m more. The plan was to show 60 games a season with the BBC paying for highlights for *Match of the Day*. The deal was put to Premier League clubs for a vote and was passed 14 to six with two abstentions. On Sunday, 16 August 1992, Richard Keys welcomed viewers to the City Ground for the first televised Premier League fixture: Forest v Liverpool. While Maxwell was throwing away millions of pounds that didn't exist for his own amusement, Murdoch had a strategy and not only won the battle but the war, the war chest and effectively a licence to print money, having seized the TV rights to the Premier League.

1984-1987
Buy Derby County shares

Yet before it all came crashing down, Derby required resurrecting as they started the 1984/85 season in the third tier. Arthur Cox was handed the most challenging of tasks. He was fresh from achieving promotion with Newcastle United into the First Division with a team featuring Chris Waddle, Peter Beardsley and the talismanic Kevin Keegan. His decision to leave the north-east for Third Division Derby was somewhat left-field, yet differences with the board and matters of principle were cited as reasons why he went. Cox set about, with Roy McFarland as his assistant, assembling a squad composed mostly of free transfers that was immediately competitive, with Bobby Davison still providing the goals. Things were going well until the turn of the year when the wins dried up and the arrival of ex-Forest players John Robertson, Trevor Christie and Steve Sutton (on loan) couldn't resurrect the listing ship, leaving Derby in seventh come the end of the season. Nonetheless, it was progress and a significantly healthier campaign than the previous one. This was better.

As for Forest, they finished in ninth and were dumped out of the UEFA Cup at the first hurdle. This was not quite what they were accustomed to, but the debut of a number nine by the name of Nigel Clough against Ipswich Town on Boxing Day, exactly 22 years after his father's playing career was effectively ended on a frozen Roker Park pitch, warmed the hearts of the football romantics.

In the summer of 1995, a young lad called Stuart Pearce arrived from Coventry City, along with the promising defender, Ian Butterworth. Most were excited about the latter's arrival while quite apathetic about the former. Clough was more determined than ever to prove to the football world that he could not only survive but thrive without Taylor and his strategy was to put his faith in youth by building a team with an average age of only 23 years and 258 days.

After a slow start to the season, Forest hit good form. Derby too began to hit their stride with Davison and Trevor Christie providing the requisite firepower as they were desperate to escape the tentacles of the third tier. The two sides were drawn together in the third round of the League

Cup, to be played at Derby. Yet football was at a low ebb and its reputation was in the gutter. On the final day of the previous season, 56 spectators died and more than 260 were injured when a fire ripped through the Main Stand at Bradford City's Valley Parade stadium during their Third Division game against Lincoln City on 11 May. Less than three weeks later, 39 spectators, mostly Italian, died during violent scenes on the terraces of Heysel Stadium in Brussels, where Liverpool faced Juventus in the European Cup Final. This resulted in English clubs being banned indefinitely from European competition, a punishment that would affect both Derby and Forest in the latter part of the decade.

Derby's League Cup tie against Leicester in the previous round had also been blighted by violence, including petrol bombings and stone throwing. As a result, Derbyshire Police had wanted the club to change the match from an evening kick-off to a weekend or an afternoon start to avoid a repeat of the trouble that marred the second leg in Leicester. They feared that the match would be used as a diversion by agitators wishing to cause trouble in the narrow streets around the Baseball Ground. Senior police officers met Rams officials for an hour, but the club would not budge. Revenue from the game was projected to be in the region of £90,000 from a capacity crowd of 26,500 fans, a figure Derby claimed they had spent on safety and surveillance facilities. 'We are looking to run a football match,' Stuart Webb told *Central News*. 'Whatever happens in Derby or Derbyshire really is not our responsibility.' Derbyshire Police issued a statement reassuring that they would do everything within their power to protect people inside and outside the ground.

'Football has had some bad publicity lately,' said Arthur Cox, looking ahead to the Forest tie. 'Some of it deserved, and it has had its effect on gates. But in our area the game is having something of a resurgence. We are averaging about 12,000 for home games and this cup tie gives us the chance to convince some more people that it is worth coming through the turnstiles on a regular basis.' Indeed, when tickets went on sale for the game on a Sunday morning, extensive queues snaked around the ground past the Baseball Hotel and into Shaftesbury Crescent. Derby's *Ram Magazine* hailed the scenes as an antidote to the grim reputation surrounding football, 'The pictures [of the queues] on this page prove more conclusively than any words can, that if football is struggling nationwide to recapture its attraction, the Derbyshire area of the East Midlands provides an oasis of hope.'

The game went ahead on Wednesday evening as scheduled. In front of an all-ticket crowd of 22,226 at the Baseball Ground, Jeff Chandler gave Derby the lead with a ninth-minute penalty yet Johnny Metgod equalised just four minutes later. From then on, Forest's new recruit Franz Carr impressed, culminating in him crowning an outstanding display by scoring the winner in the 68th minute, thus confirming their passage to the fourth round. Maxwell's Oxford United, with his daughter Ghislaine on the board as a director, surprisingly lifted the League Cup in April, defeating QPR in the final, while both Forest and Derby had their eyes on bigger prizes.

The police's fears of violence were sadly proven well founded. Following the game, windows of houses around the ground were smashed, cars were damaged and bottles thrown at the police before the trouble moved to the city centre. The problems started after the match when around 300 youths gathered at a pub, The Cambridge, and started damaging property. At one stage around 22 were penned in at the Cockpit roundabout by riot police before the mob gathered in the Market Square, halting traffic on numerous occasions. Seven people appeared before Derby magistrates charged with public order and property offences, while two from the Nottingham area were arrested during the match.

Cox continued to tinker with his squad and, among others, in came Steve McClaren and John Gregory to bolster the solid nucleus already assembled. A slow start segued into a strong showing on either side of the new year and, despite a blip around Easter, Derby required only two points from their final two games for promotion. The first of these came against Rotherham United at the Baseball Ground on a Friday night. Phil Gee eased the home crowd's nerves when he scampered through and slotted home with 13 minutes remaining, yet the visitors equalised immediately, Mike Trusson capitalising on a fumble by Mark Wallington in goal. The tension grew, increasing when John Dungworth scythed Davison down just outside the penalty area. Once Dungworth was sent for a much-needed early bath to clear the substantial layer of mud from his frame, Derby lined up to take the free kick and Jeff Chandler took his place in the Rotherham wall in an attempt to disrupt, interfere and be a general nuisance. The kick went straight down the throat of Kelham O'Hanlon in goal, but confusingly the referee awarded Derby a penalty as apparently Chandler had been manhandled in the wall. Although the decision was labelled 'brutally harsh' in commentary, Derby had a golden opportunity to clinch promotion. Trevor Christie, formerly of Forest, stepped up and slammed the ball home, thus securing third place and a ticket back to the Second Division. 'Everyone at the club should be congratulated,' said Chamber of Commerce chief executive Peter Ire. 'It has provided a boost for the whole city and I believe there will be tangible benefits for business.'

With the Central League championship trophy also on the mantelpiece, Derby were off the ropes and could look ahead to the following season with confidence. The dark days of March 1984 were now firmly behind them. They secured promotion back to the Second Division after just two years in the third tier, while Forest secured a creditable eighth in the top flight, a place higher than the previous season and with such a young team.

Maxwell, Cox and Derby wanted more and weren't done yet though. In fact, they'd only just begun and their upwards trajectory continued, irrespective of which league they were in, making light of the gap between the Second and Third Division. With Derby fourth in December and serious contenders in an open title race, Robert Maxwell pumped more cash in. Nigel Callaghan arrived from Watford in February to bolster the promotion push and, in Ian Maxwell's third season as chairman, the shirt sponsor was swapped from his father's short-lived *Sportsweek* magazine to the even less subtle Maxwell BPCC (British Printing and Communications Corporation). Early February saw Derby pull back a two-goal deficit to Birmingham City to draw 2-2 and from then on they never looked back, extending their unbeaten run to 13 and losing only once before promotion was sealed after a 2-1 win against Leeds United with two games still to play, the title coming on the final day with a 4-2 victory over Plymouth Argyle.

In a column for the *Daily Mirror*, Brian Clough expressed his delight for Derby and reiterated his long-standing respect for Cox. 'Derby was where I made my name and my reputation. A little piece of me will always be at the Baseball Ground,' he wrote. 'Arthur Cox has done more for Derby this year than the Rolls-Royce company. He's the one who has put the smile back on local faces.' Referring to the engineering company being returned to the stock market after seeing its business and assets bought by the government after voluntary liquidation in 1971, Clough urged the reader to, 'Buy Derby County shares. I don't care what they cost.'

Of course, he needed no invitation to use such a platform to put pressure on his own directors and, in doing so, take a subtle swipe at Maxwell, 'I only wish that I had bought the actual club when they hit rock-bottom three years ago. Even Cloughie's not that rich. It needed a member of the Maxwell family to pull off that deal.' Clough was effusive in his praise for Stuart Webb for facilitating the deal and supporting his manager in the transfer market, but there were no words of praise for Maxwell, 'My lot at Forest – and most others around the country for that matter – won't put in two bob. The only money Forest directors ever cough up is when they buy a golden goal ticket.'

As for his own team, they finished in eighth again, but three points down on the previous season. However, that unknown left-back signed from Coventry was now an England international, having made his debut against Brazil at a packed Wembley Stadium, while the promising central defender played only 27 games before being packed off to Norwich on loan. With Derby's promotion back to the top table, league clashes between the two clubs – and Clough and Maxwell – were back on the agenda for the first time in seven years.

1987/88
She fell for Brian Clough

Unsurprisingly, Robert Maxwell wanted more. Arthur Cox had steered Derby to two successive promotions and, although delighted, Maxwell, given his insatiable appetite for publicity and success, wasn't finished yet. The Rams showed their intent to be more than observers in the First Division and signed Peter Shilton and Mark Wright from Southampton, with the fee for the defender constituting a new club record. Shilton persuaded Wright to make the move and by his own admission was complicit in selling him the dream, having been impressed by his own meeting with Maxwell when signing his contract over smoked salmon and champagne. Maxwell was writing the cheques, but only on the proviso that the Derby crowd exhibited immaculate behaviour and that average home attendances crept above a benchmark of 20,000.

On 26 September, Maxwell helicoptered in to the Baseball Ground to watch his first game – a 1-0 defeat to Oxford United. He left before full time, but he had typically ambitious plans and, equally typically, set about publicising them. 'We are looking at the possibility, in conjunction with the city council of redeveloping one of our stands, which would incorporate facilities for community use,' he told those in attendance at the Assembly Rooms when chairing his first Derby County annual meeting. 'I was shocked to hear of the redundancies at British Rail Engineering. I will be in touch with British Rail to see if some of my engineering companies could put my facilities to good use.' He received a standing ovation from the directors and shareholders but also reminded everyone that they needed a substantial improvement in gates in order to raise funds to stay in the division. It was a curious game anyway, even without Maxwell attending, as Oxford's chairman was his son Kevin and they boasted his daughter Ghislaine as a board member. Just to add to the layers of intrigue, Oxford's Ray Houghton had rejected a move to Maxwell senior's team, while ex-Derby player Dave Langan was again left out of the Oxford side.

Derby then lost their next game 4-0 to Liverpool and crashed out of the League Cup to Third Division Southend United four days before they were due to face Forest in early October. Moreover, Maxwell's plea for bigger crowds was falling on deaf ears as attendances dropped to around 15,000. To add to the slightly sour mood, Bobby Davison was sold to Leeds and, somewhere among all of this, Maxwell tried to buy Watford from Elton John.

In the build-up to the visit of Forest, the *Derby Evening Telegraph* reported that Cox was a long-standing admirer of Nigel Clough. 'Of course I'd like to see him at Derby,' Cox admitted. 'We first tried to buy Nigel when he was in his teens and, once I've made my mind up about a player, I never lose interest.' For his own part, Brian claimed that it was not his business to be involved in his son's contracts and left that to his assistant, Ron Fenton. Brian was fully aware of Cox's admiration for Nigel's footballing prowess and general good character but was mindful of Fenton's constant reminders that to sell him such a pivotal player, even without the significance of his surname, would lead only to blame and recrimination. As Brian put it in his autobiography, Fenton did not mince his words, 'You do realise we'll get murdered if your Nige signs for anybody else.'

Prior to the game, four Rams fans aged nine and ten years old hung around outside the ground hoping to collect autographs. They politely asked Brian Clough if they could have his signature and crucially used the word 'please'. Their reward for this was not only an autograph but an invitation into the dressing room to meet the players. Furthermore, a scheme to encourage football friendship and champion the case of keeping violence off the terraces meant that members of the Nottingham Forest Junior Reds played a team of city kids from Derby's community league before a tour of the Baseball Ground and a meal with the mayor of Derby, Councillor Nancy Warman. The FIFA (Football Is Fun Again) project was the idea of Derby County and the city council and its purpose was to steer youngsters away from hooliganism. The Derby lads won the game 16-0.

The senior game was a significantly closer affair. Forest's Paul Wilkinson opened the scoring on 33 minutes and predictably, Nigel Clough was involved as he received the ball on the edge of the area and slid the ball through to Wilkinson, whose shot went under the challenge of Mark Wright and into the corner of Shilton's net, behind which were thousands of jubilant Forest fans, penned in by metal fencing. The atmosphere was as frenzied and fraught as ever. 'At Derby you could sense the hatred from the home supporters and I would wind them up by running over to the Forest fans before the kick-off to give them a clenched fist salute,' Pearce later explained. 'The tension and hostility was tremendous, much better than playing in a nicey-nicey atmosphere.' In the Forest goal that day was Steve Sutton. He recalled, 'Nothing was said in the club, but we were expected to win every game, but in your mind and in your heart, you knew it was a special game. It was always a big game. Forest fans have always been great. If you beat Derby, you were gods.'

It was Forest who were gods that day as the encounter ended 1-0 to the Reds. Although a close scoreline, it was agreed that generally Forest were the better side. This was Forest's fifth away win of the season, moving them up to fifth in the table, while for Derby, concern was growing at their inability to react when they conceded first. 'Once Derby go a goal down,' wrote Gerald Mortimer in the *Derby Evening Telegraph* an the Monday following the game, 'there is a crisis.' They had now scored only once in six and a half league and cup games and were seven without a win.

As for Forest, the exciting young team Clough had built, featuring Gary Crosby, Franz Carr, Terry Wilson and Neil Webb, was flourishing. Indeed, Webb's excellent form turned important heads, resulting in him making his England debut against Turkey in a European Championship qualifying game the following Wednesday.

The Reds maintained their good form over the Christmas period and well into the new year by the time of the return fixture at the City Ground. Although generally going well in the league, the season was all about the FA Cup for Forest as a quarter-final win over Arsenal at Highbury had the Reds through to the semi-finals where they would meet an excellent Liverpool side. Despite still being in a very healthy fifth place, their form was stuttering a little as they came into this midweek derby game in March without a win in three. In contrast, Derby found life back in the top tier tough and were in 16th, only five points clear of relegation. Notably, struggling below them were Oxford United, in their third season in the top flight but looking doomed. Now emblazoned on Derby's shirts as a sponsor was simply the name Maxwell – BPCC had been dropped – while Maxwell himself was a shadow director at Oxford, illustrating and reaffirming the complex ownership web that he spun in this period. Yet after a horrific run of ten straight defeats in league and cup, Cox's team were slowly recovering and on a run of seven games without defeat, having ended their sequence of losses with a 0-0 draw against Oxford.

'Forest have had an excellent season and their standing in the league is a true reflection of their ability,' said Cox. 'They are also in the FA semi-finals, which is good for everyone at the City Ground but also for Brian Clough in particular. I genuinely hope Forest go all the way to Wembley and win it. But that will not be on their minds tonight. I have not forgotten the testimonial we played for Ian Bowyer at the end of last season. Brian called that the championship of the East Midlands and it was played like it.' Despite mutual respect between the managers, the fierceness of the rivalry remained as undimmed as ever. 'Derby will be just as hard as Liverpool,' said Clough, 'and Derby are the only team on my mind. I almost had to ask who we were playing on Saturday. Everyone's attention is focused on Liverpool except mine and my team's. No matter when or where we face Derby, or what our respective positions in the league are, it's like a cup tie.' Clough also acknowledged Derby's recent improvement and typically reminded everyone in his programme notes about where the credit for that lay. 'The fans ought to sit down and appreciate just what he has achieved for the club,' he wrote. 'Not many people would have left Newcastle, who he had just taken back into the First Division, for Derby who were in the Third. But Arthur [Cox] was not only the best choice for the job, he was the ONLY one.'

Just before the game, which would take place on Wednesday, 30 March, Derby's oldest fan, Florence Mellor died, aged 101. For her 100th birthday, Clough and three Derby players paid her a visit in celebration of her landmark. 'At first she only really liked the Rams,' her daughter, Nellie Hodkinson, explained, 'but because she fell for Brian Clough, she extended her support to Nottingham Forest as well.'

In front of 25,017 fans at the City Ground, a couple of Nigel Clough goals were enough to give Forest the win, despite Wright scoring for the Rams. On top of his brace, it was an excellent evening for Clough as once again his touch and vision had the opposition not quite knowing how to handle him. In addition, his two goals were beautifully taken. Despite this being only Forest's third win in their last 11 league outings, it was a convincing one, exhibiting all that was good about this side. Gary Crosby was back to his best, giving the consistent Michael Forsyth a difficult evening. For Derby, Wright was a constant threat from set pieces, but for the most part any threat was easily nullified. Cox's admiration for Brian's son was extremely well founded.

Once the dust settled, this was the first Forest double over Derby since 1955 and the first double one club had enjoyed over the other since Derby's title-winning season of 1971/72, underlining Forest's entrenchment at the top of the league and illustrating how far Derby had to go to compete at the highest level, despite their impressive and high-profile signings. With Clough's young team coming to fruition and Cox's team having gained valuable experience in the First Division, the future, for once, held promise for both teams.

Through it all, though, Cox was operating under challenging conditions as, in April, Maxwell invited Johan Cruyff to be Derby's new technical director. The *Derby Evening Telegraph* reported that Maxwell met Cruyff at the Holborn headquarters of the *Daily Mirror* on 8 April 1988 and offered the Dutchman the chance to become the first foreign coach in English football. For his part, Cruyff also had another offer on the table: a £400,000-a-year job coaching Barcelona. 'I am particularly drawn to Johan,' opined Maxwell, 'because not only can he inspire the professionals, he can take the children off the streets.' Come Tuesday, 12 April, the *Telegraph* splashed with 'DECISION DAY'. The decision went against Derby and Cruyff took the Barcelona job.

Forest lost their FA Cup semi-final 2-1 to Liverpool at Hillsborough, who themselves lost to Wimbledon in the final. A third-placed finish in the league hinted that there was more to come from this young team. As for Derby, they rallied to 15th and avoided relegation reasonably comfortably, despite inconsistent form in the run-in. Their average attendance was short of Maxwell's target of 17,211 and in turn the club had run up a deficit of £817,858. An improvement was required for the following season if things were to remain on an even keel.

1988/89
Ted McMinn's nipple

Despite the promise of the previous season, Forest simply couldn't get going and by the fourth game of 1988/89, which happened to be at home to Derby on 17 September, they were yet to win, having lost on the opening day at Norwich City and drawn their next two. For Derby, Trevor Hebberd and Paul Goddard came in and helped them to an opening-day win against Middlesbrough, a defeat at Millwall and another home win, this time against Newcastle United.

Under Cox, appointed in 1984, the gap between his team and Forest was steadily closing as each season with him at the helm represented real progress and improvement in the form of higher league finishes. Yet a lower-half placing in their first season back in the First Division, given their Maxwell-fuelled rise from the Third Division, represented something of a disappointment. The gap was no longer a chasm, although matching Forest, who had never finished below ninth since Cox took over at Derby and seemed to be on an upwards curve, was no easy task. After suffering two losses to the Reds in the previous campaign, this early season meeting acted as an excellent barometer showing the extent of Derby's improvement. After all, Forest's first team was composed of established international footballers, emphasised by four players representing England at Wembley in a friendly against Denmark in midweek: Neil Webb, Stuart Pearce, Steve Hodge and Des Walker.

Clough's programme notes underlined his respect for Cox as he explained how he let his counterpart and his wife Anthea down after he and Barbara had been invited for

Empires crumble and walls come tumbling down: 1980–1993

lunch, owing to his television commitments as a pundit for the European Championship. 'I'm telling you it's the worst decision I made during the close season. I should have gone to lunch and from what I saw of the European Championship, the England side would have been better off joining us,' Clough said. England, with Shilton and Wright of Derby and Webb of Forest, finished bottom of their Euro '88 group without a point after losing to Republic of Ireland, Netherlands and the Soviet Union.

Nottinghamshire Police placed 250 officers on full alert for the fixture as 6,000 Rams fans were expected to make the short trip to the City Ground for the all-ticket game, labelled 'high risk' by the force. It was indeed high risk as the bitterness exhibited by each set of supporters was replicated on the pitch. Derby winger Ted McMinn spoke in his autobiography, *The Tin Man*, about his afternoon, 'My opposite number – England international Stuart Pearce – was the one I had most to worry about as Psycho had been bragging at a recent England game that he was going to take me out.'

The tackles did indeed fly in. McMinn clattered into Pearce, taking him out with a two-footed challenge. Wright did likewise on Crosby. Pearce thundered into McMinn. It was that sort of game. The running battles between Pearce and McMinn were a feature of such matches in this period. After a typical touchline confrontation between the two following a meaty challenge, both ended up in a heap, McMinn on top with Pearce's head around the Scotsman's chest area. 'It was a spur-of-the-moment thing but I couldn't resist the target staring me in the face,' said Pearce. 'I bit him right on the nipple as we lay on the ground. Ted jumped up and screamed at the official, "Ref, he's just fucking bit me!" I looked at him and started laughing. He saw me out of the corner of his eye and he started laughing as well. The whole thing was just too ludicrous for words.'

With just four minutes remaining, Colin Foster produced a neat volley past Peter Shilton, a day short of his 39th birthday, from a corner, putting the Reds one up and seemingly in sight of a third consecutive league win over the Rams. Yet moments later, Hebberd controlled a cross and fired sweetly into the corner for his third goal in three successive Saturdays. A suspicion of handball as he controlled the ball before volleying in was dismissed and mattered little to the travelling contingent. At the final whistle, Clough heartily embraced Cox, confirming the mutual and deep respect.

A draw was a huge step forward for Derby who could take great satisfaction from cancelling out what seemed to be a late winner so quickly away from home. Going toe to toe with the previous season's third-best team composed of international quality proved to the Rams that they could mix it with the best, which they proceeded to do. A minor blip around the turn of the year was the only blemish on an otherwise impressive season as they hovered around the top third of the table. The signing of Dean Saunders from Oxford in October would go a long way to solving their shyness in front of goal.

Forest got their act together and converted draws into wins, and by the time of the return fixture on 25 March, Clough had steered his team to the final of the League Cup and Full Members' Cup, where they faced Luton Town and Everton respectively. The Luton match was Forest's first visit to Wembley since they succumbed to Wolves in the 1980 League Cup final after a horrible and entirely preventable Andy Gray goal. They had also reached the semi-finals of the FA Cup again, where they would face Liverpool, again. Like the year before, the tie would take place at Hillsborough.

With Forest in fifth and Derby in seventh, more than local pride was on the line as they faced each other riding high in the table and in buoyant mood. Predictably, it was a niggly game with the stakes as high as ever. Derby, having not beaten Forest at home in the league since 1979, never really got going and Forest took the lead after 38 minutes through a fine goal created by Tommy Gaynor in their typical breakaway style, a feature of this team's setup. Only a few seconds after Steve Sutton had produced a good save to deny Rob Hindmarch, Gaynor escaped down the right before centring for Clough who calmly and deliberately knocked the ball back for Hodge to fire home.

The home side huffed and puffed but created little and Forest sealed the points in the second half when Wright, consistent and impressive all season, dillied and dallied before turning and directing a woefully under-hit back-pass to Shilton. Perhaps predictably, given his rather complicated transfer to Forest despite strong interest from Derby, Lee Chapman nipped in and rounded Shilton before slotting the ball into the goal backed by the away supporters, waving their inflatable trees.

With Saunders bagging 14 goals and Hebberd weighing in with a healthy total from midfield, Derby ended in fifth, their highest finish since coming fourth in 1976. Forest hit a strong vein of form after this game, winning five of their next six in the league games (the defeat was a 4-1 hammering against Wimbledon, but they always fared poorly against Wimbledon). The League Cup, for so long a feature of Clough's trophy cabinet, was once more back in his possession after a 3-1 win against Luton in early April. At the end of the month, the Full Members' Cup was claimed following a rip-roaring final against Everton, in which the Reds were on the right side of a 4-3 scoreline. In between the two, Forest faced Liverpool at Hillsborough in the FA Cup semi-final. Football, once again, became so very irrelevant.

As the Tales of Robin Hood visitor attraction opened on Maid Marian Way, East Midlands football was enjoying a resurgence, with Forest repeating their third-placed finish, alongside a haul of silverware, while Derby coming fifth, just three years after slumming it in the third tier, was an astonishing achievement. This represented a rare moment when both clubs were competing at the highest level. Indeed, not since 1902 had both clubs finished so far up in the top tier. The eye-wateringly high unemployment rates of the early 1980s had tumbled to their lowest level since 1979 while manufacturing output rose sharply by the end of the decade. Although for so long reliant on manufacturing, both Nottingham and Derby faced the task of re-establishing themselves and forging a new identity, away from heavy industry. It was a brief boom both on and off the pitch before the 1991 recession.

1989/90

Football in our neck of the woods

With Derby's rise so rapid, doubts lingered regarding its sustainability. If built on secure foundations, there was no reason why it couldn't be long-lasting, but if built on someone else's pension funds there could only be one outcome. In 1989/90, the first East Midlands derby was another early one, taking place at the City Ground before August was out and being only the fourth game of the season. Derby had drawn their opening two matches but beat Manchester United at home in their third, imparting a spring in their step ahead of their trip to Nottingham. Like their near-neighbours, Forest also opened their season with successive draws but then came a defeat away at Millwall. The season was barely embryonic, but it is always a relief to get a win on the board, especially against your rivals. Forest needed one more than Derby.

The game was all-ticket, with prices ranging from £9 in the main stand for adults to £5 for a place on either of the terraced ends. 'I've been involved in enough Forest-Derby matches over the years to know what it means to both clubs and sets of supporters,' Clough wrote in his programme notes, reflecting on the rivalry being renewed at the highest level in some time. 'I hope it's a match and occasion that does football in our neck of the woods proud – because Derby have also done their "bit" to put Midlands football back on the map. I wasn't joking when I said before a ball was kicked that clubs like Derby and ourselves were capable of putting a spoke in the wheel of the so-called Big Five.' It was all to play for.

An early tackle went straight through the back of Nigel Clough and, moments later, Derby's Paul Blades almost snapped Brian Rice in two when he went straight over the ball and into the Scot's shins. Pearce then muscled Blades away with a knee to the kidneys. Everyone involved simply got up and got on with it. No cards required.

After a foul by Brian Laws on Trevor Hebberd, Derby were awarded a free kick but close to the touchline, a few yards from the goal line. Gary Mickelwhite whipped it in towards the near post where the ball clipped Steve Hodge's head and left Sutton clasping at fresh air and ended up in the net. As Hodge walked back to the halfway line, disconsolate and annoyed with himself, a Nottingham lad, for giving Derby the lead, he heard a Cockney drawl shouting out, 'Hodgey, you facking wanker!' 'That was Stuart's [Pearce] way of making me respond!' Hodge said in his autobiography, *The Man with Maradona's Shirt*.

It worked. Forest came out after half-time in determined mood and, after some neat play around the penalty area seemingly broke down, Hodge chased down a lost cause as the ball seemed to be rolling harmlessly out of play, seemingly well shepherded by Wright. Yet somehow, Hodge managed to fire a low ball across the face of goal, resulting in a tap-in for Crosby to put Forest back on level terms. As Crosby wheeled away, the Derby defence all looked accusingly towards Wright who they felt should have taken no chances and cleared the ball.

Forest pressed further forward and Pearce found himself, as he often did, ahead of his midfielders as he received a ball from Hodge. He quickly exchanged passes with Clough before powering into the area and dispatching the ball delicately with the outside of his left foot beyond Shilton. All six touches of the ball were with his left foot, but when you have one as thunderously exquisite as his, it would be folly not to use it frequently. The services of John Sheridan, a £650,000 signing from Leeds United, remained unused as Forest won 2-1.

Come January and the first East Midlands derby of the 1990s, both teams could be pleased with their progress. Forest sat in fifth and Derby in seventh. A few weeks earlier, Forest had lost 1-0 at home to Manchester United in the third round of the FA Cup to a subsequently famous and mythical Mark Robins goal. United would go on to win the FA Cup, defeating Crystal Palace after a replay, in part helped by Neil Webb, now at Old Trafford, whose raking ball found Lee Martin to prod home and provide Alex Ferguson with his first trophy in England.

England manager Bobby Robson was in attendance ahead the 1990 World Cup in Italy. In the event, he watched five of his final squad play at the Baseball Ground that afternoon: Shilton and Wright of Derby and Forest's Pearce, Walker and Hodge. Earlier that day Clough had formally opened Ramsline Halt, a new train station at the Baseball Ground for football specials to prevent crowd trouble and keep away fans out of the city centre. The tough and uncompromising Mick Harford made his debut for Derby, a familiar figure to the Forest defence as it was he who had opened the scoring for Luton in the 1989 League Cup final. In the match programme, Dean Saunders included Pearce as one of his heroes, 'I rate Stuart as the best left-back in in the country. He's got a burning desire to win and is very dangerous when he goes forward.'

Playing in all red, Forest had to withstand some early pressure, requiring Steve Sutton to be on top form. Yet after 15 minutes, Garry Parker literally strolled forward and paused before curling a delightful through ball with the outside of his left foot for the on-running Hodge to plant a low drive into the corner of the net beyond Shilton. Mel Sage and Rob Hindmarch looked at each other in bewilderment as to how exactly it had all happened. Five minutes later, the game was effectively settled as Nigel Jemson skipped past a lunge from Wright and neatly slotted home, again finding the bottom right-hand corner.

Derby didn't go down without a fight and peppered the Forest goal, forcing Sutton to maintain his excellent form and rattling the crossbar twice. It was, though, a classic away performance as the two relatively early goals allowed Forest to sit back and see whether the home side could find a way back into the game. They couldn't and Forest were able to see the game out. Bobby Robson must have been impressed as he awarded Forest the Barclays Best Performance of the Week award. It was another home defeat for the Rams, who had now lost five of their 12 home games in the league on top of an FA Cup replay exit to Port Vale.

On Saturday, 31 March, Forest lost their customary game against Wimbledon, in which even a debut goal by Tony Loughlan after only 36 seconds couldn't prevent a 3-1 defeat. Also in London that day, Derby drew 1-1 at Chelsea. Yet neither game received much attention owing to much more significant events in the capital as an anti-poll tax protest evolved into a riot and police and protesters fought pitched battles in Trafalgar Square. Among them was a 250-strong group from Erewash and a delegation from the Derby Anti-Poll Tax Union. Back in Derby, more than 100 demonstrators heard Derby South MP Margaret Beckett and Derbyshire Euro MP Geoff Hoon address an anti-poll tax meeting, arranged to coincide with the national rally, at the Assembly Rooms. The Ilkeston Anti-Poll Tax Union organised a mass burning for the following Tuesday, by which time Erewash Borough Council would have sent out its bills. In Nottingham, a sizeable crowd gathered outside the Guildhall Magistrates Court. Activists dressed as Robin Hood invaded the City Council Chambers and custard-pied various councillors with paper plates of shaving foam.

England was changing. Margaret Thatcher, prime minister for the entirety of the 1980s, was in the final throes of her governance as the 1990s waited in the wings, her leadership dealt a withering blow as resentment towards the poll tax ran deep. Totemic figures of the decade were feeling the winds of change as the Berlin Wall tumbled. The plates were shifting. Empires built on sheer force of personality were crumbling. As the excess and boom of the 1980s gave way to the '90s, the end was nigh for Clough and Maxwell. The sun was slowly setting on their era.

Derby won only four games from 15, plunging them down to 16th. Forest, too, crumbled, enduring a seven-match winless streak, meaning they ended up in a disappointing ninth place. However, they could point to a successful defence of the League Cup as a single goal from Jemson was enough to see off Oldham Athletic in front of 74,000 people at Wembley. It was another trophy in the cabinet for Clough, his fourth League Cup triumph.

Domestic and parochial rivalries were set aside for the summer as the English team travelled to Italy for the World Cup. Pearce thought he'd given England a win against Netherlands when he scored from a free kick. Sadly, though, it was an indirect one and his effort flew straight into the net without a touch from anyone else. The game ended 0-0, meaning England needed to win their final group match against Egypt to progress to the knockout stages, having drawn 1-1 with the Republic of Ireland in their opener. Wright's deft header did the trick.

From there, Belgium and Cameroon were narrowly dispatched until the semi-final against West Germany, featuring Paul Gascoigne's tears and Pearce's penalty miss. Four of the starting XI for England at Italia '90 came from Derby and Forest: Pearce, Wright, Shilton and Walker, signalling the apparently healthy state of both East Midlands clubs. Fitting with the prevailing mood of change, English football went to Italy as an unreformed, brutish creature yet seemingly came back an enlightened, acid-dropping, ecstasy-popping, dance music-loving hippy. Of course, it wasn't quite as simple as that, yet forces were at work which set English football and its fans on a different path. Hooliganism wasn't over and left entirely behind in the 1980s, yet with new stadia, new drugs, a new decade and a new outlook, a football renaissance of sorts was under way.

1990-1993
The wrong epitaph

A week into the 1990/91 season, Robert Maxwell made it be known that Derby were for sale to anyone willing to match his asking price of £8m. Cracks were appearing. The dream was dying. The unity and harmony of Italia '90 was revealed to be a brief holiday dalliance as Manchester United fans reminded Stuart Pearce about his penalty miss when Forest travelled to Old Trafford in September. In response, Pearce slammed a free kick straight into the Stretford End goal from an outrageous distance with alarming violence and accuracy. In acknowledgement of his tormentors, he turned to face them and raised both arms before getting on with the game.

* * *

On 4 October, Brian Clough took a call that for once left him speechless. His assistant Ron Fenton informed him of the tragic news that his old mate Peter Taylor had died suddenly of pulmonary fibrosis while on holiday in Mallorca. By Clough's own admission, the hatchet should have been buried long before it came to this. He wished Taylor had popped round to see him. He wouldn't have been turned away. Perhaps a typical Taylor wisecrack would have broken the ice and they'd have taken a walk around Clough's garden, chatting, laughing and being once again, mates.

Clough wished he had asked Taylor along to Wembley as his guest and sat him in the Royal Box when his team won the League Cup in 1989 and 1990. He berated himself for not picking up the phone and returning one of his calls. At the time of John Robertson's transfer from Forest to Derby in 1983, he'd meant all the nasty and spiteful things he'd said about Taylor; he'd publicly called him a 'rattlesnake' and no doubt much worse behind closed doors. But now? Now he knew. Life is fleeting and can be snuffed out at any time, or in Hamlet's words, 'All that lives must die, passing through nature to eternity.'

Taylor's achievements in Nottingham and Derby would indeed resonate down through the ages. Yet none of this was any consolation for Clough. His 1994 autobiography is dedicated to his old friend, 'For Peter. Still miss you badly. You once said, "When you get shot of me there won't be much laughter in your life." You were right.'

* * *

Meanwhile, Derby were struggling. Yet come November and the meeting at the Baseball Ground, the proverbial form book was defenestrated.

Some typically meaty challenges established the tone. Pearce clattered into Mark Patterson, then Patterson passed the gesture on to Clough. Geraint Williams hobbled off after eight minutes, to be replaced by Craig Ramage. Steve Chettle rattled the inside of the post with a shot from distance, but he would not be denied as, moments later, another shot from the edge of the area nicked off Wright and into the corner of the net, a quite bizarre sequence of events as the defender scored only 11 times in 415 appearances for the Reds. Forest's lead was short-lived, however, as Micklewhite played the appropriately named Ramage through and he finished from a tight angle in front of the now seated away fans. Both scorers thus far were born in the city, whose teams they were playing for, maintaining a very parochial feel in contrast to the now burgeoning global game.

In the second half, Shilton booted long, Harford nodded wide to Micklewhite and he crossed for Saunders to nod home. Derby could finally sing a new song about defeating their old rivals, or at least update the one from that notorious FA Cup win in 1983. Watching from the stands due to injury, McMinn made his way to the dressing room and bumped into Brian Clough, who grabbed the winger's hand, praised the Derby performance and then wished him all the best with his recovery.

In the aftermath of the defeat at Derby, Forest sat tenth, while Derby were 17th. The Rams could take consolation from the fact that Sheffield United were bottom with a measly four points. More significantly in terms of local pride, this was Derby's first win against Forest since they returned to the First Division four years previously and their first league win since their 4-1 dismantling of the then European champions in 1979, exactly 11 years ago to the day. Despite that win, Derby were relegated that season. It couldn't happen again, could it?

In the week following, Forest's grip on the League Cup was finally loosened as Coventry City put the holders out in an epic 5-4 win at Highfield Road. Under Terry Butcher, Coventry went 4-0 up after 34 minutes with Kevin Gallagher bagging a hat-trick, only for Clough to score a treble of his own and make it 4-3. Incredibly, this all came before half-time. Parker equalised in the second half only for Steve Livingstone to finally complete the evening's scoring and leave Forest on the canvas. Forest's 22-game unbeaten run in the competition was finally over.

Derby weren't to know it at the time but they had only two more league wins in them all season. One came the following week at fellow strugglers Sunderland, and the other came in May, after relegation had been confirmed, 6-2 over Southampton. Featured in that dreadful run was the return visit to the City Ground in April.

In the meantime, supporters generally remained loyal to Cox, recognising the difficulty of managing a club being run like a circus with Maxwell the ringmaster. It was Maxwell who the fans turned against, prompting him to write an open letter in the *Derby Evening Telegraph*, 'The reason we have not maintained our progress over the last two years is that we have not had enough fans and we continue to have the local media conducting its long-standing vendetta against the club and those who run it.' As is sometimes the case with these things, the blame was apportioned outside the club and anywhere but inside. In his programme notes, Clough reminded everyone, 'Derby still means something to me because I pay my rates (or whatever it is I pay these days) in the city and from a point of view of football, it's good for our neck of the woods when we're competing together in the First Division.'

With the season reaching its climax, the game at Forest, on a Wednesday evening in April, took on huge significance in terms of Derby's fight for survival. Forest had sunk as low as 12th, while Derby were bottom with 21 points, 13 from safety but with matches in hand. They hadn't won in the league since 1 December. The omens were not good for the Rams, more like harbingers of doom as 11 years before, almost to the day, Frank Gray had fired in a solitary goal at the City Ground to confirm a 1-0 win for Forest and effectively seal Derby's relegation to the Second Division. When Ian Woan crossed and Roy Keane appeared at the back post and nodded in, history was repeating itself in 1991. Forest won 1-0 and in doing so dished out a cold spoonful of revenge for their earlier defeat at the Baseball Ground that season. For Derby, this was the first of five straight defeats, confirming a frankly miserable season and relegation.

McMinn and Pearce indulged in their usual running battle. The Derby player was substituted with seven minutes remaining and, naturally, was booed off the pitch by the fervent home support. Approaching the main stand, he was helped on his way by Nigel Clough who encouraged him to 'piss off'. 'I stopped and asked him to repeat it, but he turned away and laughed,' said McMinn. 'He was less amused when

I called him a "daddy's boy".' Having been spat at by a Forest fan as he took his seat on the bench, McMinn was seeing red and was now intent on seeking Clough out at the end of the game for a further frank exchange of views and, quite possibly, a spot of violence. Reticent at having to tackle Pearce as well as Clough in the tunnel, Wright offered to deal with Pearce, leaving McMinn free to deal with Clough.

As the Forest players headed back to their dressing room jubilant in victory, McMinn launched himself at Clough and pinned him by the throat against the wall. Archie Gemmill, now a coach at Forest, hauled him off and, after much pushing and shoving, the narrow corridor in the main stand was cleared and the Derby players were ushered into their changing rooms. Cox wasn't impressed and McMinn received a visit from Nottinghamshire Police while wrapped only in a towel.

Enter Brian Clough, who offered to sort it out. He marched McMinn into the home dressing room, replete with bottles of beer, a naked Stuart Pearce with all his tattoos on show standing on a locker and leading the choir in an anti-Derby song. Off stage was Nigel, who was taking a shower. However, he was ordered out by his father. 'Head bowed like a pupil in front of a headmaster, Nigel then explained what had happened and complained about what I'd called him,' said McMinn. 'Much to my amusement, Clough senior immediately took my side. As the Forest players began to snigger, he told his son, "Well, you are a daddy's boy and I think you should apologise to Mr McMinn. He deserves some respect after coming all the way from Derby to play a game of football." Nigel went bright red, mumbled an apology and shook my hand. His legendary father then ushered me back to the away dressing room, wishing me a pleasant trip back down the A52. What a man!'

For Forest, the win sparked a frankly remarkable run of form as they proceeded to beat West Ham United 4-0 in the FA Cup semi-final at Villa Park the following weekend, Chelsea 7-0 and Norwich 5-0, before drawing with Spurs, 14 days before they would meet again at Wembley in the FA Cup Final, and then finishing with wins against Liverpool (2-1, effectively ending any lingering hopes they had of stealing the title from Arsenal) and 4-3 over Leeds. They could go into the FA Cup Final with optimism.

Somehow, Sheffield United – rock-bottom when Forest and Derby met in November – rallied to 16th, while the Rams' fate was mathematically sealed with a 2-1 defeat at Manchester City, four games after their loss at the City Ground. A run of four wins in six between October and December was all they had to show for their efforts. The only consolation of the wretched campaign was that one of those victories was against their East Midlands rivals.

For Derby, the 1980s was one heck of a ride, from beating the European champions 4-1 just before the decade dawned, to near bankruptcy and Third Division football, back to the top division and a fifth-placed finish before ending pretty much where they had started: relegated to the Second Division. All of this was against the backdrop of Robert Maxwell's travelling show and all that came with it. In terms of their old friends down the A52, Derby enjoyed only one win against the Reds in the '80s – the FA Cup tie of 1983 – but what a seismic result it was. Yet the ride was all but over. Mark Wright and Dean Saunders were sold to Liverpool, generating much-needed cash for Derby's coffers, although ten per cent of the fee for Saunders went to his previous club, Oxford United. After much discussion and wrangling, Derby were under new ownership with Brian Fearn and Peter Gadsby joining the board and finally agreeing a sale. Maxwell was not present for the formalities – his helicopter had broken down. Six months later, his body was recovered from the Atlantic Ocean.

Forest lost the FA Cup Final as Des Walker scored the most unfortunate of own goals in a most eventful game. Paul Gascoigne rampaged around the pitch like a rhino on speed, almost decapitating Garry Parker before swinging at Gary Charles's knee with the force of a wrecking ball. Referee Roger Milford took pity on him rather than applying the rules as Gascoigne was stretchered off the pitch with his move to Lazio and possibly his career in ruins. From the resulting free kick, Pearce nonchalantly bazookaed the ball home. Mark Crossley saved a Gary Lineker penalty before Paul Stewart scored an equaliser, despite enduring a whole career and lifetime wrestling with his own personal demons. Brian Clough, by his own admission, should have retired gracefully after the game.

While *Robin Hood: Prince of Thieves* dominated UK cinemas for the duration of the summer, featuring a notoriously maverick approach to British geography since Hood apparently walked the 560 miles or so from the White Cliffs of Dover to Nottingham via Hadrian's Wall in an afternoon, Derby were in freefall as they faced the 1991/92 season in the second tier for the first time in four years. Lionel Pickering became a majority shareholder just two weeks after Maxwell's death in November 1991. The debts were tackled and, in a symbolic cleansing, Auto Windscreens became the new shirt sponsor. Marco Gabbiadini, Paul Simpson, Paul Kitson, Tommy Johnson and Steve Sutton came in, nudging the club into third and the play-offs, where they lost to sixth-placed Blackburn Rovers. A 2-0 lead at Ewood Park after 14 minutes disintegrated into 4-2 defeat. In the return leg, a 2-1 win at the Baseball Ground was not enough. In the other semi-final, Leicester City beat Cambridge United before going on to lose to Blackburn at Wembley. Then Blackburn signed Alan Shearer and their destiny took a fantastical turn.

Forest performed their ritual duty in finishing seventh and reaching the League Cup final, which they lost to Manchester United in an ill-tempered and quickly forgotten game. Although it might have seemed like a disappointing season at the time, it was a slight improvement in terms of league position on the previous two campaigns and, while losing at Wembley is never fondly thought of, it was another League Cup final. All of which makes what happened the next season even more surprising. Although in truth, the signs were there; it's just that most people simply didn't want to read them.

While 1992/93 saw Derby steady the ship in the Second Division and reach Wembley, the curtain came down on the Brian Clough era at the City Ground. The Rams finished in eighth place and lost to Cremonese in the final of the Anglo-Italian Cup, a competition for teams in the second tiers of the English and Italian leagues. Yet the real story was over by the banks of the Trent. After an opening-day win at home against Liverpool on the debut of Sky's television coverage, Forest looked to be ready to take this whole new ball game and the Premier League by storm. Yet a week later, the goalscorer against Liverpool, Teddy Sheringham, was sold to Tottenham and Forest failed to bother finding a replacement. Despite Nigel Clough and Roy Keane wrestling against the inevitable, Forest were relegated in the most messy of seasons.

Just a month after he had been awarded the freedom of the city in March 1993, Brian Clough announced he would retire at the end of the season. On the same day, Forest suspended director Chris Wootton who made several allegations regarding Clough's health. Yet the outpouring of adoration and gratitude from the fans after the home defeat to Sheffield United, which confirmed Clough's first relegation, swept away the messiness. He was 58 but looked older. He had conquered English and European football but a new game was now here. He was loved and deified by both Forest and Derby fans, and it was time to fold. He knew it too. 'I also knew in my heart that in deciding to carry on after the FA Cup Final I had made a mistake,' Clough wrote. 'It was the wrong kind of finish, the wrong epitaph.'

The boom of the 1980s was well and truly over. The model of the monolithic man at the centre of an empire was seen to be antiquated, swept away by a new broom. Short shorts gave way to baggy sleeves. Marching bands at Wembley were replaced by G-Force cheerleaders. A new era was under way and both clubs were at risk of missing out on the gravy train departing from platform Sky.

9

The short-lived Premier League years: 1993–2005

'HOW DO you solve a problem like Maria?' sing the nuns of Nonnberg Abbey in *The Sound of Music* as they contemplate the idiosyncrasies exhibited by the titular figure, who despite being generally loved for her youthful enthusiasm, drove them to distraction. A similar problem faced the Nottingham Forest board: how do you move on from such a totemic figure as Brian Clough? An answer presented itself. You appoint Frank Clark.

'We loved him – everybody loved Frank Clark – but management,' wrote Brian Clough, 'certainly team management, just wasn't in him as far as I could see.' Nonetheless, having overseen steady progress as manager at Leyton Orient before moving upstairs to take on a role as managing director, Clark was installed as the first Forest boss without the surname Clough since 1975 on 12 May 1993 after Martin O'Neill turned down the post and signed a new contract with Wycombe Wanderers. It was left to Clough's long-term assistant, Alan Hill, to break the news to him regarding his own replacement. At first, Clough was wary and completely in the dark, as Hill revealed in the fanzine *Bandy and Shinty*.

'Who is it?'

'Frank.'

'Frank who?'

'Frank.'

'Our Frank?'

Hill confirmed that the man in question was indeed the affable chap who Clough signed late in his career and won the European Cup medal in 1979. 'Well, you stop here, then. And make sure you look after him,' were Clough's instructions.

Hill promptly did just that and, while Clark was powerless to keep Nigel Clough and Roy Keane at the club, he brought in Lars Bohinen, Colin Cooper and Stan Collymore – as good a spine as any team had in the First Division that season. In Clark's first home game, Derby were the visitors.

Derby started their campaign, with, just like Forest one aim: promotion. After a 5-0 thumping of Sunderland on the opening day, they faced Forest at the City Ground on Wednesday, 18 August with their new signing, American midfielder John Harkes, going straight into the team. Forest were still labouring with Robert Rosario up front, awaiting Collymore's recovery from injury, but despite this they made the early running, stinging the palms of Martin Taylor in the Derby goal on numerous occasions. This pattern was maintained in the second half, with Taylor remaining much the busier of the two keepers. Yet it was Derby who took the lead as a chorus of boos rained down on Gary Charles, now plying his trade in the white of the Rams. His cross was headed up in the air by Neil Webb – back at Forest after a spell at Manchester United – then punched away by Mark Crossley, sporting a fetching headband after a collision on the opening day at Southend. But the ball fell to Michael Forsyth who somehow squeezed it in at the near post in front of the Trent End.

The lead didn't last long, however, as Rosario flicked on a long ball with his head to Ian Woan who danced around on the edge of the area before rifling a shot home, finally beating Taylor. Rosario might have won the game late for Forest, but the spoils were shared.

Less than a month later the two teams met again, this time at the Baseball Ground, and although it was undeniably an East Midlands derby, it was the first of its kind as the competition was the Anglo-Italian Cup, the source of a Wembley final for the Rams the previous season. Lee Glover put Forest ahead with a neat finish before Scot Gemmill pounced on a defensive error and made it 2-0 in front of a sparse crowd. Paul Simpson pulled one back with a low free kick and Paul Kitson levelled with a shot that somehow found the bottom corner, before Martin Kuhl completed a remarkable turnaround and lashed the ball home late on. A memorable evening for Derby in terms of rearranging a 2-0 deficit into a 3-2 win, yet aside from local pride, it all seemed pretty pointless really as Notts County progressed from the group of three, into another group of eight, and eventually into a Wembley final where they lost to a Brescia side featuring Gheorghe Hagi.

Besides, both teams had their eyes on the bigger prize of promotion. At the time, Forest fans would have cared little for missing out on a Wembley final against an Italian team, such was the sheer number of previous Wembley visits and, additionally, the pressing need to return to the Premier League, where they felt they belonged. Yet from the perspective of the present day, such a competition with such an outcome would be most welcome for either club.

After nine successful years as Derby manager, Arthur Cox finally called time in October 1993 and resigned owing to ill health, specifically a severe back injury that was increasingly immobilising him. Roy McFarland took over seamlessly as the team won four of their next five games, maintaining their steady campaign as they sat nicely in fifth while Forest laboured down in 17th. Pressure was building on Clark and few would have foreseen the dramatic upturn in fortunes for his side at this stage. Yet it was November when Forest's fire ignited, sparked by the arrival of Bohinen and the return to fitness of Collymore, as they put together an unbeaten run of 12 games. Conversely, November was a horrible month for Derby as they went six without a win.

On New Year's Day 1994, neither side was in the top six: Forest were eighth and Derby tenth. There was work to be done yet at both clubs. But a new year brings fresh hope and new ideas, and it was in 1994 that Jeremy Heath-Smith invited his small team of games developers at Core Design to pitch ideas for a 3D game that would work well on the newly developed PlayStation. In the back of a Victorian house on Ashbourne Road in Derby, a young designer called Toby Gard floated the idea of a third-person game, in which the player would raid mysterious tombs deep under pyramids. Work started in earnest six months later, leading to the birth of Lara Croft and *Tomb Raider*.

With just three games remaining for Derby, Forest visited the Baseball Ground on 27 April for a meeting in which the stakes were as high as they had been in a while. Forest lay second but with little chance of overhauling leaders Crystal Palace, while Derby were sixth and in the final play-off spot, just a point clear of Notts County. Both teams would have walked over shards of broken glass for the three points, irrespective of the opposition. Such was the significance of the sell-out fixture, the game was screened live at the City Ground to more than 6,000 fans.

The front cover of the programme featured Gary Charles, an apt choice given the defender's defection from Forest to the Rams at the start of the season. Inside, Charles spoke of how he was grateful that the original fixture against Forest had been postponed in December owing to a winter storm, since at the time he was injured and would have been unable to take the field against his former club. Since then, he had found his form, earning him a PFA nomination in the First Division's representative team of the season. 'I am definitely looking forward to meeting Forest again,' he said. 'I think players do like to meet their old teams.'

Colin Cooper opened the scoring with a terrific direct free kick in the first half before Charles put the game beyond his own team's reach with a bizarre own goal. The ball had seemingly bounced to safety after Collymore challenged Martin Taylor on the edge of the area, and it fell to Charles. Rather than hoofing it further away from the goal he was defending, or travelling forward with it, he decided to turn back towards his own goal, inviting Stone to come and close him down. Panicking, he tried to pass back to Taylor but instead lofted his pass, which also took a nick from Stone's boot, spooning it even higher and beyond the despairing efforts of Taylor to prevent calamity. He was helpless and the ball plopped apologetically into the Derby net. The 2-0 win effectively sealed Forest's promotion back to the top division at the first time of asking. 'I always thought I could do it, but it is not done yet,' said Clark after the game. As for Charles, it's probably fair to say that the night didn't quite play out as he had hoped.

A win at already relegated Peterborough the following weekend confirmed promotion. Despite Forest going two goals down at London Road, Collymore scored twice and Pearce steamrollered a header in to complete a remarkable turnaround. A home win against Oxford United calmed Derby's nerves and virtually confirmed their play-off place with one game remaining. In the play-offs they comfortably saw off Millwall, despite numerous pitch invasions at the New Den, but lost to Leicester at Wembley. There would be no East Midlands derby the following season as Forest left the First Division behind for the bright lights of the Premier League.

1994/95
Forest flying then the Bald Eagle lands

Forest confounded expectations by finishing third in the 1994/95 Premier League season, emulating their third-placed finishes of 1984, 1988 and 1989. It was an astonishingly good showing for a newly promoted side with Bryan Roy and Collymore forging a lethal partnership, producing an achievement that ranks joint first in terms of league finish and points garnered (77) by newly promoted sides, alongside Newcastle United a year earlier. Indeed, were it not for a torrid November, Forest might have challenged the eventual title winners, Blackburn Rovers, even harder. Yet Forest finished the season strongly with a superb unbeaten run of 13 games, of which nine were won, including a famous 7-1 win at Hillsborough in the same week that Take That released 'Back for Good', neatly reflecting the sentiment felt by many Reds fans regarding their team's stunning return to the Premier League.

As for Derby, midway through the season on 22 January 1995 there was an announcement, 'The directors of Derby County Football Club have ended 30 months of ground development negotiations by voting to build a new stadium on the site of the current Baseball Ground.' This seemed a brave move, given that other clubs were seeking a way out of their city-centre homes in favour of out-of-town new developments, invariably involving a cinema and a themed restaurant. Yet those who treasured the character of the old place could breathe easy, for a little longer anyway.

On the pitch, Paul Kitson, Gary Charles and Mark Pembridge all left during the course of the season, severely weakening McFarland's team and resulting in an underwhelming ninth-placed finish. Roy McFarland's 28-year association with the Rams was over by the end of the season and Jim Smith took the reins in June. Smith had enjoyed notable success at Oxford in the early 1980s under the auspices of Robert Maxwell and more recently replicated that with Portsmouth, reaching an FA Cup semi-final and narrowly missing out on promotion to the Premier League. Perhaps he could go one better with Derby.

1995/96

I would rather go on the dole than join them

After their successful return to the Premier League the previous season, a place back in European competition beckoned for Forest in the form of the UEFA Cup for 1995/96. This was a far cry from ties like the Anglo-Italian Cup against Derby or Notts County. Either with a cheeky sense of humour a firm grasp of history, the draw for the first round pulled Forest out of the hat alongside Malmö. They squeezed past the Swedish champions, for whom Robert Pritz featured having also played in the European Cup final too against Forest in 1979, and narrowly edged past Auxerre and Lyon before facing Bayern Munich in the quarter-finals. With Manchester United losing to Rotor Volgograd in the first round and Liverpool, Leeds United and Raith Rovers succumbing to Brøndby, PSV Eindhoven and Bayern Munich respectively in the second round, Forest flew the British flag in European competitions that season, while Blackburn and Glasgow Rangers failed to make it out of the group stages of the Champions League.

The parallels with Forest's previous European glory days continued as they travelled to meet Munich in the first leg at the very same stadium in which Trevor Francis scored the winning goal in 1979. Astoundingly, Nottingham-born defender Steve Chettle nodded Forest ahead, in the very same goal and from an uncannily similar angle to that Francis struck from 17 years earlier, but Bayern, featuring Oliver Kahn, Christian Ziege, Jürgen Klinsmann and Lothar Matthäus, kept their cool to chalk up a 2-1 win. With an away goal under their belts, Forest fancied their chances in the return leg but any hopes of a first European semi-final game since the sour taste of the Anderlecht affair were blown away by an excellent performance from the Germans.

As if facing Klinsmann and company was not intimidating enough, the Munich team flexed their muscles and brought on 1991 Ballon d'Or winner Jean-Pierre Papin in the return. Forest lost 5-1, going out 7-2 on aggregate, and Bayern proceeded to beat Barcelona at the semi-final stage before seeing off Bordeaux in the two-legged final.

Despite being on the receiving end of a schooling in the UEFA Cup, the season was, on balance, another successful one. Forest also reached the quarter-finals of the FA Cup, finished ninth in the table and started the season by extending their unbeaten league run from the previous one to 25 games. The sequence came to a shuddering halt at Ewood Park in November where they lost 7-0 to Blackburn Rovers. Nonetheless, and rather curiously, Forest's fortunes continued to mirror those of the city's famous ice skaters, Jayne Torvill and Christopher Dean, who in 1994 took the bronze medal for figure skating at the 1994 Winter Olympics in Lillehammer (just as Forest embarked on an unbeaten run that powered them to promotion) and followed that up with consecutive World Championship titles in 1995 and 1996, while Forest were tearing up the Premier League and once again gallivanting around Europe.

While the mid-1990s was a period of success for Forest, it was a time of change for Derby. A steady opening to life under Jim Smith was unfolding until a 5-1 defeat on 4 November to Tranmere Rovers at Prenton Park. Despite the result, the game was notable for the debut of new signing Igor Štimac, who scored Derby's solitary goal. It was also the catalyst for the Rams to embark upon a remarkable unbeaten run of 20 games, only ended by eventual champions Sunderland, by which time Derby had propelled themselves to the summit of the First Division. During this run, it was announced in February that a £16m stadium would be built and ready for the 1997/98 season.

Perhaps influenced by the City Ground being one of the host stadiums for the forthcoming European Championship, this was a swift U-turn from the announcement the previous year signalling Derby's intentions to stay put and develop. Yet in truth, the Baseball Ground was beyond redevelopment for the new football age. Surrounded by tightly terraced streets and difficult to access, the Rams' historic home seemed increasingly anachronistic as grounds like Middlesbrough's Riverside Stadium and Millwall's New Den sprang up, replacing wooden seats reeking of Woodbines and surrounded by the homes of the workers of the Industrial Revolution, just like Derby's home for a century.

Yet any football club that builds a new stadium runs the risk of losing a part of their identity. Without the Baseball Ground, Derby might no longer have been able to position themselves as the mud and nettles club compared to their rivals who hailed from the leafy suburbs of well-heeled West Bridgford. But the times they were indeed a-changing and a new stadium promised bigger crowds and, crucially, more revenue. Of course, the perfect coda to this seismic decision would be to secure promotion to the Premier League in the hope that they could start life in their new stadium in the top division. They duly did this, finishing second behind Peter Reid's Sunderland. After six years, the East Midlands sides would meet again in the Premier League in the year that Capital One launched its UK operations in 1996, and established its headquarters and operations centre in Nottingham. The credit card specialist would go on to sponsor Forest between 2003 and 2009.

Before the return of the provincial derby, though, the whole of England had a summer of football to enjoy as it hosted the European Championship. It was the original summer of numerous and repeated vocal claims of football coming home, which it did – in a way – to the City Ground which hosted games from Group D including Portugal, Croatia and Turkey. Forest were represented in the tournament by Pearce and Stone with England and Gemmill in the Scotland squad, while Derby fans could make the short trip to Nottingham or Sheffield to see Štimac play for Croatia.

After a slow start, England progressed to the quarter-finals where they faced Spain at Wembley, and after an uneventful and goalless 120 minutes it came down to penalties. Fernando Hierro missed Spain's first, handing the initiative to England who scored their first two efforts. Then fans were greeted with the sight of Pearce striding forward to take England's third. Thoughts immediately drifted back to the night in Turin in 1990 when his penalty found only the thighs of Bodo Illgner before Chris Waddle blasted his effort into orbit. If England fans were nervous, Forest supporters felt anxiety and, in strange way, a sense of responsibility. He was their man, their leader, their legend.

Pearce's spot-kick hit the net and years of repressed emotion came tumbling out. Of course, he never had to redeem himself to Forest fans, but with his reaction everyone instantly got it; they now fully understood why Reds revered him. Surely even Derby supporters couldn't not love him, or at least respect him at that moment, even if he famously wrote, 'If I didn't have a club to go to and Derby was my only option, I would rather go on the dole than join them.' After all, such honesty and dedication to their own fans' values is what we want from our heroes, to show the same level of passion we reserve for our rivals. Regardless, in that rare moment, both Forest and Derby fans were as one: supporters of Pearce and England. Indeed, Pearce later revealed how he received letters of support after his penalty miss at Italia '90 just from not Forest followers but also from those of a Derby persuasion too.

As usual, beating Germany in a penalty shoot-out proved a bridge too far for England in the semi-final. Germany progressed to the final at Wembley before beating the Czech Republic, lifting the Henri Delaunay Trophy and singing about football coming home, proving that reports about Germans' apparent lack of a sense of humour or irony were well wide of the mark.

1996/97
Foundation stone

While 'Wannabe' by the Spice Girls topped the charts, thoughts turned back towards the domestic season – but Forest and Derby had to wait until October before they clashed at the City Ground. After a bright opening day of the season away at Coventry City in which Kevin Campbell's hat-trick fired Forest to a 3-0 win, the Reds had yet to follow that up with another three-pointer, a fact that was not lost on Frank Clark, who, in his programme notes, declared that the clash would be 'much more special if we could clinch a home win – something we're desperately in need of at this point in time'. Emulating Brian Clough's respect for Arthur Cox, Clark heaped praise on Jim Smith, who had by now overseen more than 1,000 career games, expressing delight at him clinching promotion at the end of the previous season. Clark also found space to remind his readers of his own favourite East Midlands encounter: their previous game at the Baseball Ground, 'We won 2-0 and at that point I just knew we were destined to clinch promotion. A lot has happened since then, of course, and now we find ourselves needing the points for a different reason.'

Derby too were stuttering and were only three points and four places better off than Forest's seven points from nine games, which left them fourth from bottom. Following the well-worn path between Derby and Nottingham, Dean Saunders was now with Forest, albeit via Liverpool, Aston Villa and Galatasary, and was welcomed to the City Ground by Pearce with the customary dressing room shenanigans. The Forest captain took exception to Saunders' shoes and chucked them in the Trent before sending an unfortunate trainee to rescue them.

Fittingly and somewhat predictably, Saunders opened the scoring by finishing clinically after a cross from Jason Lee. Christian Dailly equalised in the second half with a low drive. Even if Dailly hadn't found the bottom corner, his team would almost certainly have been awarded a penalty given Steve Chettle's clearing-out of Aljoša Asanović. Ultimately, Derby were unlucky not to win as Asanović ran the show and thoroughly enjoyed himself, much to the delight of the Croatia shirt-wearing Derby fans in the Lower Bridgford End. For Forest, the game confirmed that their slow start was no blip or hiccup: they were really struggling.

A month later, on 17 November and under incessant rain, Derby chairman Lionel Pickering unveiled the foundation stone for the new stadium at Pride Park, a site a couple of miles from the Baseball Ground and previously part of the railway yards but derelict for many years. Maintaining their status as a Premier League club for the 1997/98 season, when it was hoped their new stadium would be up and running, had rarely been as important. Comfortably in mid-table, everything (apart from the drizzle) was going to plan.

By Christmas 1996, an idea hatched in a terraced house in Derby about a British archaeologist travelling the world searching for lost historical artefacts was launched on to the market and *Tomb Raider* became a national phenomenon, colliding neatly with the zeitgeist of Britpop, the Spice Girls and magazines like *Loaded*. Underlying the boorish swagger, though, the year saw Nottinghamshire post the second-highest rate of crime in the country. While the garden seemed to be getting rosier in Derby, Nottingham's was slowly withering, neatly illustrated by the Rams winning 3-2 at Manchester United on 5 April, featuring a memorable debut goal from Costa Rican striker Paulo Wanchope, and the bow of Estonian goalkeeper Mart Poom, while on the very same day Forest lost 3-1 at home to the only club below them in the table, Southampton. Now under Pearce's leadership as player-manager, having dispensed with Clark's services just before Christmas, Forest travelled to the Baseball Ground on 23 April for the very last time with more desperation than hope in their hearts.

Wanchope headed Jacob Laursen's dangerous free kick against the bar, while Chettle, again fancying his chances at the Normanton End of the Baseball Ground, rattled the crossbar from 40 yards. In the second half, Asanović stung Alan Fettis's palms with a free kick, but the night ended goalless, a somewhat disappointing final derby at the historic ground. Forest were not mathematically certain of being certain of being relegated, but to all intents and purpose, they were down. Derby remained solidly in mid-table, while Forest sank to the bottom with just two games remaining, five points from safety and with an inferior goal difference. With strong echoes of April 1980 when a 1-0 defeat at the City Ground all but relegated Derby from the top division, the roles were once again reversed.

The final game at the Baseball Ground took place on Sunday, 11 May. With Paul Durkin as the referee, Ashley Ward put Derby ahead with a header after his first effort rebounded off the foot of the post. Ian Wright equalised before Dennis Bergkamp put Arsenal ahead with a sumptuous trademark chip. The honour of scoring the final competitive goal at the Baseball Ground went to Ian Wright who celebrated his scruffy finish with an impish jig of delight. Centre-back Jacob Laursen credited the Baseball Ground with playing a key role in helping the team achieve a 12th-placed finish in the first season in the Premier League and never looking to be in any real danger of an immediate return to the First Division owing to its tightness and intimidating atmosphere. The Rams took 30 points from their home games that season compared with 16 from away matches.

Meanwhile, Forest bowed out of the Premier League and back into the First Division with barely a whimper, losing 5-0 at Newcastle. Pearce ended his 12 years at the City Ground to go on and play in the Champions League and an FA Cup Final under Kenny Dalglish at Newcastle United.

1997/98
Pride Park

Initially, Forest blazed a bright trail in the Premier League, but in the space of just three short years, at the height of Britpop and with Labour in power for the first time since before Trevor Francis stooped to conquer in Munich, the party at the City Ground was well and truly over, just when it seemed to be hitting its stride for the rest of the country. It was Derby's turn to gatecrash the premier party in town and stay there, at least for a while. Under Jim Smith's experienced tutelage, they could enjoy stability off the pitch while they took their first tentative steps on to an actual brand new pitch.

With Oasis about to top the charts with 'D'You Know What I Mean?', Pride Park officially opened on 18 July. Queen Elizabeth II and the Duke of Edinburgh did the honours and cut the ribbon, while the Derby Serenaders, the Red Devils Sky Divers and the Spice-ish Girls helped to entertain amid the celebrations. Modelled on Middlesborough's Riverside Stadium, Pride Park was officially open for business. Two weeks later, Derby played host to Sampdoria in a friendly, for which 29,041 turned out to see Vincenzo Montella score the first goal at Pride Park as the visitors won 1-0. On Wednesday, 13 August, the stadium hosted its first competitive match, against Wimbledon. The game was abandoned after 56 minutes when the floodlights failed in front of a crowd of 24,571. Ashley Ward had put Derby ahead with a trademark header, achieving a neat double as he had scored Derby's final goal at the Baseball Ground. But Chris Perry equalised for the visitors before Stefano Eranio put the Rams ahead once more. But then the lights went out.

Eventually, on 30 August, Pride Park finally saw its first competitive game played to a conclusion. The Rams beat Barnsley 1-0, but that is only part of the story. Francesco Baiano saw his penalty saved, yet Eranio, thinking he had made history in scoring Derby's first goal in their new home, converted the rebound. It wasn't so simple, though, and Paul Durkin's assistant saw something he wasn't happy with, so ordered a retake, from which Eranio did successfully score. In short, the identity of the scorer of the first goal at Pride Park remains a messy affair.

Derby finished ninth but started to feel at home in the Premier League, especially after thrashing eventual champions Arsenal 3-0 with a brace from Wanchope and another from Dean Sturridge. 'Leaving [the Baseball Ground] allowed us to play a different game, which we needed to survive,' said Laursen. It represented a third successive year of continuous progress under Smith and, just for good measure, they now had former Forest midfielder Lars Bohinen in their ranks.

With Pearce gone, Forest needed to reset entirely for their 1997/98 First Division campaign, which they did by hiring Dave Bassett. Despite misgivings from many Forest fans regarding the nature of his team's combative style, four straight wins to start the season allayed many of those fears, with Kevin Campbell and Pierre van Hooijdonk quickly striking up a prolific partnership.

Winning five of the final seven matches meant that Forest returned to the Premier League as champions, seemingly in a good position to make a decent fist of life once again at the top table. It also meant they would take their first trip to Pride Park.

1998/99
Carbonari

It was anticipated by many that if Campbell and Van Hooijdonk could pick up in the Premier League where they left off in the First Division, Forest could at least consolidate after promotion. But the sale of Campbell in late July to Trabzonspor set the dominoes tumbling, and they simply never stopped. Two weeks later, Colin Cooper was sold to Middlesbrough and the spine of the team was ripped out with the ferocity of the Predator from the movie of the same name. At some stage in the summer, Van Hooijdonk, realising that the chances of anything apart from a season of bleakness and drudgery were incredibly slim, decided that he didn't really fancy coming back, choosing instead to train with his old team, NEC Breda, and leaving Bassett's signings of Dougie Freedman and Nigel Quashie looking extremely inadequate.

At least, that is generally understood to be the story, but in an interview with *FourFourTwo*, Van Hooijdonk offered his version of events. For him, the sale of Campbell and others was a factor, but not the main one. His real issue was that he simply wasn't happy at the club, especially with Bassett's training routines, or lack of them, and was frustrated at Forest denying him a move to PSV Eindhoven back in December and then continuously setting his asking price too high, scaring off other potential buyers. But it was at Bassett's feet where he squarely laid the blame, 'We were doing f**** all in training. People say we became champions, but so what? If you were to change all the managers in the league for cats, at the end of the season there will still be one champion and three will get relegated. Does that mean the cat who is champion is fantastic and the three who got relegated are sh*t? It's about players as well. [Forest director Irving] Scholar said, "Let's see, go to the World Cup." I did, but there was still no movement. I just decided, "OK, if you hurt me, I hurt you." I didn't want to hurt the fans, they didn't create that situation, but I wanted to make a point to the people who were trying to take the p*ss. That's why I decided to stay home and train there.'

Against this backdrop, Forest opened their campaign at reigning champions Arsenal and turned in a creditable display, despite going down 2-1. This was followed by two successive wins, but a third victory would not follow until the Christmas decorations were well and truly down and stuffed back into the loft, all but forgotten about for another year. Van Hooijdonk eventually returned in November for a 1-0 defeat at home to Wimbledon, by which time Forest were second-bottom with a paltry nine points from 12 games. Up next were Derby, looking fit, functioning, and firing in seventh, at the City Ground. The gap between the teams was illustrated by each's representation at the 1998 World Cup in France. Derby boasted five players: Christian Dailly, Jacob Laursen, Deon Burton, Darryl Powell and Igor Štimac, compared to Forest's two representatives, their errant Dutchman and Scot Gemmill, who was in dispute with the club over a new contract.

It was a typically fierce derby, with Forest determined to claw their way out of an increasingly desperate situation. Van Hooijdonk almost sensationally scored one of the great derby goals from a direct free kick but was denied by the strong hand of Russell Hoult, who somehow clawed it out of the top corner. At the other end, the Dutchman cleared a Horacio Carbonari header off his own line, meaning the game remained goalless at half-time. But that was just the appetiser.

The second half was action-packed and breathless in pace. Sturridge scampered into the area only to be felled by Thierry Bonalair, and Tony Dorigo converted the resulting penalty. Forest came back and a shot from range by Nigel Quashie broke to Dougie Freedman, whose effort was well saved but squirmed free of Hoult's previously reliable grip for Freedman to shoot home at the second attempt. Moments later, Gemmill's corner was met at the near post by Van Hooijdonk who glanced it in. It took a while for any of his team-mates to acknowledge his goal but, eventually, Freedman and Bonalair trotted over to him. 'Bonalair has decided to bury the hatchet, the rest of them look as though they'd rather bury it in his back,' eloquently opined the commentator. Steve Stone then almost converted a low cross from Alan Rogers, but Hoult denied him, taking a boot to his head in the process and leaving the field on a stretcher, to everyone's concern looking concussed. With 18 minutes to go, a cross came over which Wanchope took a swing at, but his connection fell tamely to Carbonari, who made no mistake and fired home from close range to make it 2-2. All of this within the space of 15 breathless minutes. There remained time for Sturridge to twice go close to giving Derby the lead, but the game ended 2-2.

After 13 matches played, Forest were third from bottom but two points behind fourth-bottom Everton. It was a creditable and battling display by the Reds but ultimately did nothing to shake the view that it was shaping up to be a long, hard slog of a season. After all, the enmity behind the scenes still lingered. 'I am pleased for Pierre that he scored,' Bassett told the *Daily Mirror*. 'But then I am pleased when anybody gets a goal for Forest. Pierre did some good things and he did some bad things. On two or three occasions, his poor passes dropped us in the cart. He simply has to stick at it now that he's back here.' On the celebrations, or lack of them with his team-mates, Bassett said, 'I didn't really notice that our lads seemed to ignore him. That's up to them. I don't care either way.' It seems fair to say that little was being done to create any harmony, no matter how fragile, in the squad. The signs were ominous.

By the time of the return fixture against Derby in April, Stone had been sold to Aston Villa, Gemmill to Everton and young starlet Paul McGregor had been frozen out by Bassett. As for Van Hooijdonk, he had scored six goals since his return, a reasonable tally considering how dysfunctional the team was and how bridges remained very much unbuilt between him and his team-mates. It was little wonder that Forest were now rock bottom and nine points behind Southampton just above them. Not even Ron Atkinson could save them now, especially after taking his place in the wrong dugout on the occasion of his first game in charge at the City Ground – a slapstick moment that neatly epitomised Forest's season. Derby were still in seventh place and dreaming of European football.

Avoiding defeat on their first visit to Pride Park was about as much as Forest could hope for, yet at the same time, it was a huge incentive. A battling performance looked to have earned at least that until Carbonari scored the decisive goal in the 85th minute after a neat turn and fearsome shot, which just like two years previously, effectively sealed Forest's fate. 'To score against your biggest rivals away was fantastic – but I got fined for my celebration,' the Argentinian told The Athletic. 'I scored and then went to celebrate with the people. In Argentina, I was not used to that because the crowd had some form of netting or fencing to keep you apart. I was embracing everybody and shouting. The next week, Jim [Smith] told me I was fined for it. But I laughed and said, "No problem," because I scored against Nottingham Forest. The winner I scored at home was fantastic. I always remember it. It was beautiful. It was like Maradona in Derby.'

Forest were ten points from safety, with a game in hand and only five to play. They were all but doomed and they were put out of their misery two matches later after a 2-0 defeat at Villa, with the second goal the result of a cross from Stone. It was that kind of season. Derby fans couldn't have cared less about all of this, gleeful as they were with their team finishing in eighth, a fourth year of progress under Smith. The only kink in their development was the departure of Smith's assistant, Steve McClaren, to Manchester United, yet this only reinforced how impressively Derby had performed. When the team on its way to a treble of Premier League, FA Cup and Champions League wants to take your assistant manager, it is as much of a compliment as it is a disappointment.

Neither club knew it at the time, but Derby's 1-0 win in 1999 remains, at the time of writing, the final East Midlands derby in the Premier League. Forest fans perhaps knew, given the parlous state of their club, that there would be no immediate return, but the thought of a sustained absence from the top division would have found them shaking their heads in disbelief and dismissing such a thought as being overly and unnecessarily pessimistic. It is often strange how football works.

As for Derby, this was as good as it was going to get. They had reached their apex in the Premier League and although the millennium midnight failed to bring civilisation crashing down – as some thought it would owing to the world's computers being unable to distinguish between 1900 and 2000 – it did throw a bug into the previously smooth progress of the club.

1999-2002
The Bald Eagle departs

The 1999/2000 season was a difficult one for both clubs. Derby were facing an uphill struggle even before their opening game, away at Leeds United. Igor Štimac and Paulo Wanchope had departed for West Ham United and Lee Carsley had joined Blackburn Rovers. They lost 12 of their opening 19 games but improved sufficiently after the dawn of the new millennium to finish 16th.

The start Forest made to their new season and life in the First Division was little better. David Platt took charge and promptly signed three Italians, Moreno Mannini, Gianluca Petrachi and Salvatore Matrecano, at a combined cost of around £3.6m. None of the trio made any notable impact and the 3-1 defeat on the opening day of the season at Ipswich Town was a clear indicator as to which way the wind was blowing. The Reds finished 14th and were seemingly going nowhere fast, yet supporters could at least turn their feet to skating should they wish as, on 1 April 2000, the Nottingham Arena and Arena Rink of the National Ice Centre were opened to the public by Jayne Torvill.

The following season saw more of the same stasis for both clubs. Derby took 14 games to register their first Premier League win of 2000/01, which didn't arrive until 18 November against Bradford City, and they finished just above the relegation zone, albeit eight points clear. Forest showed some signs of progress under Platt and finished in the top half of the First Division table, but patience was wearing thin. At the end of the campaign, Platt was appointed manager of England's Under-21s. Only 33 years old when he took his first managerial post at Forest, and tasked with dealing with the fall-out from a disastrous relegation from the Premier League, it was too much too soon for Platt. By his own admission, he would have done things differently were he to have his time again. Being handed a sizeable chunk of transfer money by the ambitious owner, Nigel Doughty, was oddly unhelpful for a rookie manager. 'It was very much, "This money's here because we want to bounce back into the Premier League,"' he told The Athletic. 'If I could do it again, it would have been better in a funny way if that money was not available.' In stepped Paul Hart, promoted from youth academy director to nurse and nourish the young talent coming through.

In an effort to jump-start their fortunes, Derby signed Fabrizio Ravanelli in July 2001, but owing to their financial problems a year later they had to defer his wage payments, which they ended up paying for several years. The walls were closing in. Despite an opening-day victory against

Blackburn, Derby then went ten games without a win. Midway through this terrible run, Smith rejected an offer to become director of football and resigned from his post as manager after more than six years in charge, during which, for the most part, steady progress was made year on year. 'We wanted to continue to use Jim's vast experience in football for the benefit of Derby County,' said chairman Lionel Pickering. 'He thought carefully about the new role but decided it would be better to leave.'

Smith's assistant Colin Todd, a former Derby player, stepped in but could do little to lift the mood or results and found himself being replaced in January 2002 by another ex-Ram, John Gregory, after a spell that included a humiliating home defeat to Bristol Rovers in the third round of the FA Cup. Results improved a little, but a run of seven consecutive losses towards the end of the season meant that Derby were relegated after three years of decline. Like the life of Jarvis Cocker in the 1990s Britpop anthem 'Common People', the Premier League slid out of view of the East Midlands.

Forest slid down to 16th in the First Division, but gradually improved under Paul Hart, with youngsters such as Michael Dawson, Andy Reid and David Prutton gaining valuable experience in the first team. They had little choice but to trust in youth given the collapse of ITV Digital in March 2002. The £3m per year that First Division clubs were promised would not be forthcoming. This also hit Derby particularly hard given their wage bill was shaping up to be one of the highest outside the Premier League after their relegation. The largesse and excess of the 1990s were truly over for both clubs and they would once again lock horns, but this time in the second tier of English football.

2002/03
Together again

As the season kicked off, Queen Elizabeth and Prince Philip visited Nottingham as part of their Golden Jubilee celebrations and officially opened the Ice Centre before watching a special ice gala, choreographed, of course, by Torvill and Dean. In September 2002, The Screen Room, the world's smallest cinema according to the *Guinness Book of Records*, opened on Broad Street in Nottingham (it would later be renamed Screen 22 in 2011). With Forest just about in a play-off spot and Derby in mid-table, they met at Pride Park in late October, with the Reds looking to consolidate their lofty place and score at their rivals' new home for the first time. They achieved the former but not the latter with a goalless draw.

Forest striker David Johnson saw his seemingly legitimate goal ruled out for offside against an equally young and inexperienced Derby side, whose youth was emphasised by the fact that Gregory had covered the walls of the dressing room with posters highlighting the importance of the fixture in the East Midlands. 'In the first half we never got to grips with Forest,' Gregory told *The Guardian*, 'But in the second half it was virtually one-way traffic. At one stage our goalkeeper was in danger of getting frostbite.' Perhaps, but Forest rose two places to fourth, as their ambition to qualify for the play-offs for the first time looked increasingly sound.

Little had changed for Forest by the time of the return fixture at the City Ground in March 2003. They were again in sixth place, but Derby had dropped to a worrying 20th, with Gregory coming under increasing pressure. They were without a win in seven and had lost their previous three. A Wednesday evening trip to Nottingham had rarely looked more intimidating.

In the 13th minute, Andy Reid's deep cross found Marlon Harewood who headed into the corner. Forest were just getting started and, from another Reid cross, David Johnson's header hit the bar before Nottingham-born Manchester City loanee Darren Huckerby was on hand to nod the Reds into a 2-0 lead after only 15 minutes. In the second half, Steve Elliott bundled Johnson over in the area and Harewood converted the resulting penalty to make it 3-0.

'There is a lot of flak coming my way, but I'm determined to achieve what Forest have done here,' Gregory told *The Guardian*. 'I'd be lying if I said I didn't care about our league position because obviously teams are creeping up on us, but I'm determined to see this through and I will not let my head go down.' He didn't get the chance to make good on his promise as, two days later, Gregory was sacked for alleged misconduct. The allegations related to training methods and treatment of players, prompting Gregory to launch legal proceedings. The case was eventually settled in his favour for an undisclosed sum. George Burley took charge of an increasingly desperate club, which was financially insolvent in part due to the high wages of Ravanelli and Georgi Kinkladze. Derby were left struggling in 18th place, their closest brush with the third tier since 1984, and Pickering's millions were dwindling away. Just to add to the turmoil, BBC Radio Derby's Graham Richards, while commentating on a local derby between Leicester City and the Rams earlier in the season, had claimed that Foxes striker Brian Deane 'collapsed like the World Trade Center, only less spectacularly', three days after the first anniversary of 11 September. All the while, Forest were safely ensconced in the play-off places.

Forest did indeed reach the play-offs and after a 1-1 draw with Sheffield United at the City Ground in the first leg of the semi-final, they looked to be home and dry when they took a 2-0 lead at Bramall Lane. United pulled a goal back almost immediately and found an equaliser moments later. In extra time, Paul Peschisolido put United ahead and an own goal by the unfortunate Des Walker seemed to mark the end of things for Forest. A last-minute own goal by United's Robert Page after a Huckerby shot meant that fingernails were bitten down until the final whistle, but ultimately it was Neil Warnock's United who went through to the final to face Wolverhampton Wanderers after this chaotic and frankly bonkers game. To offset the disappointment experienced by both sets of fans, Derby-born Sat Bains's restaurant became the first restaurant in Nottingham to win a Michelin star.

2003/04

Coffee cup

Things settled down a little for 2003/04. Derby continued to labour against financial strife and underachievement, while Forest reverted to the mean of mid-table. The two teams met in Nottingham on 27 September and played out a 1-1 draw. Without striker Johnson, who was ruled out for a long spell with a broken leg, Forest lacked a cutting edge. Both goals came in a hectic two-minute spell in the first half. Derby youngster Tom Huddlestone, born and raised in Nottingham, knocked the ball in from the left for Mathias Svensson who headed it into the path of

Júnior. The Brazilian made no mistake in slotting his shot low past Darren Ward. This prompted a quick reply from the home team as Reid squeezed an effort through Andy Oakes's hands.

Hart lamented the loss of Johnson and was in the market for a replacement. 'I'm interested in a lot of players, but I can't always get them,' he told *The Guardian*. 'Today I didn't think we played as well as we can but we still got something. I expected a tough game and we got one. Having said that we had some gilt-edged chances to win the game, but then Derby could say the same.' George Burley had no option but to embrace the future potential of his youthful prospects. 'I'm pleased with the improvement of the side. We always said this was going to be a hard season,' he said. 'Forest are a good side. They showed last season they are capable of promotion, but we matched them today and the draw was a fair result.'

He was right to foresee the season being a hard one. When it came to Forest visiting Pride Park in March – still looking for their first goal there – Burley's team were third from bottom and, despite having played a game more, they were three points behind Gillingham who sat just above them. Still struggling to overcome the disappointment of their play-off defeat and the loss of Johnson, the season had petered out somewhat for Forest. They lay in 17th – probably safe but not quite certain – while they had also dispensed with the services of Hart and replaced him with Joe Kinnear.

Ian Taylor put the Rams ahead after only three minutes, a pattern that would become common at Pride Park in the future. Then came the notorious coffee cup goal. In Forest's penalty area, Barry Roche horribly sliced a simple back-pass up into the air for Paul Peschisolido – now tormenting Forest fans in the white of Derby after having done so for Sheffield United previously – who casually tapped home. In an effort to explain his error, Roche pointed to an errant plastic coffee cup that lay discarded and in tatters on the spot where his boot, the ball and the drinking vessel had triangulated together in a strange collision to heap embarrassment on him. He was right to do so: the ball had indeed taken a nick off the cup and bounced upwards just before Roche was about to hoof it clear.

Peschisolido's second goal, and Derby's third, was much more conventional as he slotted home after being set free by Marcus Tudgay. There was just enough time remaining in the first half for Gareth Taylor to bundle home a cross from Mathieu Louis-Jean and, in doing so, score a somewhat underwhelming first Forest goal at Pride Park. Hopes of taking something away were a real possibility when Gareth Williams prodded home after some penalty area pinball, and with 23 minutes remaining Forest started to believe. But in the closing stages, Peschisolido broke down the left and squared for Tudgay to slot home and secure a famous 4-2 win.

It was little consolation, but Forest had finally broken their duck after 247 minutes at Pride Park, although they had yet to enjoy a lead. The table looked much healthier from Derby's perspective after this bizarre game, but the focus was firmly on the first half's freak goal. 'The coffee cup flew on to the pitch at just the right time for me,' said Peschisolido. 'It acted as a kind of golf tee and I had little to do. I did feel a bit for Barry Roche but not too much; I was too excited about scoring that goal. I went on to score another and the atmosphere was electric.'

The emotions were somewhat different for Roche. 'For it to happen in any game it would have been bad enough, but for it to happen at Pride Park against that lot, it made it all the more difficult,' he said. 'I'll be honest, it took me quite a bit of time to recover from it.' But he did recover and went on to enjoy a long career, making over 600 appearances in total after also having long spells with Chesterfield and Morecambe.

Once the kerfuffle over the coffee cup died down, both clubs avoided relegation although it was a close call for Derby who finished just one point clear of the bottom three. It was a tumultuous season for the Rams as, in October, the parent company of Derby County went into liquidation. 'If you've got £8m, you've got Derby County – but I'd listen to £5m,' said Pickering as reported in *The Telegraph*. Reacting to unrest among fans at the lack of investment in the squad, chairman Lionel Pickering told BBC Radio Derby, 'If you can do better where's your money – and if you don't like it, go and watch Forest.' The money had run dry and Pickering wanted out as the Co-operative Bank were owed £27m. Up also stepped John Sleightholme, a barrister, who led a consortium comprising Jeremy Keith and Steve Harding. Yet doubts soon arose regarding the size of their wealth after they claimed all shares in the club and had paid just £3 for the ownership of Derby County.

* * *

On 20 September 2004, a spokeswoman for Derby City Hospital had a very sombre announcement to make, 'It is with the deepest sadness that we announce that Brian Clough has died peacefully at the age of 69. Brian was an

Artist's impression of Leonard Benbow scoring Forest's second goal in the 1898 FA Cup Final at Crystal Palace.

Forest's Ian Storey-Moore strikes at goal at the Baseball Ground in November 1969. Forest won 2-0.

Ian Storey-Moore acknowledges the cheers of the Derby County fans as he is introduced to the crowd by Derby secretary Stuart Webb and assistant manager Peter Taylor as the club's new signing. However, his old club Nottingham Forest refused to countersign the transfer forms and Manchester United stepped in to sign the England international. March 1972.

Derby County players show off their league championship medals for the 1971/72 season under Clough and Taylor. John McGovern, Terry Hennessy, Alan Hinton, John O'Hare, Archie Gemmill and trainer Jimmy Gordon all represented both Derby and Forest.

Manager Brian Clough and assistant Peter Taylor leaving Derby County after a meeting with the board in October 1973.

Derby County's Archie Gemmill after scoring the opening goal against Forest from a free kick in January 1983.

Derby County chairman Robert Maxwell lines up with his team before the English League Division One match against Chelsea at the Baseball Ground in November 1987.

Ted McMinn on the receiving end of a tackle from Des Walker in April 1991.

Colin Cooper celebrates the opening goal in a 2-0 win at the Baseball Ground in April 1994 which saw Forest gain promotion.

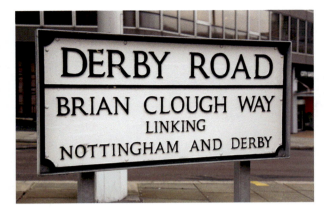

A Brian Clough Way sign on the A52, renamed after the Forest and Derby manager in 2005.

Derby County's Kris Commons celebrates his goal against his former club during their FA Cup fourth round replay match at the City Ground in February 2009.

Nathan Tyson celebrates with a corner flag after Forest beat Derby at the City Ground in August 2009.

Billy Davies and Nigel Clough clash on the touchline at Pride Park in January 2010.

Derby County's Jeff Hendrick is congratulated on scoring the winning goal in September 2011 at the City Ground despite his team being reduced to ten men in the first minute.

Derby's Craig Bryson celebrates his third goal in the resounding 5-0 'deforestation' in March 2014.

Derby-born Ben Osborn celebrates scoring his late winner against Derby at Pride Park in January 2015.

Stuart Pearce celebrates Ben Osborn's late winner at Pride Park in January 2015.

'Welcome to our Forest Kingdom'. This display was unveiled at the City Ground by the fan group Forza Garibaldi for the game in January 2022. The tip of Robin Hood's arrow reads 'Ramslayer'. Credit: OurGloriousBanners

in-patient at Derby City General Hospital, and his family were with him when he passed away in hospital.' On behalf of the Clough family, she added, 'The family would like to express their heartfelt thanks to Dr Jan Freeman and the staff of Ward 30 for the wonderful care they gave him.' In reference to the ten-hour liver transplant that Clough received on 13 January 2003, the spokeswoman continued, 'They [Clough's family] would also like to thank the donor family for allowing Brian to have 21 months of health and happiness. The family would naturally appreciate privacy at this sad time, and kindly ask members of the media to respect this.'

Six days later, Forest faced West Ham at the City Ground on a bright Sunday afternoon. The songs of Frank Sinatra, Clough's favourite artist, serenaded fans before the game, tributes were paid, silences were observed, and tears were shed. Now with West Ham, Marlon Harewood apologetically rolled the ball home to give the Londoners the lead. With six minutes remaining, Paul Evans's low shot found the corner of the net to put Forest on level terms. In the final minute, Reid released recent signing Marlon King, who paused, turned inside and unleashed a beautiful curling shot into the Trent End goal. It was a deeply cathartic moment.

On 21 October, fans of both Derby and Forest united to mourn him at a memorial service at Pride Park Stadium. Originally to be held at Derby Cathedral, the venue was switched due to the demand for tickets, resulting in more than 14,000 people braving the torrential rain and gales to attend. Perhaps Martin O'Neill articulated the deep sense of loss felt not only by Derby and Forest fans, but by all football supporters – in fact, anyone with only a passing interest in the sport, 'I remember hearing that his career as a player was over, ended by a knee injury. That was the first time I cried over Brian Clough, but it was not the last. He was the legendary manager of Nottingham Forest and Derby County, two rival clubs set apart by history, colours, tradition and a 15-mile stretch of tarmac, but one common thread and memories of sharing the greatest-ever manager. He is a unifying factor and is being mourned at both ends of that road equally.' At the risk of cliché, English football had truly never seen anyone like him, and never would again.

2004/05
Third tier

For the 2004/05 season, the Football League rebranded its competitions. The First Division was now the Championship, underneath which was League One and then League Two. For Derby, this jump-started them out of their malaise, while Forest stumbled under Joe Kinnear. Unusually, the teams had to wait until December to renew their antipathy towards each other, by which time the Rams were in 11th place and going reasonably well with new free signings Iñigo Idiakez and Grzegorz Rasiak hitting the ground running.

The Kinnear experiment had gone very wrong very quickly at Forest, who were third from bottom and struggling on many levels. His promise of 'sexy' signings turned out to be Andy Impey. As if he couldn't quite possibly make himself any more unpopular with Forest fans, Kinnear somehow managed to do exactly that by calling the derby 'just another game' on the eve of the meeting at Pride Park.

The game played out as predicted. Tommy Smith finished an exhilarating flowing move to put Derby ahead after just three minutes, mirroring Ian Taylor's goal the previous season. Taylor soon blazed a penalty into orbit after a handball by Impey, but in the 75th minute the game was well and truly up for the visitors as Smith curled over an inviting cross from the left for Rasiak to connect with at the far post and guide the ball home with his head. Just for good measure, the Pole made it three from close range after the Forest defence oddly decided to go on a collective walkabout. Forest had still not experienced the feeling of leading at Pride Park, despite four games there.

Kinnear skipped his post-match press duties, leaving David Johnson to face the inquisition. 'We never gave ourselves the chance,' he correctly surmised. At one stage in the game, Reid and Kinnear seemed to exchange some frank views with each other and, somewhat predictably, Kinnear was sacked days later, replaced by Gary Megson in January. Oddly enough in such turbulent times, Nottingham had a gross domestic product per capita of £24,238, the highest of any English city apart from London.

Come 26 February, Forest were one place off the bottom and six points from safety. Admittedly they had two games in hand, but such things are of little use if you have little chance of winning them. Derby climbed to fourth and although automatic promotion looked to be a three-way contest between Wigan Athletic, Ipswich Town and Sunderland, they were right in the thick of the play-off race. A win for the Rams would represent seven consecutive away victories, and would be their first at the City Ground since 1971. Derby's poor record in Nottingham offered small crumbs of comfort for Forest fans in the face of their equally awful record at Pride Park and their perilous league position. Maintaining their long unbeaten home record against their rivals would at least be something.

After stinging the palms of Forest keeper Paul Gerrard, Rasiak looped a header that apologetically plopped into the far corner to put Derby ahead after 11 minutes, maintaining their ludicrous record of taking the lead early on in such games, this being the third time in succession they had done so. This was the fourth time in a row that Derby had taken the lead since their 3-0 mauling at the City Ground back in March 2003. On 34 minutes, Kris Commons danced his way into the heart of the Derby defence but was felled. Gareth Taylor slotted the resulting penalty past goalkeeper Lee Camp.

In the second half, Rasiak and Peschisolido continued to cause Forest more problems, yet the Reds improved and their efforts were rewarded when Taylor stooped to head the ball powerfully into the net from a corner right in front of the visiting fans. Perhaps Forest might yet find a way out of the relegation woods. However, it was not to be as with 12 minutes remaining, Rasiak somehow arched his frame to convert a Chris Makin cross towards the top corner of the Trent End goal. It was a fair result with Forest showing some sorely missed fight, yet the point was perhaps more useful in maintaining Derby's play-off push than in banishing Forest's relegation woes.

'We looked like a team that wasn't used to being in that position,' Megson admitted. 'If we'd managed to turn round a goal in front [at half-time], we'd probably have won the game,' Burley said. 'Full credit to Forest, though, they were determined and came back at us. We knew they would close us down and try to stop us playing.' Despite it being an encouraging performance by Forest, and certainly an improvement on their collapse at Pride Park, they were still staring down the barrel of relegation to League One, while Derby consolidated their play-off ambitions in fourth.

And so it came to pass at Loftus Road. Forest were relegated to the third tier for the first time since 1957 and, in this way, became the first European Cup winners to suffer such ignominy. A proud and long unbeaten home record against Derby meant little in the face of such a crushing relegation, especially while the Rams fought it out for a place at the top table where the riches were gifted with gay abandon and clubs feasted on caviar and champagne. Pies in the rain at Southend United and Yeovil Town was all Forest that fans could look forward to while their team repeatedly hoofed the ball up into the air at the behest of Megson.

Derby reached the play-offs after finishing in fourth but lost out to Preston North End, who themselves were beaten by West Ham at Wembley. Preston had impressed in their first season under Billy Davies and he guided them to the play-offs again in 2006 – a feat that did not go unnoticed in the Derby boardroom. As for Forest, it would get worse before it would get better.

10

Hopelessly intertwined: 2005-2014

ALMOST DIRECTLY between Nottingham and Derby, the M1 runs vertically. It is the main road connecting the north of the country with the south, running as it does between London and Leeds. Just beside the motorway on the Nottingham side sits Long Eaton which lies on the Midland Main Line railway. Like the M1, it vertically dissects the two cities as trains run north and south from London to Sheffield. Around seven miles on either side of these major trunk routes sit Nottingham and Derby, constantly staring at and grimacing towards each other.

Long Eaton station also serves as a stopping point between Nottingham and Derby should you catch a train. From Nottingham, the track follows the route of the River Trent in a south-west direction, past the Attenborough Nature Reserve until it reaches Long Eaton, which is in the Erewash district of Derbyshire yet has a Nottinghamshire postcode. From there, the rail track meanders north-west, under the M1 and through Draycott until it hugs the River Derwent at Borrowash before reaching Derby. Breaston and

Risley sit astride the quaint countryside in no man's land, both boasting proud cricket clubs, country pubs, rolling hills and nature trails. Like genial uncles, they sit directly between two tempestuous football clubs that measure their success and failures against each other's. They are not the only two clubs to do this; they are just two of many. Yet few others which share such a fierce rivalry can be so hopelessly intertwined as these two.

'Maybe it's the aspirational attitude of Nottingham that holds them back a bit,' says Derby-based award-winning writer, poet, lyricist and educator Jamie Thrasivoulou. 'I've had some intense jealousy from Nottingham poets just because I come from Derby, and Derby doesn't have the infrastructure for the arts that Nottingham has. Derby was a contender for the City of Culture award [for 2025, which ultimately went to Bradford], but Nottingham would never be on that list as it doesn't need to be, the city is already culturally rich and sophisticated. Nottingham is, as much as it pains me to admit it, more cultural. It's got Rock City. It's got the Theatre Royal. It's got so much more fandangle than Derby. It has two proper universities too. It has such a vast city centre, compared to Derby.'

Yet despite this, perhaps it is the case that Nottingham and Derby exist in the Goldilocks zone of having just the right level of differences and similarities between them to stoke the fire of a fierce rivalry.

2005/06
Pearce in a Derby shirt

In September 2005, the A52, which links Newcastle-under-Lyme with Mablethorpe but more pertinently Nottingham with Derby, was renamed Brian Clough Way. Signs marking the rebranding beside the dual carriageway at various intervals were erected, only to be taken as souvenirs by either Derby or Forest fans, or maybe people simply fascinated by Brian Clough. In December 2016, the latest appeal was made for their return. 'As much of a fan of Brian Clough as I am, I would never consider stealing them,' said Kal Singh Dhindsa, who previously campaigned for a statue of Clough and his assistant Peter Taylor at Pride Park Stadium in Derby. 'In my opinion, if you are such a big fan of Brian Clough, you should just leave them there for other people to appreciate. If Mr Clough was here today I think he would probably give someone a good telling off.' Signs had gone missing from Stapleford in Nottinghamshire and Risley, Borrowash and Ockbrook in Derbyshire.

After three consecutive seasons of the two clubs slugging it out with each other in the second tier, both counties' police forces could enjoy a period of not having to plan for the East Midlands derby as Forest started 2005/06 in League One, having slipped ignominiously down. Their struggles continued as they recorded only one win from their opening six games. Derby manager George Burley resigned in June as relations between him and the board – and especially the director of football, Murdo Mackay – broke down irreparably. Already bristling at the sale of youngster Tom Huddlestone to Tottenham Hotspur in January (but loaned back immediately), apparently without his knowledge, Burley felt it was time to sever ties. Phil Brown stepped in, but lasted only until January 2006 and was sacked after a 6-1 defeat to Coventry City and being dumped out of the FA Cup in the fourth round by Colchester United of

League One. Former Forest striker Stern John briefly rocked up at Pride Park, but his eight appearances yielded neither goals nor wins. Paul Peschisolido and promising goalkeeper Lee Camp were frozen out as Brown brought in 42-year-old Kevin Poole as goalkeeping coach and as a temporary replacement for the Derby-born stopper. The young keeper's father publicly voiced his anger at how things were being done behind the scenes, while Brown succeeded in little more than annoying most people connected with the club.

Academy manager Terry Westley stepped in as caretaker until the end of the season and the deeply underwhelming campaign finished with Derby in 20th, just about winning their battle against relegation, but it was off the pitch where another battle was rumbling on. Deeply angered by the way things were being run, a group of local businessmen joined forces with a view to wrestling the club back into local ownership. Peter Gadsby, John Kirkland, Don Amott, Mike Horton, Peter Marples, Jill Marples and Mel Morris took control for the final game of the season, seeing off interest from SISU, which would later take charge of Coventry City. In 2009, Mackenzie and Mackay were found guilty at Northampton Crown Court of fraudulently claiming thousands of pounds in 'commission, claiming cash totalling £440,625 after brokering a loan for the club'. They were sentenced to three years in prison, while former chief executive Jeremy Keith was sentenced to 18 months having been convicted of false accounting. But back in 2006, with new ownership, the Rams could start to look up again.

Forest had little reason to gloat about the circus at Derby as League One life was proving to be rather unkind to the Reds. Defeats to Chester City, Woking and Macclesfield

Town in various cup competitions besmirched their season. A run of seven games without a win culminated in a 3-0 defeat at Oldham Athletic on 15 February. This, along with some desperate football and the shenanigans at Yeovil Town where two fans were invited by the manager into the dressing room to air their views to the players, saw Gary Megson relieved of his duties. On that incident, captain Ian Breckin said to fanzine *Bandy and Shinty*, 'We were all just a bit ... the fans didn't really know what to say. They were more surprised than us really.' Ian McParland and Frank Barlow took over and almost managed to gatecrash the play-offs as they oversaw an unbeaten run of ten games, including six straight wins. But the late surge was not quite enough to make up the ground lost under Megson and Forest finished just outside the top six. However, a little pride had been restored and some hope was created for the following season.

The closest thing to an East Midlands derby in 2005/06 was Ted McMinn's testimonial on Monday, 1 May at 3pm, between Derby and Rangers which attracted a spectacular 33,475 spectators to Pride Park Stadium. A mysterious infection picked up the previous year had resulted in McMinn having most of his right leg amputated. The Derby XI featured Nigel Clough and was captained by Stuart Pearce, and Clough, wearing the white of the Rams, scored with a well-executed volley to make the score 1-1. Pearce, then manager of Manchester City, marauded forward from left-back at every opportunity and got his chance to score when Stefano Eranio slid him clean through. The left-back made no mistake and finished neatly with an arrowed shot from the outside of his trusty left foot. Arms out in celebration, he then ran towards the Derby fans, living up to the pantomime villain he no doubt was for the home fans. As if such sights were not jarring and surreal enough – with Pearce too in Derby white – he later displayed a wry sense of humour beyond the psycho façade and kissed the badge in jest. 'In terms of kissing the badge, there was a bit of sarcasm in that which wasn't lost on the fans,' he told talkSPORT.

2006/07
Scots in the hotseats

The new broom of management swept through both clubs for the 2006/07 season, depositing two Scots into the hotseats: Billy Davies at Derby and Colin Calderwood at Forest, and both had a positive impact.

Before appointing Davies, Derby sounded out former Forest player Martin O'Neill for the post, yet he turned the job down since his wife was recovering from illness. So Davies took the helm and the first thing he did was tell Terry Westley, who had prepared a whole pre-season schedule, that he was no longer wanted at the club. 'I didn't think it was true but when I went in for pre-season, Billy told me it was impossible for me to stay here,' Westley said in *Pride: The Inside Story of Derby County in the 21st Century* by Ryan Hills. 'But having said that, he also replaced the cook, the cleaner and every other member of staff. He was paranoid about anyone who had been there.' Former Forest youth player Giles Barnes, who enjoyed a strong season under Davies at Derby, also vouched for Davies's paranoia, explaining how he would sometimes play games with the press and opposition managers regarding his team selections, 'There would be times he'd throw spanners in and he'd go to a player and say, "I'm going to make it look like you're not playing all week but you are, I just want to see if they know my team." A lot of the time he would be right as well!'

Despite the unorthodox methods, Davies was incredibly successful in building an excellent team spirit, propelling Derby to an epic play-off semi-final with Southampton, a tie with more sub-plots than *Line of Duty* and *Lost* combined. Burley was now the Saints' manager and his side boasted former Rams Iñigo Idiakez and Grzegorz Rasiak, while Derby captain Matt Oakley had served Southampton for 12 years. Idiakez missed his penalty in the shoot-out in the pouring rain and Derby were through to Wembley – one game away from the Premier League.

It wasn't all plain sailing, however. Although they were six points clear at the top in February, trouble was brewing behind the scenes. Recent signings would apparently not be eligible for win bonuses paid out to other players. And that wasn't all: tensions within the squad went deeper, and upwards, between Davies and managing director Mike Horton. The Professional Footballers' Association were called in to settle the dispute and although Derby slipped out of the automatic promotion positions, they overcame first Southampton, then West Bromwich Albion in the play-offs to secure an improbable promotion. It was a joyous moment, but that's when the problems really began.

When it was put to Davies on the Wembley pitch in his post-match interview that he was now a Premier League manager, the Scot chose not to provide the standard response one might expect about looking forward to competing with other top bosses and teams. Instead, he darted out of shot, muttering something about the plan being to 'enjoy the night'. 'After the play-off final,' he told *FourFourTwo*, 'what

I said was, "I don't know if I'll be here next season." The press never clarified with me why I said that. I was trying to say that something's going on. They tried to make it out that it was the Davies Show, but it wasn't – Davies had a knife in his back.'

Aside from the third-person response – for which Davies would become notorious – the squad he had built wasn't ready to compete at the top level: it was essentially an ageing team that had punched way above its weight under the inspirational leadership of the former Preston North End manager. It needed strengthening, perhaps even major surgery, if the club were to do anything beyond battle for survival. Davies said, 'I gave the board options for new signings and the board decided they would pick the cheaper options. We were chasing guys such as Matthew Etherington and Carlton Cole in their heyday, and yet we weren't getting them in. If I say that there are six or seven options, and options one to four are players who'll help to make Derby a competitive Premier League club, but the owners opt to bring in options five, six and seven, they can't complain too much about the outcome. You can't spend only £10m in the Premier League and expect to compete.' All of this was rather unhelpful when it came to preparations for a first season back in the Premier League since 2001/02. But for now, Derby's joy at being back in the top flight was there to be savoured.

Forest also had their own play-off experience, but it was substantially less successful. They didn't make it to Wembley, but somehow contrived to lose to Yeovil, despite winning the first leg of their semi-final 2-0 away from home. Anything that could go wrong in the second leg did, meaning that for

Forest fans the mere mention of the town in Somerset will always conjure up deeply traumatic memories that are best forgotten. To find any silver lining in the whole experience is difficult, but the signing of Chris Cohen from the Glovers was one. The release of *This is England,* the film written and directed by Nottingham-based Shane Meadows and starring Nottingham's Vicky McClure, also offered some consolation.

2007/08
The Brian Clough Trophy

Before the 2007/08 season started, there was the small matter of the inaugural Brian Clough Trophy game, a friendly – if there is such a thing – played at Pride Park on 31 July in front of 25,059. Derby won 2-0 with goals from Jay McEveley and Craig Fagan. 'Brian would have thoroughly approved of this trophy, to be played between two clubs he loved so much,' said Barbara Clough. Proceeds from the game, which raised approximately £100,000, went to local charities in the East Midlands. Forest donated £25,000 to go to the Dannielle Beccan Memorial Trust – in memory of a teenager who was tragically murdered in St Anns in 2004 – while Derby split their £25,000 donation between ten designated charities. Both clubs agreed to give £12,500 to the East Midlands Air Ambulance.

If that night seemed to bode well for Derby's return to the Premier League, it was the falsest of omens. If Forest fans were still nursing their Somerset-sized Yeovil trauma, Derby were about to be the ungrateful owners of their own deep and lasting anguish as their team embarked on the very definition of a nightmare season. A mere 11 points accrued tells only part of the story; everything else is just a deep pit of misery. Davies was replaced by Paul Jewell in December, but like a boxer nursing a hangover and getting pummelled in the ring, they were simply too far gone, utterly beyond salvation.

The animosity behind the scenes between new chairman Adam Pearson and Davies was palpable. 'It didn't help, that's what I'd say. It took us a while to settle down and a lot of that team, Billy had bought,' former Derby defender Michael Johnson told The Athletic. 'Then, the new manager [Paul Jewell] comes in and doesn't fancy them.' As if losing match after match wasn't slapstick enough, a sex tape featuring Jewell materialised in March. Although filmed six years previously, it didn't seem to matter and simply reinforced the tragicomedy that was Derby's season. They posted the lowest-ever Premier League points total, along with the fewest wins and goals scored in a season, plus the most defeats in a season, and the most goals conceded since the Premier League was reduced to 20 teams. They were the first team to be relegated in March. There are simply no silver linings or consolations to be found.

Whether the road signs remained in place or not, things were better down the A52. Forest dusted themselves down and achieved promotion from League One, despite only breaking into the top two on the final day of the season. Sitting third going into the final game and a point behind Doncaster Rovers, Forest needed to better whatever Donny did against Cheltenham Town. Naturally, fans were full of hope, if not expectation. After all, Forest's opponents at the City Ground were their old foes, Yeovil.

Forest went 2-0 up inside the opening 20 minutes, the first scored by Nottingham-born Julian Bennett and the second by Kris Commons, but when Yeovil pulled one back hearts were sent wildly fluttering. Lewis McGugan extended the lead in the 28th minute and, despite conceding again in the second half, Forest ground out a 3-2 win. All eyes switched to Cheltenham where the home side chalked up a 2-1 win, helped by a future Derby captain, Richard Keogh in defence, thus condemning Doncaster to the play-offs and handing Forest automatic promotion back to the Championship after three seasons in exile. With Derby ingloriously relegated and Forest surprisingly promoted, the two would be back together again the following season. The respective police forces started digging out their derby plans and procedures which had been stuffed into a drawer for the last three years.

Yet while the celebrations on the pitch continued, led by Commons, other things were on his mind. Despite Calderwood's insistence that a new contract was in the offing, it had failed to materialise. According to Commons, Forest were dragging their heels with talks about not knowing which league they would be in the following season and, consequently, being unsure what their budget would be. The noises coming from the club were that they wanted to tie up a new deal, yet the reality was that nothing solid had been put forward and Commons went into the final stretch of the season almost certain he would be leaving come the summer, promotion or not.

Interest came from QPR and, intriguingly, Derby in May, but Commons and his partner Lisa had far more serious and important matters on their minds than silly football transfers. 'What people did not know is that we had only just cremated our daughter in March,' Commons told The Athletic. 'We had a full-term baby, Lola, who was born in Nottingham and I still did not take any leave. I missed one game. I remember coming back into the dressing room after that and the lads asking if I was all right. I just told them that I wanted to get back to playing football. But looking back, there wasn't anyone, managerial-wise, who gave me much support. My missus had just had to give birth to a stillbirth baby and there was no realisation of this in the football world.'

Rather than uprooting and moving to London to join QPR and add another layer of stress to an already impossibly sad situation, the couple decided to stay near to their extended family in the East Midlands, which meant Commons signing for Derby. He knew that at least two games a year, he would be on the receiving end of some abuse from Forest fans, but reasoned it was a small price to pay for his partner being close to her family and her support bubble.

Although not a direct replacement, Forest had already lined up a big signing of their own: Derby striker Robert Earnshaw. The Welsh forward joined the Rams a year previously from Norwich City for £3.5m but struggled to make an impact at Pride Park during their disastrous season, making only seven starts in the Premier League and clearly not featuring in either Davies's or Jewell's plans. 'Derby was disappointing but that's the way it goes,' he told Forest's website. 'I'm just looking at is as a chapter closed and will learn from it.' Looking back on the transfer in conversation with former BBC Radio Nottingham presenter Robin Chipperfield, Earnshaw was a little more forthcoming, 'I went to Derby. I spent a year at Derby. I needed to leave to progress, football-wise. Things weren't quite right; the club, behind the scenes, it wasn't quite right.' Given these two transfers and their first competitive meetings for three seasons, the derby games for 2008/09 were shaping up to be rather tasty.

2008/09
Scarf-twirling

The fans would have to wait until November to renew acquaintances, by which time neither club were in a good place. Forest struggled to adapt to life back in the Championship, chalking up only two wins from their opening 14 games, leaving them second-bottom and with pressure mounting on Calderwood. In an effort to banish the severe hangover of the previous season, Derby brought in nine players over the summer, Commons being one of them, alongside the likes of Steve Davies, Paul Green and Rob Hulse. Despite a poor August, they improved significantly and lay comfortably in mid-table by the time of the first East Midlands derby of the season at Pride Park. The game not only lived up to the usual hype, but surpassed it by some distance. With Forest fresh from promotion and Derby still suffering the after-effects of tumbling from a cliff, they collided like particles smashed into each other in a Hadron Collider.

The final score was 1-1, but simply stating this is akin to describing Leonardo da Vinci's *Mona Lisa* as a nice portrait or Pablo Picasso's *Guernica* as a bit odd. Forest took the lead in the 55th minute when a corner led to a scramble and the ball pinballed off Emanuel Villa's head. It took six games but Forest had finally taken the lead at Pride Park. It was short-lived as, just ten minutes later, Derby drew level when Villa produced a deft flicked finish from a free kick. With 15 minutes remaining, the visitors were reduced to ten men when McGugan was shown a red card for a rash challenge. Yet all this drama was just a mere B movie ahead of the main event in added time.

Two minutes beyond the 90, Nottingham-born Miles Addison rose to head in what he thought was the winning goal, yet the referee, Stuart Attwell, awarded a penalty instead as he spotted an infringement that nobody else in the ground did. In Forest's goal was Lee Camp, born in Derby, with 97 appearances for his hometown club under his belt and a former recipient of the Rams' Sammy Crooks Young Player of the Year Award. Nacer Barazite stepped up with glory on his mind, but Camp dived superbly down to his right and turned the spot kick around the post. It seemed that Forest would somehow get away with a point – one they would be thankful for, given their dreadful record at Pride Park. They had yet to win there.

Implausibly, there was time for more. In the 94th minute, recent history bizarrely repeated itself as Addison planted a splendid header into the net from a corner, only for Attwell to once again disallow the goal. Multiple bodies rose to challenge and meet the cross, but only one person in the ground spotted an infringement. While Derby players and fans argued the toss, Forest charged up the field and very nearly snatched a truly improbable three points, yet Paul Anderson dallied too long and the chance went begging, although Attwell blew his whistle to call play back too. Somehow the game ended 1-1, thanks in no small part to Camp. 'I was in Littleover that morning and I drove over to Nottingham to meet the bus,' Camp told the *Talk Derby to Me* podcast. 'When I got to the City Ground, there were four or five Forest fans there – and you wouldn't mess with them. They weren't in suit and tie. It was almost like a hit job. I remember walking out and it was like, "You remember who you're playing for today, son." They came out of nowhere. I remember thinking: It's not a day to drop one today. Funnily enough, I've got off the bus after the game and they're there, arms open, jumping up and down, saying, "You're one of us now." But I'm thinking you four are all right now, but there's another 10,000 I've got to deal with when I get back to Derby. That was a crazy day, a surreal day.'

Unsurprisingly, Jewell was deeply unimpressed by Attwell's performance. It was Attwell who had already achieved infamy for awarding Reading a goal at Watford just six weeks prior to this game when the ball went nowhere near the net, but instead innocently bounced two yards to the right of the post, to the bemusement of pretty much everyone concerned. As a result, he was stood down by the Professional Game Match Officials board, although in fairness, it was his assistant, Nigel Bannister, who signalled for the goal. 'His sending-off was harsh, some of his bookings were harsh, I'm not sure it's a penalty, then why he doesn't give the goal I don't know,' Jewell told *The Guardian*. 'He gave the most unbelievable decision at Watford. He's 25, he's meant to be the next best thing since sliced bread, then he's taken out of the Premier League and he's given a game of this magnitude. It beggars belief.'

Calderwood couldn't quite believe his luck. 'Obvious push, there were probably three or four fouls in there,' he remarked with a mischievous grin. 'It wasn't a penalty, but I'm very glad it was given against us. The referee judged the game really well. That's twice we've had him and I've no complaints.' In the studio, Archie Gemmill felt that a draw was, despite everything, a fair result and as the debate, inquest and dispute raged on, Barbara Clough presented the Brian Clough Trophy to both captains.

An away point was not good enough for Calderwood, though, and his side continued to struggle up to Christmas until he was relieved of his duties a day after Boxing Day, which saw third-bottom Forest humbled 4-2 at home by Doncaster Rovers, who were just below them and managed by Sean O'Driscoll. Forest owner Nigel Doughty had someone in mind – none other than Billy Davies – and on New Year's Day the ex-Derby boss was appointed manager of Nottingham Forest.

Not to be outdone in the dugout stakes, Derby sacked Jewell five days later with his side 18th and replaced him with Forest's second-highest scorer of all time, Nigel Clough. He also happened to be the son of a rather famous ex-Forest and Derby manager. 'I know the club inside out. It has always had a special place in mine and my family's heart and I know that this is one of the most exciting jobs in football', said Clough. Beyond the East Midlands, perhaps this seemed like a surprise, but between junctions 25 and 28 of the M1 and the surrounding area, few eyebrows were raised: this sort of thing happens. The ferocity of the East Midlands rivalry was suddenly turned up to 11.

As if things couldn't get weirder, Derby and Forest came out of the velvet bag together in the draw for the fourth round of the FA Cup in January, coinciding with the closure of the Tales of Robin Hood visitor attraction on Maid Marian Way. So the situation now was ex-Rams Lee Camp, Robert Earnshaw and Billy Davies were now at Forest, while Derby were managed by a Forest legend, whose assistant was also the much-loved former City Ground winger Gary Crosby. Just for good measure, they also had the recently departed Kris Commons who had left Forest in acrimonious circumstances. For Commons, it would not be just two tricky games against his former club this season – it would now be three.

It was a busy night for Derbyshire Police. Around an hour before kick-off, two sheeps' heads were thrown at two pubs in Alvaston. One was thrown through the window of The Lodge in Grange Road, smashing a downstairs window. Half an hour later, a lamb's head was thrown through the window of The Mitre. A second sheep's head was later found outside the same pub in Osmaston Road by police. A spokeswoman for the Derbyshire force said, 'Bar staff at both pubs said they had had Forest fans in there that evening, but they had not had any trouble in there at all.'

Elsewhere, violence broke out at the Florence Nightingale pub, leading to jail time for six Forest fans and five Derby supporters. It was reported that a hearing at Derby Crown Court was told how innocent bystanders were left 'terrified' as the trouble raged.

In front of a crowd of 32,035, the teams repeated their 1-1 scoreline with both sides scoring remarkably similar goals. Derby took the lead in the 35th minute after a low cross from the right was dummied inside the box by Paul Green for Rob Hulse to unleash a skidding shot into the corner of the net. Forest equalised in the 64th minute after a low cross from the right was dummied inside the box by Nathan Tyson for Earnshaw to unleash a skidding shot into the corner of the net. It had to be Earnshaw. It couldn't really have been anyone but Earnshaw. Commons had an opportunity to get his name on the score sheet but blazed over, and he would now face his former club not the initially envisaged two times in 2008/09 – or even three – but four times. A replay at the City Ground on a wet Wednesday evening beckoned.

Newly installed manager Billy Davies would have to wait a little longer to judge the reception he would get from Derby fans as he missed the game to be at the side of his teenage son's bed after kidney surgery at Glasgow's Gartnavel hospital. After the operation, his son stabilised.

After only 37 seconds of the replay, Forest took the lead through Chris Cohen, while Commons was loudly booed with each touch. By the 14th minute, Forest were two goals up and sailing towards the fifth round after Tyson was felled by Stephen Bywater in the Derby goal. Tyson dispatched the resulting penalty. Commons was enduring a truly torrid evening on his return to Nottingham.

Hulse reduced the arrears before half-time with a smart header and on the hour, Green equalised in front of the travelling Rams. Garath McCleary should have restored Forest's lead but squandered a very presentable chance before Commons strolled forward unchallenged and unleashed a shot that cracked back off the post. It was a warning that Forest failed to heed. With 15 minutes remaining, Commons's defining moment arrived as he again took aim from range. His shot nicked off Wes Morgan and looped into the net. Unbelievable, yet somehow quite believable. This was an East Midlands derby, after all.

There was just enough time for Forest youngster Mark Byrne to squander another excellent chance before the final whistle blew, and Commons could afford himself more than a wry smile. 'I always knew I was going to get abuse,' he told The Athletic. 'But there was a moment when I went to take a corner in front of A-Block where there was a hail of lighters chucked at me. One of them was a Zippo and I thought to myself, "Blimey, that is an expensive bit of kit, that." I don't mind the cheap ones, they would just bounce off ... but that thing would have knocked me out.'

The abuse was relentless, fuelled by a perceived sense of betrayal on the part of Forest fans when only a few people were party to the tragic back-story behind Commons's move to Derby. 'In that moment, it had gone beyond abuse, singing songs and all the rest of it. This was proper hatred now. They wanted my blood. I just thought that these people did not know everything; they did not have all the facts ... and it started to wind me up. There was an explosion of emotion that came out when we had come back from 2-0 down to win 3-2.'

Robbie Savage took it upon himself to somehow increase the drama levels and performatively twirled a Derby scarf around after the game, serving to celebrate with his own fans but he was also quite happy to antagonise the home crowd too. Such a gesture was noted by those of a red persuasion. First the demise of the Tales of Robin Hood Centre, and now this.

Derby's famous win – their first at the City Ground since October 1971 under Brian Clough – earned them a plum tie against Manchester United in the next round, just a month after facing the Red Devils in the semi-final of the League Cup. They lost out in both competitions.

Just 17 days later, the teams met for the fourth – and final – time that season at the City Ground for their return league fixture. By this time, the initial sharp improvement under Davies had subsided. Forest were still looking nervously back over their shoulders towards the relegation zone. Under Clough, Derby's pattern was similar: initial lift followed by more drift, yet they seemed clear of any relegation worries.

In the end, it proved to be a comfortable win for the Rams. Lewin Nyatanga opened the scoring with a predictably early goal in the fifth minute. Hulse scored his third in three games against Forest to make it 2-0 and Steve Davies put the game beyond Forest's reach in the 67th minute. Earnshaw bagged a consolation goal in the closing stages, his second against Derby that season. Billy Davies was unusually magnanimous, 'Individual errors cost us dearly. We were outmuscled and outfought in too many departments. Derby deserved their victory – there is no argument at all.' Perhaps even he understood that, for the time being, Forest's battle for survival was more pressing than ratcheting up the ante in the derby stakes. All of that could wait until the next season, once safety was secure. For the time being though, he had a different fight on his hands.

With those two wins at the City Ground on his first two visits back to his old manor, Nigel Clough had extended one of the rivalry's stranger records. No Derby manager not named Clough had won at Forest's home since George Jobey, as far back as September 1925.

When the cards of the 2008/09 season were turned, Derby finished 18th and Forest survived in 19th:

disappointing but not unsurprising places for a team promoted from League One and one relegated from the Premier League. Although unknown at the time, both clubs would remain in this division for the foreseeable future, locked together 'as two spent swimmers, that do cling together and choke their art', as the Captain puts it in *Macbeth*. The pattern was established: drama, red cards, squabbles, ex-players scoring against their old clubs, former managers taking their new employers to their old homes, early goals and grudges – all in the second tier.

Fuelled by mediocrity as mid-table Championship clubs and seeing other supposedly less famous and established names replace them in the top division, the rivalry between Forest and Derby was fully reignited. That's not to say that the intensity of feelings had diminished much prior to 2008/09, but more to emphasise how meeting each other four times in four months in the circumstances that they did was akin to throwing paraffin on to an already burning bonfire. It didn't seem that long since that both clubs were going to Old Trafford in the Premier League and coming away with three points, yet now here they were scrapping it out towards the foot of the Championship, while Fulham finished in seventh in the top flight and qualified for the Europa League. Wigan Athletic, Stoke City, Bolton Wanderers and Portsmouth, who had even won the FA Cup the previous season, seemed comfortable in the top tier. Even Hull City survived their first Premier League season. If this was what the new century was going to be like, neither Derby nor Forest fans liked it very much and would quite like to go back to when both were duelling in the top division, thank you very much.

Consequently, that frustration and anger at the state of things required an outlet and, given the similarities in recent achievements, the proximity to each other (neither ever really cared too much about Leicester City), the sudden increase in fixtures and, naturally, the connections of the two managers to the opposing clubs, and the players they signed, the bitterness of the rivalry went up a notch or two. The rise and continued evolution of blogging allowed fans an outlet for their frustrations, a perfect way to take a swipe at your rivals from the safety of the sofa along with the emergence of a small social media website called Twitter. In many ways, this season was the big bang of the modern rivalry between the clubs, rebooted to V2.0 for the digital age.

It is worth contemplating just where Leicester sit in terms of the East Midlands derby. The short version is that Leicester are not really in the conversation. In his poem *Derby Day*, Jamie Thrasivoulou makes it quite clear regarding this situation, 'It's Derby Day, It's Derby Day, Step aside Leicester, Out of our way.' He went on to elaborate, 'Leicester had always been the odd one out in this conversation. They really hate us and also really hate Forest. But apart from those Derby fans at the 1994 play-off final, when we were all over them but still lost the game, I'm not personally bothered about Leicester because it's not the traditional rivalry.'

Geographically, Leicester is indeed the odd one out, left standing without a chair when it comes to the East Midlands. It is approximately 30 miles south of both Nottingham and Derby but somehow seems even further away. Agreeing on where the north starts and the south ends in England is a fool's errand, yet in some ways Nottingham and Derby seem like 'The North' and Leicester seems like 'The South', at least culturally and socially. Despite Leicester boasting its own proud railway and industrial heritage, alongside it being a stronghold for radicalism in the Victorian era, the 30-mile journey south makes it seem much more distant than it is from the north end of the East Midlands.

As for the Foxes, given their slightly isolated geographical location, they have arguably always lacked a sustained and definitive rival with which to develop a deep and long-standing historical grudge. Coventry City are perceived as rivals, certainly to Foxes fans south of the city, but who they reserve their greatest ire for depends upon how well Derby and Forest are doing in relation to their own fortunes. Antipathy towards Derby peaked around the 1994 play-off final at Wembley and was stoked again when former Forest favourite Stan Collymore suffered a horrific leg break at Pride Park while playing for Leicester, spawning a song delighting in his misfortune.

Yet geography mattered little to Derby and Leicester fans who formed an alliance of sorts and caused chaos when they clashed with Forest supporters in Nottingham city centre on 23 June 1984. Approximately 400 people hurled bricks, bottles and glasses at each other and, presumably, anyone who got in the way. It started in the afternoon and went on until the evening on a day when there wasn't even a football match involving any of the teams happening. 'Members of the public were terrorised,' said a police spokesman, 'and various witnesses described the scene as the worst violence they had ever experienced in the city centre.' Initially, officers used truncheons to charge the gathering mob, but the numbers swelled. The alliance was herded to Broadmarsh Bus Station where buses were hastily commandeered to get them out of the city. In the aftermath, 75 youths were interviewed, with charges ranging from public order offences to possession of an offensive weapon leading to a number of custodial sentences.

It is certainly true that Leicester fans have little time for Forest, but since their club's astonishing Premier League title in 2015/16 and their subsequent success in establishing themselves as a major force in English football, the Foxes have never seemed so distant from the Championship grind that Forest and Derby endured between 2008 and 2022. The Foxes orbit a different planet to that which the Reds and Rams circle; they have never felt so far away from the finely balanced equation.

2009/10
The corner flag

After the intensity of the games the previous season, a little more decompression time might have been welcomed by all but the computer that spews out the fixture list was deaf to such a concept and seemed to have developed sentience by pairing the teams together in late August at the City Ground, the fifth league game of the season. Forest were yet to win, while Derby already had seven points on the board in Clough's first full campaign in charge. It was another thoroughly bonkers game, which, if it were possible, somehow managed to elevate the distaste and bad blood between the clubs even higher.

'I remember going on the bus,' says former Derby defender Shaun Barker, 'and Forest fans were throwing stuff at the coach, kids shouting horrible things and parents and dads encouraging it. I find it quite strange but also understand that that is part of people's footballing life.' Born in Trowell, on the border of both counties, Barker grew up following Forest as a child but played with distinction for Derby between 2009 and 2015, making 98 appearances for the Rams, and was scouted meticulously by Nigel's brother, Simon, who was chief scout from 2009 to 2013. He almost joined Forest before signing for Derby. Barker recalled, 'Billy Davies tried to sign me for Forest at the same time that Nigel tried to sign me for Derby, and obviously having followed Forest as a kid, people presumed I was going to sign for Forest. I ended up signing for Derby because of Nigel. I remember speaking to Billy Davies and he was selling the dream: getting promoted, earn this much money, how much you could earn next year, all these bonuses. I then spoke to Nigel and he sold it the opposite way, he said the club was in a mess and we need people like you and players with a team mentality and hard-working. That sold it to me. I told him Forest were interested but he said straight away, you're not signing for them.' The contrasting styles of approaches between Davies and Clough is telling and gives an indication of the tension and friction simmering between the two managers.

Radosław Majewski blasted Forest ahead inside the first minute with a bona fide rocket of a shot that almost broke the crossbar in two before bouncing down and settling in the net. It had only been six months since Forest took the lead at the same end inside a minute in the FA Cup replay, but still contrived to lose 3-2. The game was far from over and, besides, Commons was once again in the white of Derby and, as Forest fans well knew, capable of a goal.

Throughout, Savage and Commons were loudly jeered each time they touched the ball or went vaguely close to it and, in the 28th minute, the inevitable happened: Hulse scored again with a header, but this time in the wrong net – 2-0 to Forest.

Hulse predictably went and planted a header in at the right end, but it was ruled out for pushing Wes Morgan, perhaps harshly. If everything went right for Commons on his previous visit to Nottingham, the opposite was true here. He was dispossessed in midfield by Cohen who put Tyson through to round Bywater and make it 3-0 just before halftime. Surely the game was over. Sure, Derby had form for coming back from 2-0 down at the City Ground, but from *three* goals behind? Such a deficit was surely beyond them, even with Hulse on the field.

They almost went and did it. This being an East Midlands derby, they almost pulled it off. Six minutes after the interval, Miles Addison finally scored a legitimate goal – a rather odd overhead kick that wrong-footed Camp and might have nicked off Morgan. Ten minutes later, Jake Livermore's shot took a deflection before nestling in Camp's net. It was on. Another famous comeback really was on. All the while, Clough maintained his composure on the touchline from where his father surveyed the pitch for so long and so successfully. He stood impassively while Derby fans started to believe. The tension grew. Savage was at the centre of some pushing and shoving, and being Robbie Savage, incited a push from Tyson who received a yellow card. Finally, after nine minutes of added time, the whistle blew, but somehow the after-party even managed to surpass the breathless game.

Tyson decided to help the ground staff out by picking up and taking in a corner flag, but rather than dump it into a dusty old storage room, he instead ran past the Derby fans ensuring the little red flag with a tree on it fluttered in celebration. No doubt Savage's scarf-twirling and his own tussle with him during the game inspired such a gesture. Once the Derby players clocked this, all hell broke loose, with more scuffles breaking out than it was physically possible to count while stewards and police officers did their best to intervene.

'I remember the last time Derby were here and Robbie Savage was waving a Derby scarf around,' said Billy Davies. 'There was very little made of that and we hope it will be the same for this. We never complained about it or made a fuss because we understood that Derby should enjoy the victory they had here.' Forest were fined £15,000 and Derby £10,000, but for the Reds it seemed a small to price to pay for gaining some sort of revenge for their collapse when two goals up the previous campaign and for bagging their first three points of the season. Indeed, the win sparked Forest's season into life while Derby spiralled and lost their next three games.

Tyson would later, perhaps inevitably, move to Derby and reflected upon his role in the flashpoint with a degree of embarrassment. 'I picked up the flag, waved it in front of the A-Block and then I was actually running across to the other side, where our fans are, but it just happened to be where the Derby fans were,' he told Sky Sports's *EFL Rivalries* programme. 'Then it all just kicked off and I remember thinking afterwards, "Oh my God, what have I done?" I regret doing it. That just shows how much passion is running through your veins in that game. You want to go out there and enjoy it but hopefully nothing like that will happen again. My dad was not happy and my family were just like, "What were you doing?!"

In many ways, Tyson was simply maintaining the long and established tradition of winding up the opposition as much as humanly possible in a Forest-Derby fixture. Yet there was even more needle to come.

The teams met again at Pride Park on 30 January 2010 for the first derby of the new decade. Prior to this, the opening of the Nottingham Contemporary in November, one of the largest contemporary art spaces in the UK, signalled its arrival with an exhibition of works by David Hockney and Frances Stark. Built on Garner's Hill, the oldest site in Nottingham and in the centre of the Lace Market, its unveiling perhaps added weight to Nottingham's perception of itself as being more sophisticated than its city neighbours. Forest were 19 games unbeaten, winning 13 and in second, in as good a position for a trip to Derby as they had ever been. Yet to win at Pride Park, the game represented an excellent opportunity to rectify that, especially since their hosts were struggling in 19th.

Derby threatened from set pieces in the first half, while Forest improved in the second. Yet the most natural of occurrences played out in the 78th minute when Hulse crashed in a header from a Commons free kick to give Derby the points and end the Reds' unbeaten run. Just as headline writers were preparing to report this narrative, another presented itself. With the clock ticking down, Chris Gunter and Jay McEveley clashed over a throw-in, sparking a melee on the touchline, in which everyone from both sides got involved. Davies claimed that Clough kneed him in the back of the leg during the scuffle.

Clough denied the allegation. 'Staff and players from both sides were involved, and, if there was that many bodies, there is likely to be physical contact. But it was purely accidental,' said Clough. 'I don't think I've got anything to apologise for. I've explained the situation as it happened. As far as I'm concerned, that's it. If someone else wants to take it further, they can.'

The enmity between Davies and Clough now matched that of the supporters. After the August fixture at the City Ground, it was reported that Clough and his backroom staff were not invited in for a post-match chat. Understandably and predictably, Derby did the same after this game. 'In our last four or five meetings, Billy hasn't spoken one word,' Clough told *The Guardian*.

'It's in the hands of the lawyer now,' said Davies once the dust settled. 'They are in the process of gathering evidence at the moment and I'll let them deal with what they've got to deal with.' Nothing more came of the incident. 'There's a lot of poison in and around this fixture,' Davies said. 'I've played in Old Firm games and I've never come across anything like it – not what happens on the field but the stuff that goes around it. The Old Firm game is the worst in the world, but what goes on here is petty. I've been involved in Old Firm games that have never had this kind of pettiness and I'm quite surprised, to be honest.'

In truth, the pettiness rained down from both sides, with key protagonists in each camp and Davies's use of the word 'poison' was apt. 'At the time we had Billy Davies as manager and he didn't like their manager, Nigel Clough, who didn't like Billy Davies,' Guy Moussi, the former Forest midfielder, told the *Nottingham Post* in April 2021. 'Robbie Savage, people had issues with him. Everybody hated Kris Commons because he signed for Derby. The atmosphere was crazy. I remember fans coming to me and saying do what you want, lose some games, but this game you are not allowed to lose. Fans came to me saying if you break Kris Commons's legs you will be a legend. The Derby game was different.' Fever pitch had indeed been achieved.

Despite the loss, Forest went on to finish third and reached the play-offs, but lost out to Blackpool, who defeated Cardiff City in the final and took their place in the Premier League. Derby's season was quite a frustrating one as they ended up in mid-table. The repercussions from 2007/08 were longer and deeper than first suspected as the club was still recovering financially, meaning Clough was severely limited in terms of the transfer market and, each year, was having to shave more and more off the wage bill.

2010/11
The most parochial of derbies

The 2010/11 season played out in a very similar way to the previous one – come May, Forest had lost another play-off semi-final and Derby were still in mid-table. But it produced two memorable derby games for those on the east side of the M1.

The Reds started their campaign with seven draws from the opening ten games, but were hitting their stride with McGugan and Earnshaw regularly finding the net. After an excellent run of form in autumn, Derby had lost their last four as the teams prepared to meet in the final game of

2010 at the City Ground as the mist did indeed roll in from the Trent on a damp Wednesday evening.

It was a perfect stage on which to perform under the lights in a crucial festive fixture. 'There is a different aura going out on to the pitch for a derby,' said Barker. 'You feel more pressure. You understand what the game means, perhaps more than the fans appreciate, the build-up, the excitement. You want to be part of that game. That's the game you look for. If you don't want to play in those games, then you are not really made to be a footballer. You've got to enjoy that pressure, being a hero or a villain.'

Forest heroes were indeed created. With a degree of inevitability, a goal occurred before anyone had eased into their plastic seats: Luke Chambers put the hosts ahead in the second minute with a powerful header from a deep corner. 'They started like a house on fire,' admitted Barker. 'It was crazy. You had to get through the first ten minutes. It was Forest at their best really: pace, energy, aggressive, the crowd were fully behind them. There were a few players that got picked out by Nigel in that game. I thought I was one of the culprits really. Chambers scored early and he was my man at the back post.'

The mould for these games remained very much intact and most expected Forest to double their lead, before losing it or almost throwing it away. Yet Derby's Luke Moore had other ideas and, he after being put through by Alberto Bueno, smashed in at the Trent End past Camp, in the 14th minute, to level. This wasn't in the script.

Just ten minutes later, spurred on by Aaron Ramsey on loan from Arsenal, Earnshaw produced some lovely work wide on the right before crossing for Marcus Tudgay to power a header in off the bar and restore the home side's lead. This was a case of two ex-Derby players combining to score against their former club. In added time of the first half, Tyson crossed for Tudgay to put Forest 3-1 ahead with a solid header, straight out of the Rub Hulse playbook.

Tyson was having a whale of a time and it was he who again crossed from the left for Earnshaw to make it 4-1. From the kick-off, Commons sparked into life and embarked on a direct run but was halted unfairly outside the area. To a cacophony of boos, he planted his free kick into the net past Camp to make it 4-2. Naturally, Commons's celebrations involved much shushing of the home crowd, pointing out his name on the back of his shirt and pointing to the badge. Derby weren't quite out for the count yet.

But in added time, Earnshaw capitalised on a defensive mistake and buried Forest's fifth goal, neatly making the scoreline resemble that of the main road that links Nottingham and Derby. 'I wanted to create a history at Forest,' Earnshaw told former BBC Radio Nottingham presenter Robin Chipperfield. 'I wanted to leave people with memories that they can hold on to forever, the memories that in 50 years' time or whatever, they can always go back to and feel that moment. We were lucky enough to beat them 5-2 – a moment that the fans could really enjoy.' He certainly achieved that.

Assisting Nigel Clough on the bench was former Forest player John Metgod, while the Reds had two former Rams in their team and were managed by the Scot who had guided them to promotion to the Premier League. It was the most parochial of derbies.

Naturally, Billy Davies was delighted with the win. 'I don't know if it's as well as we've played this season, but that was a very good three points,' he said. Clough's mood was significantly less chipper. 'I'm very angry, very upset, because this was a massive setback,' said Clough. 'There was a lack of desire individually and collectively. I thought we were further down the road than this. The players can't hide, they either do it or they don't, and if they don't, at some point you move on to the next group. We can't afford to have nights like this.'

Just four games later, the teams clashed again at Pride Park for the return fixture. In that short time, Derby had suffered one of the most humiliating results in their history in the third round of the FA Cup on 10 January, losing 2-1 to non-league Crawley Town. Forest had a spring in their step and were surging up the table, while Derby languished in 14th. With 11 minutes remaining, the Reds took the lead; Earnshaw expertly dispatched the ball home and took great pleasure in conducting the away fans in a song about how the Welshman was now metaphorically red while holding a particular displeasure for his former club.

Davies, too, was not backwards in celebrating his side's win at full-time. 'I celebrate the same way on the touchline and I go to the fans, there's no difference. I have no issues at all with coming back here,' he said. 'I have no problems with what took place in the past, I am not bitter in any way, I have great memories from here and had some great times at this club. As the Forest manager, I expect a bit of stick.'

On his side's seventh defeat in nine games, Clough appealed for people to look at the bigger picture. 'It's got to be put into perspective, you can look at the last eight weeks or two years,' he said. 'Is there any other Championship club in that time that's brought in more money than it's spent and reduced the wage bill by nearly half? We are still just about keeping our heads above water. If there's any other Championship club that's done that in the last couple of seasons, we would like to know who they are.'

This was Forest's first win at Pride Park at the eighth attempt, and of course, it had to be Earnshaw who scored the decisive goal, one in which he took great delight, 'It does mean more. When something has not been pleasant at your old club, what you want to do is go back and show what you are actually about and show them what you do. This is actually the way we play football and score goals so for me, it was about that.'

The goal itself come from of hours on the training field. 'It was repetition, the times in training, repeating the chance, repeating that shot,' said Earnshaw. 'I did that shot from the edge of the box so many times in training that when it came to the chance, that's the moment and that's what it felt like. When Nathan Tyson went down the left, I was thinking about positions and where I was supposed to be in the box and where the defender is. So I'm breaking it down in-game. When the ball went a little too far, to [Paul] Anderson, I knew to pull back – same as training. I gave the signal to Anderson: nod it down here.'

Anderson did precisely that and Earnshaw did the rest. 'Sometimes the football gods give you a moment. Is it fate? It just happened to be this game where I scored the winner,' he said.

Despite this, the Reds had led at Pride Park for only 22 minutes over nine games, or 810 minutes of football.

Just for good measure, it was Forest's first double over their rivals since the 1989/90 season. It was a sweet moment for Forest fans, but ultimately their team fell short as they were outwitted by Brendan Rodgers's Swansea City in the play-offs.

2011/12
Ten men

Despite his achievements on the pitch in leading Forest to two consecutive play-off campaigns, Billy Davies's race was run. Perhaps Nigel Doughty grew weary of hearing the same cracked record from Davies concerning his demands for ever more funds to splash in the transfer market, notwithstanding the prickly nature of the Scot. He was replaced by Steve McClaren, who had endured a troubled time in charge of England and later VfL Wolfsburg, but enjoyed an excellent two-year spell at FC Twente, where he led the relatively small Dutch club to their first Eredivisie title in 2010, playing an expansive and attractive style of football.

Following Davies out of the exit was Nathan Tyson who trundled off down the A52 to Pride Park. 'I'd heard rumours that Derby were interested,' said Tyson in *Pride*. 'But Forest threw me under the bus. We lost at Swansea in the play-offs and I was sat there and the chairman Nigel Doughty came around and said "Unlucky guys". The chief executive [Mark Arthur] was going around shaking all the players' hands, saying, "Unlucky, see you next season" and he gets to me and says, "Unlucky, all the best."'

Given his desire to stay local and not uproot his three children, Tyson took the call from Derby, especially since all Forest could offer was a contract through the post, without a phone call or chat to follow it up. Rumours that Guy Moussi would also join Derby proved to be unfounded.

The Rams won their opening four games of 2011/12, but then lost the next two before coming to Nottingham for the first derby of the season on 17 September. Forest, despite sporting some rather snazzy stripey socks, were struggling under McClaren and had lost their previous two games. It was in the early stages of this season that riots broke out in London and were replicated nationwide. In Nottingham, cars were set alight in Basford, Radford and Mapperley, while petrol bombs were hurled at Canning Circus police station as Forest played out a thrilling 3-3 draw with Notts County in the League Cup, going through after a penalty shoot-out. It was a similar pattern in Derby as incidents were reported in Alvaston and Normanton.

Both sets of fans were now accustomed to the notion that pretty much anything could happen within the opening two minutes of this fixture, and this occasion was no different. After 66 seconds, Ishmael Miller was put through by Andy Reid only to be bundled over by Fielding in the Derby goal. Despite the protestations, referee Scott Mathieson brandished a red card and awarded a penalty, which Reid converted. Derby had 88 minutes to play with ten men and were a goal down. It didn't look good.

All was not lost though. They did, after all, have a manager with the surname of Clough in charge, who felt the red card was more of a collision than anything else and put it down to one of those things. So Derby got busy. In the 29th minute, Chris Cohen went down after attempting to make a tackle and stayed down clutching his knee. Mathieson allowed play to continue, despite Matt

Derbyshire chasing the official around the park in an attempt to get him to pause the game until, eventually, the ball went left and found Jamie Ward, whose loan spell with the club was now made permanent. It seemed he had few options. Regardless, he skipped past Majewski and found himself on the touchline and outside the penalty area, with Chris Gunter bearing down on him and even fewer options. He promptly bamboozled Gunter but still had Camp to beat and hardly any angle from which to do so, his boots flecked with chalk dust from the goal line. The only option was to cheekily slip the ball through Camp's legs from the tightest of angles, which he promptly did. At which point, and not for the first time in this fixture, chaos reigned behind both goals and the stands in between.

'I wouldn't have stopped, I would have played on,' McClaren said. 'It's up to the referee.' Some may point out that the Derby players might have taken responsibility when a fellow professional lay prone on the ground. 'It's not our job to stop play,' Clough observed. 'We play to the whistle.' Either way, Derby were level and Cohen suffered the first of three long-term knee injuries. 'I wish Chris Cohen never would have had that knee injury because it is a terrible injury in the football world,' Ward later told *The Rampage*. Yet he remained unrepentant about playing on. 'People can talk about sportsmanship,' Ward said. 'But three or four of their players surrounded the referee to get Frank Fielding sent off [at the start of the game]. Yes, it was a sending-off, but they didn't need to surround him because he was always going to get sent off. As I was celebrating, Matt Derbyshire tried to grab me, but it's part and parcel of the game. You just have to get on with the game and defend better.'

For all the huffing and puffing from Forest, Derby still created chances to go ahead and they did just that when academy product Jeff Hendrick slotted home from outside the area to seal a famous 2-1 win. As the song goes, they only needed ten men to do so. The outcome piled even more pressure on McClaren and frustration was unleashed towards him and the chief executive, Mark Arthur, regarding a supposed lack of spending. Not many managers last long in the face of such a humiliating result in this fixture.

Indeed, the former England boss lasted only another two weeks until 2 October, when he resigned after a painful home defeat to Birmingham City, with the team fourth from bottom and only eight points from ten games on the board. Doughty also announced he would step down as chairman at the end of the season but would continue to support the club financially. 'Part of the role of chairman is to accept responsibility for what happens at the club,' said a Forest statement. 'As such Mr Doughty accepts responsibility for his personal decision to recruit Steve McClaren as our manager in the close season. Given our very poor start to the season and Steve's resignation, Mr Doughty feels it is only right to do so.' The McClaren experiment lasted 111 days with the only tangible benefit being the return of Andy Reid to the club.

The year was one of contrasting fortunes for Derby. The Industrial Museum, which occupied part of the Silk Mill in the city, closed as it struggled to entice visitors in. Denied lottery funding, it was challenged to reapply with a more ambitious plan for development and trumpet the region's reputation for innovation. It would be another ten years and a complete overhaul before, in May 2021, the radical

Museum of Making opened its doors to the public after an £18m makeover, boasting – among many fine displays and interactive experiences – an entire room devoted to a 1951 model railway landscape. While the museum closed its doors, the club set about opening its own doors much wider and submitted plans to the council to develop the land outside Pride Park. In 2007, the club had submitted development plans to the tune of £20m, but the latest ones were somewhat scaled down. Cafes, restaurants, office space and convenience stores were featured in the plans, all with an eye on the looming financial fair play regulations due for implementation in 2012.

The new year brought tragic news. On 4 February, it was announced that Forest owner Nigel Doughty had been found dead in the gym at his home. Obsessed with Forest, he ensured he had internet or radio access to a game wherever he was in the world. From a working-class background and a solid Labour supporter, Doughty made his fortune in private equity and since 1999 had pumped millions into the club he loved, knowing that the chances of recouping his investment were slim. Forest's academy now takes his name.

A month later, Forest made the trip to Pride Park, buoyant from breaking their Pride Park duck the previous season but saddened by the owner's death. Each pre-season, Doughty would invite anyone and everyone attached to the club to his house for a party. 'I remember him being a really, really nice bloke who loved football,' former Forest captain Ian Breckin told *Bandy and Shinty*. 'I knew he was a successful businessman, but he liked to be in and around the club and he made you feel as though you were his friend. He used to have a party once or twice a year and invite us all to his house – all his family and friends, wives and kids – it made it feel a bit more like a family club. He was a lovely, lovely man.'

On top of that, Forest were struggling at the foot of the table under Steve Cotterill, brought in to arrest the slide. In their favour, Derby had also lost their way. November saw the Rams chalk up five straight losses and a further three in a row in February. Forest mirrored this with four successive defeats in November and December and three in January. They even managed to go seven games without scoring a goal to round off a miserable 2011.

The fixture was originally scheduled to take place on 5 February, a day after Doughty's death, but was postponed due to snow and eventually took place on Tuesday, 13 March. With Tyson now in white, the usual scuffles and mass confrontations played out in a game most notable for the horrific injury suffered by Derby defender Shaun Barker, who in a seemingly routine collision with his own goalkeeper dislocated his right kneecap and ruptured his medial ligament, posterior cruciate ligament and damaged his patella femoral ligament. Tudgay, stood nearby, knew something was seriously amiss and urgently signalled for aid. Despite the innocuous nature of the collision, it was the type of injury more commonly seen in rugby or American football.

In the eight minutes of added time, Tudgay, maybe suffering from shock, was sent off for a second yellow card and there was still time for Derby to claim a late winner as Nottinghamshire-born Jake Buxton headed home a career-defining goal from a free kick to give Derby the points and their first double over the Reds since the 1971/72 season, exacting quick and effective revenge for being on the receiving end of the double the previous season. This was the first derby after Nigel Doughty's death, prompting some unsavoury chants from a minority of home fans. Notwithstanding the win from a Derby perspective, it was a pretty miserable and sad evening.

The season played out unspectacularly for both clubs. Cotterill brought in Sean O'Driscoll as his assistant, which saw an upturn in the team's fortunes and just about steered the club to safety, finishing 19th. Derby posted a 12th-placed finish, their first in the top half since 2007 when they won the play-off final. It wasn't necessarily pretty, but it was certainly progress and with Sam Rush replacing Tom Glick as the face of the owners, General Sports and Entertainment, optimism for the season ahead grew.

On 11 May, a fire broke out in a semi-detached house in a residential street in Osmaston, resulting in the deaths of six children. Images circulated in the media showed the father, Mick Philpott, wearing a Derby shirt, and this combined with his previous criminal history led to some deeply distasteful chants from a minority of Forest supporters in future games. 'Both fans were firing off unnecessary insults towards each other in the name of banter which is not acceptable but unfortunately is part of football and terrace culture,' said Derby poet Jamie Thrasivoulou. 'But fans get lost in the moment. The etymology of "fan" is "fanatic". Another commonality that Forest and Derby fans have is that they are fanatics; they are obsessed; they live and breathe their football clubs. Not every supporter can say that, and the majority of Derby fans are from Derby and the majority of Forest fans are from Nottingham.'

With Forest mired in uncertainty regarding ownership and long-term financial security, they welcomed the decision of Fawaz Al-Hasawi to complete his purchase from the estate of Nigel Doughty on 11 July. He installed his cousin as chairman. As is traditional in such situations, they stamped their authority and made changes: Cotterill was sacked and Sean O'Driscoll was given the job. Several signings were made to improve a struggling and depleted squad that only narrowly avoided relegation.

2012/13
Eye test

Just like the previous season, Forest received Derby at the City Ground in September and, once again, Derby came away with the points owing to a controversial sending-off. This time, though, it was the home side who were reduced to ten men, giving an air of inevitability to Craig Bryson's well-taken winner on the same day as Nottingham's Robin Hood marathon.

Derby were without Barker, still recovering from his serious injury sustained against Forest. 'A few of the Forest lads came to see me after the game to wish me all the best and although it was a tough time back then, it was great to know that both clubs were there supporting me,' he told the Forest programme. On their previous visit to Nottingham, Jamie Ward scored that improbable goal and was relishing the prospect of inflicting more pain on Forest fans. 'I want to go and win on Sunday to make the Forest fans unhappy,' he said.

Surprisingly, there was no explosive start to the game: no red card, no dramatic opening goal, and no flashpoint. The first half passed without much incident, yet the afternoon sprang into life just 20 seconds into the second half. Dexter Blackstock, a key protagonist in the notorious Tyson corner flag scuffle, was sent off after his elbow was judged to have caught Richard Keogh's face as the two contested a high ball. Within ten minutes, Derby took the lead as Bryson slotted home to secure a 1-0 win. Despite a red card and the obligatory jostling as both sets of players converged after Gareth Roberts clattered into Cohen, it was, by this fixture's standards, a relatively sedate affair. Derby had now secured their third consecutive victory over Forest; the Brian Clough Trophy was starting to feel at home at Pride Park.

'I don't think the referee was perhaps strong enough on the day, although please don't think I'm implying that his performance was an excuse for the result,' said Forest captain Danny Collins. 'The red card has been debated long and hard since Sunday. Once the referee had made his decision I asked him whether he had seen it clearly and he was adamant that Dexter had committed an offence worthy of a red card.'

Derby trundled along quite nicely and cultivated strong home form, while Forest picked themselves up and kept in touch with the top six, seemingly making good progress under O'Driscoll and starting to play more expansive football, the hallmark of their manager's teams. Yet after a 4-2 home win against Leeds United on Boxing Day, leaving his side in eighth place and one point off the play-offs, Hasawi sacked O'Driscoll, leaving many fans' jaws on the floor. The vast majority were as bewildered as the rest of the football world, and angrier than most. He appointed Alex McLeish as manager a day later. There was a strong suspicion that the Kuwaiti owner was starting to lose the run of things and making it up as he went along, chasing only shiny objects with not a care for, or understanding of, what is required to run a football club.

When the teams met at Pride Park on 19 January, Forest were in ninth and Derby 12th, making the sacking of O'Driscoll even more baffling. Somewhat fittingly, Chris Cohen, now fully recovered from his knee injury sustained against Derby in 2011, opened the scoring after having initially swung an air shot at Billy Sharp's cross before neatly converting. It was Forest's first goal away from home since late November.

In the second half, Simon Gillett was dispossessed in midfield by Conor Sammon, who slipped Ward through to equalise. Him again. It was Ward's first game back after injury. 'That's his first start for three months and he's been our major goal threat when he's started this season, so to not have the partnership we wanted out there for three months has been hard for us,' said Clough.

McLeish was looking to expand his options with a view to a push for the play-offs. 'I am going to try and be as busy as I can. I spoke to the owners today after the game and they are very keen for us to add players to the squad,' said the Forest boss. 'I think these guys have got a good chance of climbing further up the table, but I would like to have an even better chance by adding new players.'

It didn't go well. McLeish, under the impression that funds would be made available, tried to strengthen in the January transfer window, and felt he had secured the signing of George Boyd from Peterborough United, only for the deal to fall through due to Boyd apparently failing an eye test. There seemed no logical reason for the explanation and fans wondered whether it was simply a case of Hasawi not wanting to spend money. Some even speculated that he had a new manager in waiting who didn't fancy Boyd and so pulled the plug on the deal. Either way, Peterborough owner Darragh MacAthony was far from impressed with the way Forest had gone about their business, a sentiment shared by most Forest fans.

Once the January transfer window closed, McLeish was ushered out of the manager's swivel chair – by mutual agreement it should be added – and back came Billy Davies. On the one hand, there was a logic to such an appointment. Hasawi wanted promotion yesterday and Davies had not only achieved this with Derby but had gone close on two occasions with Forest. Perhaps with Hasawi's financial support to secure those much-desired stellar signings that Davies regularly coveted, the final step could be made, and everyone would win. Yet on the other hand, putting two very combustible characters together was asking for trouble. It was the equivalent of Forest going all in at the bottom of the night with a risky and daring hand.

As the season drew to a close, on 2 April, Mick Philpott, his wife Mairead, and a friend involved in the plot, Paul Mosley, were all convicted of manslaughter after setting their home ablaze, with the intention of blaming the fire on Philpott's former lover, who left him. Instead, the fire caused the deaths of six children aged five to 13 years, including five of Philpott's 17 children and a son of Mairead from a previous relationship. It was the saddest and grimmest of cases.

Davies had engineered a strong close to the season and went into the final game with an outside chance of gatecrashing the play-offs. They needed to beat Leicester City at home and hope other results went their way. They lost 3-2 and Leicester faced Watford in the play-offs, but lost out in the most dramatic of circumstances when Anthony Knockaert missed a penalty in added time and Watford went straight up the other end and scored to make it to Wembley, all in the space of 19 seconds. Derby improved their final position for the third consecutive season and finished tenth. The groundwork put in by Clough was finally starting to yield tangential progress.

2013/14
Deforestation Day

For the third year running, Forest were required to grudgingly welcome their rivals to Nottingham for the first derby of the season. Forest were going well under Davies, having won their opening three games and lost only one by late September. Davies had persuaded Hasawi to back him, which he duly did, splashing out for Jamie Mackie and Jack Hobbs while also bringing in more unfamiliar faces such as Djamel Abdoun. Derby were inconsistent, with some fans growing weary of Clough's pragmatic football and the seemingly glacial rate of progress. Yet they had won three and drawn one of their four away games thus far. A stalemate seemed likely.

A Hobbs header from a pinpoint Andy Reid corner shortly before half-time was enough to secure the 1-0 win for the Reds, going some way to easing the pain of successive defeats at home to Derby in the two previous seasons.

But now, Davies's agenda in returning to Forest was transparent – to put as many noses out of joint as humanly possible. 'It is a good win for us and I am very pleased,' said Davies. 'I have to say, it was against a side that, they tell me, are making very good progress – and this one is a shambles. I am absolutely pleased about what we are doing so far and now we move on to the next one.' Such barbed comments, alongside his paranoia, rudeness and apparent mission to sack most of the backroom staff, including finance director John Pelling, operations manager Brandon Furse and head of media Fraser Nicholson, under the battle cry of 'unfinished business' was all becoming very tiresome and tedious.

In addition, upon his return, Davies brought with him Jim Price, previously a solicitor at Ross Harper in Glasgow, to work in a senior role. What didn't sit well with fans was that Price had been suspended by the Law Society of Scotland because of the alleged financial irregularities that led to the law firm closing down, resulting in him being found guilty of professional misconduct and struck off in 2017. Together, they went through a period of hosting question and answer sessions via Price's Twitter account on Friday evenings and, on one occasion, they enigmatically claimed that 'the innocent shall not be harmed'. This cast a large shadow over Price's ability to pass the fit and proper persons test. The kicker here was that Price was Davies's cousin and agent/adviser.

All of this, alongside Fawaz's personally commissioned portraits of him alongside Brian Clough, late payments to staff and the indignity of having Fawaz's refrigeration and air conditioning business on the shirts under the two stars and famous tree, was very testing for Forest fans who could really only see one way this was all heading.

As for Clough, patience had worn thin with steady but slow progress from the almighty mess he inherited after the traumatic season in the Premier League and the sweeping-up of Davies's and Jewell's mess. After the 1-0 defeat he said, 'We caused our own downfall again with the goal. We should have cleared the ball first of all and then we lost the man from the corner. It is a small mistake, but we didn't get away with it and it has cost us the game. We are not getting away with the mistakes we are making and a lot in the opposition penalty area is not going our way either, and we are certainly not getting a lot of breaks from the officials.'

His time was up. 'After much consideration, the board feel it is time to move Derby County forward to the next level,' read a club statement in the hours after the match. Defeat in the East Midlands derby had claimed yet another managerial job. Derby's start to the season had been indifferent, but not disastrous. But losing to that lot down the road was only forgivable in certain circumstances and, against a backdrop of finishing no higher than tenth and no lower than 19th for four seasons, defeat at the City Ground suddenly seemed unacceptable.

'The season he [Nigel] got sacked, we were a good footballing team,' said Barker. 'I thought we'd get in the top six that year. Leicester turned up and sat pretty much 11 behind the ball to frustrate us because we were a good footballing team [the Foxes won 1-0 at Pride Park in August 2013]. Burnley did the same [when winning 3-0 later that month]. They were two teams that came to Pride Park to sit back and soak up our style of play.' Indeed, until the Forest game, the only defeats Derby had suffered that season were at home to the two teams that went on to dominate the league and win promotion by a distance. It was Clough who signed Craig Bryson, Johnny Russell and Chris Martin and effectively laid the very solid foundations for success. 'We were one of the biggest clubs in the division and one of the lowest paid,' said Barker. 'Our average age went down from 31 to 23. There were four or five academy players in there. There were players coming from League One and Two and the only money he spent really was on a few players here and there.' Whoever took the helm had a sound platform on which to work.

When Derby opted for Steve McClaren a few days later, one started to wonder whether any managers or players beyond Nottinghamshire and Derbyshire actually existed.

The second coming of Billy Davies was unravelling in spectacular fashion, while the appointment of McClaren proved to be a roaring success. He tinkered with the formation by bringing in John Eustace as ballast in the midfield, allowing Bryson and the highly rated youngster Will Hughes to play further forward. The impact was immediate as his side turned in seven straight wins in November and December. Like Derby, Forest enjoyed a run of 14 unbeaten between December and February, but also like Derby, they went into the return game struggling for form, having not won in six. Amid the tension and paranoia and banning of journalists, the wheels were falling off. And then the whole wagon smashed to the ground in one unholy mess as Derby smashed Forest 5-0 on 22 March.

Naturally, there was an early goal. Craig Bryson opened the scoring after six minutes and added another after half an hour, quickly followed by Hendrick making it 3-0 – all before half-time. Forest's record at Pride Park was woeful, but this was off the scale. Johnny Russell made it four with a stunning strike before Bryson completed his hat-trick from the spot in the 69th minute. The Scot's treble was the first for a Derby player in this fixture since Steve Bloomer's in a victory by the same scoreline in 1898. It was their biggest win since the 4-1 spanking in November 1979 and, frankly, their biggest and most decisive win ever over their rivals. While the form book is often said to be defenestrated on the occasions of such derbies, it was the Reds who were well and truly thrown out of the window on what became known as Deforestation Day for Derby fans.

A makeshift team owing to injuries meant that Forest had Danny Fox and Jonathon Greening in central defence and winger Jamie Paterson up front. But this was light years away from any kind of excuse, especially since the options on the bench allowed Davies to play a more balanced team. Besides, it could easily have been more than five. For Forest fans, it was a simply horrific sight, while to Derby supporters it was a piece of art that could be hung in some Berlin art gallery and Davies's business remained resolutely unfinished. Just to add painful insult to long-lasting injury, Derby's attack was spearheaded by Patrick Bamford, who laid Hendrick's goal on a plate for him and won the penalty for Bryson's third. Bamford was with Forest's academy from the age of eight and is Nigel Doughty's godson.

Such a resounding victory gave the city some consolation, for earlier that month a fire broke out on the top floor of the car park next to the Assembly Rooms, damaging the ventilation system and leaving the future of the iconic venue in the balance.

'We knew if we kept doing the right things the end product would come and there's no better day to do it than today in front of 33,000 fans,' said McClaren. 'I think this win is for the Derby fans.' Davies left his assistant, David Kelly, to face the press, and he said, 'It was a disappointing catalogue of goals we gave away and what we were working on during the week was disappointing in how it was executed on the day.' Such comments reeked of Davies's tactic of shifting the blame away from him and his management. 'It's a huge, huge game in the season and we're disappointed we've let the fans down. We only had a fit group of 18 we brought today but that's not an excuse, it's just the facts of what's going on,' said Kelly.

Two days later, Davies was gone. His sacking was inevitable from the moment he returned and started firing backroom staff. Only a remarkable charge to the Premier League would save him, but his arrogance and paranoia combined with Hasawi's naivety and tendency to sack managers was only going to bring about one outcome: this. Davies hasn't managed since. He has claimed that a smear campaign by the press is responsible for this, while others would say that the reason lies squarely with one individual. Forest's miserable run continued until they got some points on the board under caretaker manager Gary Brazil and finished in 11th place. The place needed fumigating if the club was to move on.

McClaren steered Derby to third position and a play-off final against QPR at Wembley. They bossed the game and, when Gary O'Neil was sent off for bringing Russell down after an hour, it seemed only a matter of time before the Rams would score and return to the Premier League. Yet the football gods had other ideas and, in the final minute, Bobby Zamora pounced on an error by Keogh to score just his fourth goal of the season, with Rangers' only shot on target giving manager Harry Redknapp another promotion. It was cruel on Derby and McClaren, yet the Rams were in a solid position to bounce back, especially since local businessman Mel Morris, who earned a large portion of his fortune from backing the firm behind the ludicrously successful mobile phone game, *Candy Crush Saga*, bought a 22 per cent stake. He was a very rich man ready to help his local football club. As for Forest, the disconnect between their fans and the club under Hasawi was now a chasm. Something special was required to mend that bond.

11

Local heroes and villains: 2014-2022

2014/2015
More than a job

With Nottingham Forest now cleansed of the aura of Billy Davies, the club still needed something special to rebuild the bridges so spectacularly burned under his management. Fawaz Al-Hasawi still presided over matters, but he needed to pull something special out of the hat in order to convince supporters that he really was a capable and knowledgeable owner, and not just someone who made decisions based on which way the wind of public opinion was blowing.

He duly pulled Stuart Pearce out of the proverbial headgear. 'This club probably has more of a pull than any club in the country,' Pearce said. 'I've represented five professional clubs and I would like to think I've given them good service. The honour of coming back into this club is massive. By the time I've finished with management if ever I felt I had the opportunity to become manager here and turned it down, then I would not be fulfilled.'

With Steve McClaren about to enter his first full season as head coach at Derby, under Andy Appleby as chairman, this meant that both clubs were led by former England managers with Pearce having not only led the under-21s but also assisted Fabio Cappello as coach for the senior team; he even took full charge in a caretaker capacity for a game following the Italian's resignation in 2012. The summer saw England return home from the World Cup in Brazil with their tails tucked firmly between their legs after gaining only a solitary point from their three group games and being eliminated before the knockout rounds. Having international pedigree in management with England was not the shiny badge it had once been.

McClaren's preparations were hit by new signing George Thorne suffering an anterior cruciate ligament injury in a pre-season friendly against Zenit Saint Petersburg, which ruled him out for most of 2014/15. Forest's preparations went more smoothly as in came Michail Antonio from Sheffield Wednesday and Britt Assombalonga from Peterborough United for a club record fee. The negotiating process with Peterborough must have been tricky, given the lingering bad blood between Forest and Posh owner Darragh McAnthony after the aborted signing of George Boyd.

When Pearce walked out of the City Ground tunnel for the opening game of the season against Blackpool, anything and everything seemed possible. His team started brilliantly, remaining unbeaten in the opening five games and winning four of them. Derby began more hesitantly, with eight points accrued from the 15 available. The sixth match of the season dictated that Derby would travel to Nottingham to face their old foes, the first meeting since the legendary 5-0 defeat at Pride Park, a result immortalised by shirts proclaiming 'NFFC 5-0' emblazoned across the Rams' megastore at the time. With the match to be played on 14 September, it fell very close to the tenth anniversary of Brian Clough's death and was to be marked by both sets of supporters in the tenth minute with a standing ovation.

A typically tense encounter broke into life in the 71st minute when Antonio powered through the middle of the park and slipped the ball to Assombalonga who deftly swivelled and planted his shot into the corner of the Trent End goal. The joy for the home side was short-lived, however, as nine minutes later a Derby free kick from the left was met with a thumping header by Richard Keogh before the ball was poked home. It could have been either Ryan Shotton or Leon Best who got the final touch and little clarity was forthcoming from McClaren after the game as to the identity of the scorer, 'Shotton has claimed it, but Best is trying his hardest to pinch it from him.' Just for the sake of another layer of East Midlands intrigue, Best was born in Nottingham.

After the equaliser, there was just enough time for Jake Buxton to receive the game's customary red card before the shares were spoiled. 'He [referee Paul Tierney] was a little inconsistent,' said McClaren. 'I wasn't quite sure what he was going to do. He was a bit inexperienced for a local derby and we ended up with ten men and had to hang on for a draw.' His opposite number was equally frustrated. 'I'm a little disappointed with the quality from both teams – although I can only speak for Forest,' said Pearce. 'It was scrappy. We didn't get on the ball and pass it enough. The atmosphere was as good as I have ever known it and maybe the occasion got to one or two.'

A point for Forest was fine, albeit slightly disappointing given their impressive start to the season. But the day was blighted by the sight of Chris Cohen once again hobbling off the field against Derby. After 15 minutes Cohen got his foot caught in the turf, twisting his knee in the process. He rejected the offer of a stretcher but was seen wiping a tear from his eye as he hobbled down the tunnel. It was the third cruciate ligament injury of his career. 'In the changing rooms after I said to the physio about ten times, "That's got to be it, I can't just keep doing it,"' he told *The Guardian*. 'And then I got in the car, and the first thing I think I did was ring my mum and just said, "I know what I've got to do."' It took a while, but Cohen did eventually make his way back to full fitness.

Despite an excellent start, things went downhill for Pearce quickly with a flurry of draws and defeats, while Derby settled into a nice groove by going seven games unbeaten, including five wins. Pearce's job in arresting the slump was made even more difficult in December by Forest being placed under embargo for breaching financial fair play rules in the 2013/14 season. It meant that they were prohibited from signing any new players – either on permanent or loan deals – unless they had 24 or fewer 'established players', defined as those aged 21 or over who had made at least five starts for the club. The way out was to demonstrate they had stayed within the maximum permitted losses of £6m – £3m losses plus £3m covered by shareholder investment – for the current season. Under the ownership of Hasawi, this seemed an unlikely outcome in the short term.

Even the loan signing of Tom Ince from Hull City failed to spark any kind of life into Pearce's team. Ince later claimed that while with Forest, 'I started the first few games and got man of the match in a few of them but then found myself not playing.' This was much to the bemusement of Forest fans who don't recall any particularly memorable performances.

With a team struggling for form and under a transfer embargo, Forest fans travelled to Pride Park on 17 January 2015 fearing the worst. With his team labouring, they expected to see Pearce unleashing his inner Psycho by ripping heads off his players and banging them together like a marauding Viking. But instead they got Pearce the corporate manager, calmly sipping coffee from a polystyrene cup after games. This would have been lapped up if results were sound, but with every game doubt crept in. Indeed, they arrived at Pride Park without a win in seven and having lost their last three in miserable circumstances. In among all this, they had found time in their underwhelming schedule to squeeze in an FA Cup defeat to Rochdale of League One.

When Henri Lansbury nodded into his own goal from a Johnny Russell corner in the 16th minute in front of Derby's biggest home crowd of the season, 32,705, the form book seemed well and truly intact and far from being ripe for a severe shredding. Three points would have sent Derby to the top of the table prior to the afternoon games and, given Forest's form and morale, such an outcome seemed inevitable. The evidence overwhelmingly pointed to a home win and yet another East Midlands derby claiming a managerial casualty and, given the head that looked set to roll, a major scalp from a Derby perspective.

But something changed. Forest improved significantly in the second half and equalised when Assombalonga reacted quickly to fire in from a scramble caused by a set piece. The Derby fans, who were set to bury their old enemy with taunts about Pearce being sacked in the morning put them on ice. A draw would have salvaged some pride at the most hopeless of places from a Forest viewpoint and, from there, perhaps they could rebuild their season.

But Ben Osborn had other ideas. Born in Derby and son of a big Rams fan, he was signed for the club's Under-8s but not retained at the end of his first season. He was then invited for a six-week trial at Forest and so successful was he that he ended up staying until he was 24. Despite that, he followed Derby until he was around 17 but knocked it on the head when he got closer to the first team. 'Towards the end of my time at Forest it had completely swung the other way, to the point where I'd dislike Derby as much as any Forest fan,' Osborn said.

In the 92nd minute, Robert Tesche slipped the ball to Osborn in the middle of the park. He ran forward and kept going until he reached the edge of the Derby penalty area. With little on, he chanced his arm and fired a low and hard – yet straight – shot towards goal, which Lee Grant seemed to horribly misjudge. The ball arrowed into the net.

'I didn't know what to do – as you can probably tell from my celebration!' said Osborn. 'I'd scored my first professional goal in the biggest game of the season, at the ground where all my mates had season tickets and who my whole family had supported all their lives. It sank in after the game and I suppose that's when the penny dropped that it was a pretty special moment.' It was complete pandemonium in the away end.

On the touchline, Pearce's mask slipped and out popped the old Psycho who celebrated with the glee and redemption of his penalty kick against Spain in 1996. Frankly, it was frightening. 'I'm entrenched in Nottingham and this is slightly more than a job for me,' he said. 'I enjoy football at the all-or-nothing end. Yes, I enjoyed today but I probably enjoyed it more for the fans who have been so loyal to me. I respect loyalty.' Whatever happened next, he and Forest always had this. Even at a low ebb, they had vanquished their old foes at the most unlikely of times and places.

No doubt utterly frustrated and annoyed, a Derby supporter ran on to the pitch at full-time and appeared to swing at Forest defender Kelvin Wilson before being tackled to the ground by Jack Hobbs, and then being dragged away from the field by stewards. Derbyshire Police said a 23-year-old Derby man was arrested in connection with the pitch invasion and released on bail.

In another incident, Fawaz Al-Hasawi claimed that a club car had been vandalised, with two tyres deflated, windscreen wipers broken, and a personalised number plate wrenched off. The club owner tweeted pictures of the Mercedes-Benz Viano with the words, 'Very professional! But in the end I don't mind at all! The three points are more important!' Derby issued a statement from club president Sam Rush, 'I know that the vast majority of Derby fans are equally appalled by the callous act of a thoughtless individual seeking to attack a player on the pitch and similarly those who chose to vandalise the Forest chairman's car after the match. We can only apologise for those individuals who mistakenly call themselves Rams fans. To these people Derby County Football Club will not tolerate this type of behaviour, under any circumstances. We will seek to permanently exclude from our club anyone who thinks this is even close to acceptable.' All in all, it was a typically eventful East Midlands game and only Forest's second win in 13 at Pride Park. They had still only spent 43 minutes in the lead from 1,170 minutes played.

'It's important that we now move forward from here and follow it up with another good result in the next game,' said Pearce. They didn't. Just four days later, Forest travelled to Fulham and found themselves three goals down after only 35 minutes, victims of a Ross McCormack hat-trick. They recovered to only lose 3-2, but a 1-0 defeat at home to Millwall followed. Despite the chaotic state of the club under Hasawi and the transfer embargo, the team seemed to lack cohesion and Pearce was sacked on a dark, miserable Sunday evening.

Within minutes of the announcement, another followed, declaring the appointment of former player Dougie Freedman. This resulted in the most typical of new manager bounces as Forest won five games from their next six. In among the managerial comings and goings, the Reds were hit with a full transfer embargo on 4 February over the non-payment of a fee to Peterborough for the signing of Assombalonga. This was in addition to the restrictions placed on them for breaching financial fair play rules. Just for good measure, Tom Ince signed on loan for Derby. Taking the chair of a club legend is the most thankless of tasks and Freedman could have been forgiven for running for the hills at this juncture. Under him, Forest then plateaued to finish the season without a win in eight games and limped to the end, finishing 14th. A lot had happened in a seemingly very short period of time.

It wasn't a case of bunting and street parties in Derby, though. A seven-game winless run straddling March meant that they fell agonisingly short – just a point off – the play-offs in eighth place. Although no consolation, their final three games of the season looked incredibly fun for the neutral, drawing 4-4 with Huddersfield Town, 3-3 with Millwall and then losing to Reading 3-0 on the final day. It felt like a great opportunity wasted as a two-point lead at the top of the table at the end of February had disintegrated into dust in two short months, leading to the accusation of Derby lacking the required and elusive 'bottle' to get the job done.

With speculation linking McClaren to the vacant post at Newcastle United, Derby took the front foot and sacked their manager. Under him, the club had taken steps forward. 'Attendances were up to the highest average for a season since the team was in the Premier League and the largest in the Championship during the past season,' McClaren said. 'I wanted to remain with the club and was confident of leading the side to a successful season next year.' But the board, under Mel Morris as chairman now, couldn't see past the failure to reach the play-offs. 'However, I have to accept the club's owner, Mel Morris, wants to take a new direction,' admitted the former Forest and England manager. As for the board, they believed that 'the appointment of a new head coach is required to continue the club's on-field progress and the search is now under way to appoint a successor'. Morris had put a clear maker in the sand for future bosses: play-offs or nothing.

So in the blink of a Championship season, both clubs had fired former England managers, while key goals were scored by players born in the cities they scored against. In many ways, it was just another season in the latest round of East Midlands derbies.

2015/16
If I was picking the team...

Although Freedman now had a pre-season in which to prepare for the campaign ahead, Forest were still under a transfer embargo. Nonetheless, he was able to entice Jamie Ward whose contract had expired at Pride Park and was thus able to join since he was a free agent. 'What's in the past is in the past. I like to wind people up,' he told the BBC's *East Midlands Today*. 'It was to spice up the local rivalry and it got me a bit more stick than I wanted. I enjoyed it at the time, but hopefully the fans can see past that and get behind me.' Ward was one of three free transfers and six loanees brought into the club before October was out. This certainly wasn't going to be a tilt at the play-offs, more of a trudge towards mid-table.

The approach to recruitment could not have been more different over at Derby. Morris started writing cheques, and big ones, too, as he completed a full takeover from the GSE group in August. By the end of the month, approximately £20m had been spent on Andreas Weimann, Jason Shackell, Jacob Butterfield and Bradley Johnson, while Ince's loan move had been made permanent. Such spending represented almost 90 per cent of the club's turnover for the 2015/16 season and wages rocketed too. With Paul Clement now in the dugout, Morris seemed keen to ensure that the former assistant to Carlo Ancelotti at Real Madrid had all the materials he needed to achieve promotion. He was essentially going all in and a stunning start to the season offered vindication of his approach as the Rams went ten games unbeaten – including eight wins – before the first derby came along on 6 November at the City Ground. In contrast, Forest had only three wins under their belt and were without a win in eight with a side comprised of free agents and loanees. Avoiding defeat would have been satisfactory; anything more, a most wonderful surprise. But then again, derbies exist in a vacuum.

An early goal from Nélson Oliveira – on loan from Benfica – was enough to swing the game Forest's way on a Friday night. After just five minutes, his shot nicked off the posterior of Richard Keogh and ended up in the Bridgford End goal. Apart from that not a lot else happened. 'We had chances too and it was a well-deserved victory,' said Freedman. 'The crowd played a huge part in getting us over the line in the last ten minutes.' Clement had no complaints, 'We're to blame for not getting the right result tonight for the way we played. We lost a bit of identity.'

Oddly, the result boosted both teams. Despite losing their next game at Brentford, Freedman's bunch of hired guns then put together a run of 13 unbeaten. The football might well have been devoid of interest or excitement, but in the circumstances, it was more than acceptable. As for Derby, they picked up right back where they left off, stringing together another impressive unbeaten run of eight, winning five until the new year kicked in. From then, results suddenly dropped off, prompting Morris's visits to the changing rooms after games to grow more frequent. More signings followed, expanding an already bloated squad. Yet it was not enough to halt the slump and on 8 February, Clement was sacked after a run of six without a win and replaced by academy director Darren Wassall – a former Forest defender under Brian Clough – with Harry

Redknapp later brought in to oversee proceedings and share his experience.

Although frustrating, Derby's results and league position hardly merited a crisis: they were fifth at the time, a wobble but hardly a sacking offence. Indeed, one might daringly describe Morris's move as Fawazean. 'Every player he has wanted, he has had,' Morris told *East Midlands Today*. 'All the signings were all signed off by Paul. We put a lot of money behind him, even up to the last couple of weeks. At any point, Paul could have embraced the plan we had. Put it this way, if I was picking the team, he wouldn't have been playing some of the players in some of those games.' It seemed that Morris was keen to shovel any blame for this apparent failure as far away from his own door as humanly possible.

Of course, Hasawi had his own reputation to uphold in the firing managers stakes and he promptly consolidated this by sacking Freedman on 13 March. The encouraging run had come to a shuddering halt at the time that Clement was clearing his desk as Forest endured five defeats in six games. With the club still under a transfer embargo, Freedman could have been said to be doing a reasonable job, but this was Forest under Hasawi when a managerial sacking was de rigueur, even if the timing was not, with this one coming not after a loss to their rivals but bucking convention by pulling the trigger five days before a game against the Rams, leaving former Derby player Paul Williams in temporary charge. The owners of each club were developing quite a reputation for themselves.

Ahead of the game, *East Midlands Today* recorded a feature called 'The Ultimate Derby' in which Brian Laws and Craig Ramage took charge of their respective teams on the *Championship Manager* computer game. While Ramage took the game quite seriously, Laws was significantly more laid-back, dispensing managerial wisdom such as deciding to 'give it ten minutes' with his team a goal down at the start of the second half. It was a portent of things to come.

All of this meant that the latest East Midlands derby featured a former Derby player in charge of Forest and a former Forest player in charge of Derby. As it was, Martin Olsson's goal in the 79th minute for the Rams was the difference in a forgettable and lacklustre game, meaning Forest's sixth defeat in eight matches. They went on to lose their next three too, yet for Derby, things were ticking along nicely now. 'I wanted Harry [Redknapp] in the dressing room before the game, at half-time and at full-time,' said Wassall. 'He chose to sit in the directors' box because he hasn't seen us play recently and he gets a better view. Harry's input is just as much as anyone else's, and I welcome that because if he can improve us in our promotion push by three or four per cent we will be delighted.'

Under Wassall, Derby recovered from their miserable January and reached the play-offs, but lost out to Hull City at the semi-final stage, the damage done after a 3-0 defeat in the first leg at Pride Park, temporarily renamed the iPro Stadium for sponsorship reasons. Naturally enough, such an achievement fell short of the target in Morris's eyes and Wassall wasn't given the job on a full-time basis, returning to his academy role. Morris's first full season as chairman turned out to be rather eventful, but ultimately provided little return for £25m spent. Having tried an internal and inexperienced appointment overseen by a mentor, Morris predictably switched lane and put his eggs back in the basket labelled 'experienced' as Nigel Pearson was appointed on the basis of his credentials as a successful Championship manager and boasting experience in the Premier League. Once again, it seemed like a case of all or nothing.

Forest limped to a 16th-placed finish, seemingly their spiritual home since if one were to calculate their average league position since 2000, it would be around 16th place in the second tier. The only real optimism came in the transfer embargo being lifted in May, yet few trusted the owner to spend the money wisely, if at all.

2016/17
The Derby way v the Forest way

From out of nowhere, Philippe Montanier was appointed manager of Forest. Having enjoyed varying degrees of success in Europe, most notably with Real Sociedad who he guided to fourth in La Liga 2012/13, it was a still a gamble. Even more so when the summer recruitment saw eight free transfers/undisclosed fees and three loan deals for players most had to embark upon a deep internet search to find out anything about them. Such random business was crowned with the signing of free agent Nicklas Bendtner in September. After a few performances in the red shirt, it quickly became apparent why he was previously without a club. It was shaping up to be another trying season.

Derby laboured under Nigel Pearson in the early stages of the season, posting only one win in their opening nine games. Ahead of a midweek trip to Cardiff City on 27 September, a furious argument between Morris and Pearson occurred at the training ground, leading to the manager being suspended. Apparently, Morris had concerns about Pearson's general approach and, more specifically, the poor start to the season. Quite why Morris felt that tackling a man who would later fight off a pack of wild dogs while hiking in the Carpathian Mountains was a good idea is anyone's guess. Derby won 2-0 in south Wales, only their second victory of the season.

Pearson left by mutual consent and was replaced by Steve McClaren, who emulated Billy Davies and returned for a second spell in charge of an East Midlands club. Where one club went, the other seemed to follow. This precipitated an immediate upswing as Derby recorded five straight wins coming into the visit of Forest to Pride Park on 11 December. Bizarrely, Forest were on a mini winning streak of their own, having won their last three fixtures. But the team lacked cohesion and a clear structure and more often than not looked like a bunch of random players chucked together and told to get on with it, which is pretty much what it was.

The game was barely a contest as Derby ran out 3-0 winners. In true slapstick fashion, Bendtner headed into his own net from a corner before Ince danced through the Forest defence to make it 2-0, taking particular delight in scoring against a club he had endured a tough loan spell with two years previously. Will Hughes deservedly made it three, rounding off a torrid afternoon for Forest fans. If you had tried to pick three goalscorers that Reds fans would least like to see, it would have been precisely this trio, which seems a little unfair on Hughes given that all he did to attract the ire was to be raised in Derby and be rather talented. But that's how rivalries work, something that McClaren knew all too well, 'It's a huge win for the supporters and will make their week and a huge three points for us that puts us up there, but I'm still not looking at the table.'

As for Forest, the performance and result confirmed what most suspected, that the recent mini improvement under the Frenchman was no major turning point or a sign of things clicking into place, but merely an isolated run of decent results. 'During a derby game you need to play a full game at 100 per cent and at 1-0 you can come back, but we needed to play at a good level,' said Montanier. 'We had no opportunity of scoring and it was easy for Derby County to score because we did not have a good discipline.' Playing at a good level, or even a reasonable level, was proving to be quite difficult.

There were mixed feelings among the 32 runners, composed of Forest and Derby fans, who spent the morning running from the City Ground to Pride Park to raise money for Prostate Cancer UK, wearing T-shirts highlighting the charity's Men United campaign. For those of a Derby persuasion, the aches in their legs floated away, while for the Forest fans among the runners, walking out of the stadium felt like doing the 20 miles course all over again. The Nottm2Derby run raised approximately £8,000.

Unsurprisingly, Montanier was relieved of his duties in January, the fifth consecutive season that Forest had changed manager midway through and typically between Christmas and March – all under Hasawi's watch. Nobody really knew whether Montanier was any good as a manager, given the frankly unplayable hand he was dealt. Once again, Gary Brazil dusted down his chalkboard to take temporary charge until Mark Warburton was given the job just in time for the return visit of Derby in March.

In the run-up to the game, Derby endured a horrible February consisting of four defeats and two draws from six. A 3-0 defeat at Brighton & Hove Albion was the final straw and McClaren was sacked again, six days before the derby. He was replaced by former Rams player and coach Gary Rowett, a capable and highly respected manager but one whose football was more pragmatic than easy on the eye. Besides, yet another sacking meant another step away from Morris's 'Derby Way' – a vague soundbite that espoused sustainability and faith in youth. Such things are difficult to grow when new managers keep walking in and swiftly out of a club.

Warburton's appointment was confirmed just four days before the game and, in an open letter to the fans at the end of the season, new chairman Nicholas Randall stated, 'We can assure you as a supporter and everyone else who cares about Nottingham Forest that Mark will be given the precious commodity of time to turn matters around and to build something special at the club again.' His first task was to steer Forest away from the threat of relegation as they sat fourth from bottom just one point above the line.

The game was a pulsating one in which Forest put up a fight, something sorely missing from the encounter in December. Zach Clough put the home side ahead after only five minutes in yet another case of an early goal for the home side in this fixture. Yet after the break, Matěj Vydra equalised and then David Nugent put the Rams ahead in the space of eight minutes. Under Warburton's insistence that his team play out from the back, Forest were wobbling as the home fans mocked Rowett's trainers in an effort to distract from the way the game was panning out. Yet in the 94th minute, Forest earned a corner and, predictably, chucked everyone up. Left-back Daniel Pinillos headed powerfully in to rescue a point and immediately earn cult status with his one and only goal for the club.

Rowett was left deeply frustrated. 'To get the goal so early in the second half, at that point we were in complete control and really dominant and moved the ball fantastically well,' he said. 'The disappointing thing from there, having been in control, was that we have to see things out. But I'm not going to be critical of the players because I don't know what we want completely yet.' For Warburton, it was something to build on, 'We have been with the players for three days, you ask them to do certain things, you don't want to change too much at short notice, but you ask them to get on the football, to be brave and pass the football. In the first half, they showed they can do that. We challenged them, they dealt with it and that is very pleasing.'

The point proved to be vital. Going into the final game of the season, Forest were required to better Blackburn Rovers' result. A 3-0 home win against Ipswich Town just about did the job, but only by the slimmest of margins. Forest and Blackburn finished with the same number of points, but the Reds enjoyed a marginally better goal difference of -10 to Blackburn's -12. Pinillos's goal against Derby really did matter. Come the final whistle against Ipswich, Forest fans spilled on to the pitch to celebrate survival, much to the delight and catcalls of Derby supporters, yet the jubilant scenes went beyond just survival. They were just as much an expression of relief since the club would be under new ownership in a matter of days, signalling the end of the disastrous and at times farcical Fawaz Al-Hasawi era. The fact that it was Chris Cohen who scored the third goal was fitting, given his seemingly omnipresent battles against injury.

Derby's ninth-placed finish was well short of the play-off places, yet Rowett would get another shot the following season. But it was behind the scenes at both clubs where significant changes were taking place. On 30 April, Derby confirmed that Rush was 'taking time off', but that soon evolved into a sacking, according to their statement, 'Derby County Football Club has today dismissed with immediate effect, president and chief executive officer Sam Rush on the grounds of gross financial misconduct and breach of fiduciary duty.' As the modern parlance puts it, that escalated quickly. Previously enjoying an excellent working and personal relationship, things got ugly between Rush and Morris rather abruptly. It would take another 18 months before any further light would be shed on the matter, and even then it was minimal. After a series of allegations and counter allegations, eventually a club statement was published, 'The club and Mr Rush have settled their respective differences on agreed terms, they are now moving on with their lives and no further comment will be made.' Morris had the helm to himself.

Just 18 days news of after Rush's departure, it was confirmed that Nottingham Forest were under new ownership with Hasawi selling 100 per cent of his stake to Evangelos Marinakis, founder and chairman of a major shipping company and owner of his hometown club, Olympiacos, since 2010. Shortly after this formalisation,

Randall's open letter was published in which allegations of match-fixing in Greece were dismissed on Marinakis's behalf and it was acknowledged that, as it stood, the club was 'in intensive care'. Furthermore, 'stability' was identified as 'one of the most precious commodities in football' and there was also strong intent to improve the club's community work and to 'build on the social solidarity that was epitomised by Brian Clough and which is also a unique part of what may be called "the Forest Way."' Suddenly, 'ways' were very important in the East Midlands. Yet putting the constant search for identity aside, it certainly seemed that Forest were in much more knowledgeable and capable hands.

2017/18
Nugent and Vydra. Repeat

Unusually, Forest went into the first derby of the season in better shape than their rivals. Under Warburton they played football that was easy on the eye and leaned on youth, but any good results were invariably followed up by a couple of poor ones. As for Derby, they were struggling to find any consistency, meaning that they went into October's derby at Pride Park in 17th place, below Forest in 13th. After just 24 seconds – surely the earliest goal ever scored in this fixture – Vydra fired the Rams into a lead that they never looked like relinquishing. Nugent bagged a second early in the second half, meaning that the same strikers who scored against Forest in the previous fixture once again hit the target and in the same order. Regardless of the moral support offered by former Forest defender Julian Bennett in the away end as a punter, the Brian Clough Trophy remained with Derby, who promptly won their next three games and enjoyed a 12-match unbeaten run from December to February. Rowett felt that the better team won, 'But after the second goal I thought we started to control the game and should have added to the two goals.' Warburton accepted that possession and pretty football cannot be separated from results, 'I thought we were very good for long periods, but that's not what our supporters or our players want to hear.'

The year finished in predictable style for Forest – with a managerial sacking. Warburton's dismissal was the sixth consecutive season in which the club had sacked a manager, all of which adhered to the apparent unwritten rule that this must be done between Christmas and March. It seemed that the stability which chairman Randall spoke about was a way off yet. In came Aitor Karanka, who was assistant to José Mourinho at Real Madrid and had won promotion with Middlesbrough in 2016. He swiftly brought in six players in the January window and oversaw a memorable FA Cup third-round win over Arsenal, dumping the holders out 4-2 at the City Ground. Five days later, a fire broke out at Nottingham Railway Station, causing £5.6m of damage, apparently set off by a drug addict's lighter in the toilets.

Forest were in their seemingly natural habitat in the lower half of the table, while Derby had lost their way a little but still sat fifth by the time of the return league fixture at the City Ground. The teams played out a reasonably entertaining goalless draw, the first such scoreline between the sides in 31 meetings at the City Ground, stretching back to April 1906. Rowett felt his side had done enough to win the game, despite Huddlestone being sent off late on for two fouls on Lee Tomlin, while Karanka took solace in his team's improvement. For Forest fans, it was just nice to get through a game without seeing Vydra or Nugent scoring against them.

Derby reached the play-offs for the second time in three seasons but lost to Fulham, despite taking a 1-0 lead into the second leg at Craven Cottage. Although once again they flirted with promotion, the season became defined by another collapse, owing to a run of 12 unbeaten between December and February giving immediate way to an eight-game run without a win and three consecutive defeats in April. Sometimes it takes an outsider to identify and articulate the nature of the problem. 'Derby is such a fragile place that if one thing went wrong, everybody would jump on it,' said Cameron Jerome, who Rowett signed for Derby in January 2018, in *Pride*. 'National press, local press, everyone. It was no fault of their own but it's just such a great narrative for everyone to look at.' He could easily have been speaking about Nottingham Forest too.

As for Rowett, his achievements hadn't gone unnoticed at Stoke City who were facing up to life outside the Premier League for the first time in ten years. They made eyes at him and he reciprocated by asking for permission to speak to the Potters about their vacant managerial position. Talks were successful and Morris was once again left looking for a new manager. He didn't look around for too long and, in May, the manager's parking space had a new name on it: Frank Lampard.

But before domestic football, with its ceaseless transfers and squabbling, cranked up again, there was a World Cup in Russia to be consumed. England reached the semi-finals before losing out to Croatia, prompting trouble in Mickleover after fighting broke out among football fans.

In Nottingham, the worst trouble came after the quarter-final win against Sweden as fans flocked to the Market Square and damaged bus stops, signs and vehicles. The only representative of either club at the World Cup was Iranian midfielder Ashkan Dejagah, who made just one appearance for the Reds from the bench in a 2-0 defeat at Fulham. Also in the Iran squad was future Forest forward Karim Ansarifard. This was all a very far cry from Italia '90 and the last time England reached a World Cup semi-final. Back then, four of the starting 11 who played the semi-final against West Germany plied their trade in the East Midlands.

2018/19

(We are) Derby v the rebel city

With Lampard in charge, Derby's squad featured several future internationals and young talent as Mel Morris attempted, once again, to reduce the age of the squad. To achieve this, Lampard's connections would prove invaluable. In came Chelsea's Mason Mount and Fikayo Tomori alongside Liverpool's Harry Wilson, all three on loan. In theory, the budget had a little wiggle room, given the sales of Vydra and Andreas Weimann and the departures of several players as free agents or for undisclosed fees. Yet the wages of such hot young talent and Lampard himself were not insubstantial.

With Christmas looming, Forest travelled to Pride Park on a Monday night feeling optimistic about getting a rare result in Derbyshire. Indeed, with Derby fifth and the Reds seventh, this was a rare case of both teams being in good form and both having eyes on the play-offs. It had all the ingredients for a memorable encounter, yet was soured by a vulnerable Derby fan, Charlie Harrison, being taunted for wearing a Rams shirt in the build-up to the game. Footage was posted on social media, prompting universal condemnation. For their next fixture against Bristol City, Charlie was invited into the Derby dressing room to meet his heroes.

Just before kick-off, award-winning Derby poet Jamie Thrasivoulou read a rousing rendition of We Are Derby to a montage on the big screen. Written after being asked by Rams bosses to come up with something to motivate fans and players, the poem pays tribute to the history of the city of Derby and the club. A sample stanza reads:

> *We're engineers with dirty fingernails*
> *Graft and sweat pump through our veins*
> *We're Rolls-Royce engines, Belper nails*
> *Toyota motors, Bombardier trains*
> *We are Derby*

'That was the first time I did it live on the pitch,' said Thrasivoulou. 'It actually got commissioned in the summer just before the start of that season by Frank Lampard and his communications team. They just wanted to do something different, and they put the word out asking if there was a poet who lives locally who does stuff nationally. At that time I had won an award for my poetry – the Bread and Roses Culture Award in 2018 for song writing and spoken word collaboration that celebrates working-class life.'

The poem struck a resounding chord with Derby fans from its inception. Thrasivoulou said, 'I did a gig on Normanton Park for the Jo Cox Foundation and the theme was we have more in common than that which divides us. The Friends of Normanton Park, who look after the place, said to me, "We've got a chalkboard on the park, would you mind chalking a stanza on the chalkboard?" That very day I was debuting a very recent poem I had written about Derby County that was to do with Frank Lampard coming in. In that original poem was the stanza about Steve Bloomer and the old Baseball Ground. So I chalked that up on the chalkboard as it represented the area and Steve Bloomer was from Pear Tree and lived near the Baseball Ground.' To his surprise, the poem was still there a few weeks later, despite him fully expecting it to be at best scrubbed away, but more likely defaced with childish drawings. A member of the Punjabi Rams supporters' group took a walk with their dog around Normanton Park, saw the stanza, took a photo and posted it on Twitter. Events snowballed from there, culminating in the club contacting Thrasivoulou.

The poem was played in the dressing room for the first home game of the season, a 4-1 defeat to Leeds United. But owing to entrenched superstitions of footballers, it did not get a repeat airing in the bowels of Pride Park. However, for the next home game, the poem aired on the big screen, resulting in Jamie's phone lighting up with congratulatory messages.

In the December 2018 meeting, neither team could break the deadlock and once again a goalless draw was the outcome. Both teams worked the opposition keeper and a fine effort from Forest's Joe Lolley rattled the crossbar, while Derby felt they should have had a penalty for Tendayi Darikwa's challenge on Tom Lawrence, prompting Lampard to claim, 'I think the most staunch Nottingham Forest fan in the far side of the stadium saw that was a penalty.' Naturally, Karanka saw it differently, 'I don't know if it was a penalty. The referee was closer than me and if he made that decision it's because he felt it was the right decision.' Ultimately, though, a draw was a fair result and meant both sides could forget about each other for a while and concentrate on reaching the play-offs at the very least as Derby maintained their iron grip on the Brian Clough Trophy.

'Both teams were pretty rubbish that day; it was a really boring game,' admitted Thrasivoulou. 'I had 3,000 Forest fans chanting "wanker" at me as soon as I started the poem. But fair play to them since if someone did that at the City Ground, we'd do the same.'

A slight dip in Forest's form coming into the game developed into a severe wobble and, a mere six days later, some were reporting that the special Christmas sack reserved for Forest managers was back under the tree as the Reds somehow contrived to draw at Norwich City on Boxing Day despite being 3-0 up with 13 minutes remaining and still 3-1 up in added time. A miserable and customary defeat at Millwall followed before a home game against Leeds United on New Year's Day in which it was received wisdom that the Forest hierarchy were just waiting for the right moment to do what they do best – fire a manager between December and March. A 4-2 win delayed the inevitable, but on 11 January, Karanka cleared his desk. The parallels with Sean O'Driscoll, fired by Hasawi after a 4-2 win at home against Leeds on Boxing Day in 2012, were eerie. On the surface, the Spaniard had the team moving in the right direction and playing exciting football, including a memorable 5-5 draw at Aston Villa, but behind the scenes, all was not well as it was reported that he alienated some members of his squad and the management above him.

European Cup winner Martin O'Neill was appointed four days later, finally taking the role after almost doing so back when Brian Clough retired. Assisting him was another former Forest favourite, Roy Keane. The noises emanating from the boardroom were of pushing for the play-offs, but such an upheaval seemed to derail the form of the team. Meanwhile, Ashley Cole joined Derby on 21 January, adding another layer of stardust to the first team and another big name to the wage bill.

Both teams were still very much in the mix when they met again in Nottingham on 25 February, with Derby in seventh and Forest ninth. On the Saturday prior to the Monday evening game, around 20 Forest fans ran from Pride Park to the City Ground in the return leg of the Nottm2Derby run for Prostate Cancer, raising an additional £7,000.

Forest fan group Forza Garibaldi organised and choreographed a huge display in the Trent End, paying tribute to the city's reputation as a 'rebel city'. Banners celebrating Eric Irons, Helen Watts, Alan Sillitoe, D.H. Lawrence, Ned Ludd and, naturally, Brian Clough were revealed just before kick-off. If the intention was to express pride in the city and its achievements while also whipping up a frenzied atmosphere for the visit of their fierce rivals, it worked a treat as the deadlock was broken by that most typical of things in the history of the fixture – a ludicrously early goal. This time, it was Forest's Yohan Benalouane who poked home from around a yard out inside the first minute. The game ended 1-0, finally ending Derby's record run of holding the Brian Clough Trophy as after 1,073 days, the silverware took up residence in Nottingham.

Charlie Harrison led the teams out, representing Umbrella, a Derby charity that supports children and young people aged five to 30 with any special need. Supporters of both clubs had raised around £1,000 for Charlie since his story was circulated. His father, Stuart, said he would buy a football kit for his son and donate the rest to Umbrella.

Forest never gained the momentum they had under Karanka and finished ninth, a position flattered by winning their final three games of the season. For Derby, it was the most eventful run-in to the end of a campaign in a long while.

Back in January, a Thursday afternoon training session at Moor Farm ahead of their visit to Leeds was suddenly interrupted by the sight of police vans careering up the road, followed by sirens and then a 20-year-old intern with a backpack and wire cutters being apprehended. It transpired that Leeds boss Marcelo Bielsa liked to send his staff to watch other teams train and saw nothing wrong with such a practice, going as far as putting it down to good preparation. The EFL saw it differently and Leeds were fined £200,000. Football being football, Derby then faced Leeds in the play-offs.

The Rams lost the first leg 1-0 at Pride Park, but overcame Leeds by winning 4-2 at Elland Road in one of the all-time epic semi-finals. The players celebrated wildly in front of their travelling supporters, as did Morris, by mimicking looking through binoculars in reference to the spying shenanigans. However, Derby lost 2-1 to Aston Villa at Wembley, meaning another season of Championship football and another gargantuan amount of funds poured into the first team with little reward.

The city was buoyant after Derby City Council approved further development of the site at Infinity Park Aerospace Campus in March. The site was already home to Airbus and the advanced aviation company VRCO and, as a result, the city's reputation as the home of innovation seemed to be in rude health; it just needed a football club to match that innovation and success, yet despite coming close the club itself was on somewhat less firm footings. The ramifications of not reaching the Premier League this time would run deep.

2019/20
#wounded

With both clubs posting a top-nine finish – the first time both had been in the top ten since 2013 – changes of manager would seem perverse and unnecessary. Yet the respective owners had proven that they were far from averse to chopping and changing when it comes to the hot seat. Forest decided to bring an end to their habit of replacing a manager mid-season by getting it done before the new campaign started and sacked Martin O'Neill on 28 June, a week after his assistant Roy Keane left his role as he wanted to be a manager again in his own right. It was reported that the mood among key players was negative and irreparable and so the owner acted swiftly, replacing O'Neill with the former Rennes and Ivory Coast coach Sabri Lamouchi. Nobody really knew what to expect.

Derby, too, replaced one manager with another, but for very different reasons as Lampard left to take the role of head coach at his beloved Chelsea on 4 July. It was an opportunity that was too tempting to turn down for the former Blues player so Morris, now with a taste for a big name as manager, turned to another and appointed former PSV Eindhoven boss and 100-cap Netherlands international midfielder Phillip Cocu.

The sense of anticipation at Derby grew exponentially as a few days after the season started, it was announced that Wayne Rooney would join as a player-coach in January from MLS side DC United. This was a major coup since Rooney had acquitted himself well with DC, scoring 25 goals in 52 appearances. Yet the deal was a curious one, with more than a whiff of commercial interest behind it. 'On the back of Wayne joining the club, we have just been offered a record-breaking sponsorship deal with our principal shirt sponsor, 32Red,' said Mel Morris. Presciently, Rooney's shirt number was to be 32. Reportedly earning £100,000 per week at Derby, whichever way the deal was looked at, it represented a huge commitment on the part of the club to funding the wage demands of their crown jewel of a player. This was either extremely clever business acumen from Morris or overstretching Derby's resources. Only time would tell.

Fans of either side didn't have to wait too long to find out what their new cosmopolitan managers were all about as the teams met at the City Ground in round two of the League Cup in August. Despite being in the increasingly derided competition, this was Forest v Derby and 27,000 turned up to see the home side take a two-goal lead before half-time with goals from Albert Adomah and Joe Lolley. A third goal in the second half from João Carvalho gave the Reds a resounding win to retain the Brian Clough Trophy. Cocu named a relatively young and inexperienced side and while Lamouchi's team wasn't quite at full strength, it was picked with one thing in mind: to win.

Derby failed to register a shot on target, yet Cocu defended his selection. 'It was not [a gamble], because Forest's team was the same,' he said. 'We face each other two more times in the league and it is up to us to give an answer to this and a good feeling to our fans.' Although the league meetings take precedence over the early rounds of the League Cup, beating your rivals always reflects well on the manager, while losing can easily become a stick to beat them with. However, a double over Forest in the league and no doubt this result would be brushed off by Rams fans. As for Lamouchi, he leaned into the East Midlands rivalry. 'Derby is always a difficult game to play. But it was a very good performance and very good result,' he said. 'I wanted to win this game, not only for our fans but because I know it is important. The atmosphere was important.'

In typical fashion for such a game, a skirmish broke out after the final whistle between Rams captain Richard Keogh and a member of the Forest ground staff as the player warmed down. Keogh eventually departed the playing surface bloodied and angry. Unbeaten in six games in all competitions, Forest started the season surprisingly well as, once again, they signed a host of relatively unknown players. In contrast, Derby had not won any of their past four fixtures.

It wasn't only in the men's game where Forest were enjoying superiority over their rivals. On Sunday, 8 September, Forest Women recorded a 1-0 win over Derby County Women at Pride Park. Former Derby forward Precious Hamilton nodded in the deciding goal with just seven minutes remaining in front of a record attendance of 2,318 for the FA Women's National League North Division. The previous best had been set the previous season when 2,109 saw local girl and Derby fan, Amy Sims, head the only goal of the game to secure the points against Forest. Forest Women were officially founded in 1990 by the NFFC Community arm and changed name from Nottingham Forest Ladies to Nottingham Forest Women in July 2019. Similarly, 1990 was also the year that Derby County Ladies FC formed after previous iterations of Derby County Women FC and Beacon Wanderers, though they would eventually return to the Derby County Women name. Like their male counterparts, the women's teams also seemed to be joined at the hip, moving cheek by jowl in a series of close contests defined by former players.

Yet a slow start on the field for the men's team was to be the least of Derby's concerns. On Tuesday, 24 September, a team bonding evening went horribly wrong. After a game of ten-pin bowling, the players gathered at the Joiners Arms pub and, although most went home around 8pm, a small group continued drinking after a team dinner. Later that evening, Tom Lawrence crashed into the back of Mason Bennett's car on the A6 north of the city and proceeded to collide with a lamppost. Club captain Richard Keogh was in the back seat of Lawrence's Range Rover. Lawrence and Bennett left the scene, leaving an unconscious Keogh behind. The two did return to the scene 45 minutes later by which time Keogh had been treated by paramedics. A club statement made its disappointment and anger clear, 'The players were out as part of a scheduled team-building dinner with staff and, while the majority of them acted responsibly and left at around 8pm and were not involved, a small group, including the team captain Richard Keogh, continued drinking into the night. They should have known when to stop and also ignored the opportunity to be driven home using cars laid on by the club and chose to stay out.'

A month later, Lawrence and Bennett were ordered to carry out 180 hours of unpaid work and given a 12-month community order and banned from driving for two years. District judge Jonathan Taaffe was at pains to point out that a prison sentence was a viable option. Lawrence and Bennett were also fined six weeks' wages by the club.

As for Keogh, he was unable to play owing to extensive damage to his medial collateral and anterior cruciate ligaments that would keep him out for up to 15 months. On top of that, he was subsequently sacked for gross misconduct on the basis of his failure to wear a seatbelt in Lawrence's car and because the players had ignored the opportunity to be driven home using cars laid on by the club. In an interview with *The Guardian*, Keogh disputed this, pointing out that there were no club cars outside the pub at any point, only a club employee who had a number to call for a driver. 'The way they put it was as if the club had officially laid on cars and we ignored them, that we walked straight past the chauffeurs to get into our own cars,' said Keogh. 'It's just absolute nonsense. The car thing annoyed me and it annoyed the other lads as well because there were no cars.'

Keogh later won a compensation battle against Derby, who were ordered by the EFL's Player Related Dispute Commission to pay up the full value of the remainder of his contract, over £2m. He was also found to have been wrongly dismissed by Derby and not to have committed gross misconduct or brought the club into serious disrepute. Given that incident still relatively early into his tenure, Cocu's cup was suddenly overflowing with problems.

By the time Cocu took his team back to Nottingham for the first league derby of the season in November 2019, he had managed to steady the ship a little and picked up three wins from the previous five games, sitting 15th. Forest were proving to be the surprise package and had climbed to fifth by playing a highly effective counter-attacking style under Lamouchi, who played against the Reds for Auxerre in the UEFA Cup in 1995.

The tight game hinged on a mistake. Ten minutes into the second half, Derby's Jayden Bogle played an errant and casual pass across the face of his own penalty area, on which Lewis Grabban pounced and dispatched the ball into the Trent End goal. The game finished 1-0 to the Reds. 'The second half was much better,' said Lamouchi. 'They made a big mistake and our striker, Grabbs, played a fantastic game one more time with great finishing. That is what we wanted to see from him.' Cocu also pointed to Bogle's mistake as being the difference between the two sides. 'In the big games, in many games but especially in games like this, a detail, a mistake, bad judgement or sometimes class can make the difference,' he said. 'Today, the mistake of Jayden cost us the result. That is tough because I think we played quite a good game.' Derby had now failed to win on any of their past eight visits to the City Ground in all competitions, with their most recent victory coming in September 2012. For the first time in seven seasons, it seemed likely that Forest would enjoy a more fruitful season than their fierce rivals.

Few were prepared for what the new year would bring. In January, Derby were charged by the EFL over breaches relating to spending rules centring around their amortisation policy and a review of the sale of Pride Park from the club's ownership to Morris and, more specifically, the value of the ground. Derby vehemently defended themselves and vowed to strongly contest both charges. Yet football and all its attendant furniture were pushed back to the far recesses of the world's living room as, within the space of two weeks, it lost its status as the most important of the trivial things to simply being a trivial thing. On 27 February, Marinakis's Olympiacos travelled to Arsenal for the return leg of their Europa League tie. The Greeks scored a last-minute winner to progress to the last 16. Eight days later, Forest hosted Millwall on Friday night for a league fixture, yet succumbed to a hat-trick from Matt Smith who scored three goals in the space of 13 first-half minutes to inflict a 3-0 defeat on the Reds. Marinakis was still in attendance come Monday morning, the Forest website announced, 'Mr Marinakis was diagnosed after showing the first symptoms on his return to Greece. During his stay in Nottingham he did not show any symptoms of the [Covid-19] virus.'

In between the Millwall victory and the club statement, Derby comfortably beat Blackburn 3-0 at Pride Park, lifting them to 12th while Forest sat in fifth. Two days later, Arsenal announced that they had closed their training centre as a result of head coach Mikel Arteta receiving a positive Covid-19 test result. At that stage, the weekend's fixtures were cancelled, with Forest scheduled to play Sheffield Wednesday at Hillsborough and Derby due to travel to Millwall. It was later reported that the earliest known person to contract Covid-19 within the UK was identified to be a 75-year-old woman from Nottinghamshire. Analysis of samples by the University of Nottingham showed she tested positive on 21 February. The world quickly went into hibernation.

Eventually, football cranked back into gear and both teams resumed the season on Saturday, 20 June in front of empty stadiums and to the sound of coaches barking instructions. Forest took the lead at Hillsborough through a typical Joe Lolley effort, but a 93rd-minute header from Connor Wickham prevented them from taking three points. Derby enjoyed their trip to Millwall and came away with a 3-2 win featuring a hat-trick from Louie Sibley.

Despite their lower position, it was Derby who adapted to football behind closed doors better than Forest. Going into the meeting at Pride Park on 4 July, the Rams had won all their three games, while Forest recovered from the disappointment at Hillsborough to chalk up two wins from successive home games. It seemed like Cocu was starting to get a tune from his squad. 'I think we are heading in the right direction, but there is still room for development and improvement as individuals and as a team,' he said. 'I think we did quite well in the games against them [earlier in 2019/20], but many teams have had the same feeling when playing Forest. I think that is one of their greatest strengths; you feel like you are doing well against them but at any moment they can score a goal. They have good organisation and defence and, when they go ahead, they are difficult to beat.'

Just like at Hillsborough, Lolley put Forest ahead and, having effectively nullified Rooney from pulling the strings from a deep position, the Reds looked set to come away with a huge and satisfying win in the most unusual of circumstances, this being the first East Midlands derby to take place with no fans present. When Derby's Martyn Waghorn saw red in added time for a dangerous challenge on Ryan Yates, the game was Forest's to throw away. Yet in the 96th minute Rooney delivered a final hopeful ball into the box from a free kick, at which keeper Brice Samba flapped and, after some six-yard box pinball, Chris Martin nodded in to rescue a point for the home side and puncture Forest's progress to the play-offs. The similarities with the Reds' first game back at Hillsborough were as striking as they were frustrating for Reds fans. Indeed, the draw took one particular Forest fan by surprise as Nottinghamshire's British Transport Police reported a person in the canal opposite Nottingham station and announced on Twitter, 'A Forest fan had jumped in to celebrate a win over local rivals, unaware of the late equaliser. #wounded.'

Lamouchi was furious. So furious in fact that he sent out his assistant Bruno Baltazar for press duties. 'We had chances to score the second goal and at this time of the season, we can't miss so many specific chances,' Baltazar said. 'And then we are playing against ten men, it's unacceptable that we lost these two points at this stage of the game. We need to work on this really quickly.'

They didn't. Forest failed to win any of their five remaining games and with each game, the pressure grew to secure the play-off spot everyone thought they would and culminated in the now infamous collapse against Stoke City. All they needed from their final game was a point as they sat in fifth place, level on points with Cardiff City, but crucially three points and five goals better off than seventh-placed Swansea City who travelled to Reading more in hope than belief. Inconceivably, Forest managed to turn such an advantage into a farce as late goals rained in both at the City Ground and the Madejski Stadium. In the 94th minute, Wayne Routledge scored Swansea's final goal of a 4-1 win, while in the 96th minute, Forest's Nuno da Costa put through his own net, thus ensuring his stay at the club yielded a minus-one goal contribution. Both Cardiff and Swansea leapfrogged Forest to take the final two play-off spots as Forest dropped out of the top six for the first time that year, with only moments of the season remaining.

Much hilarity ensued from the western side of the M1, while much gnashing of teeth commenced east of it. Despite losing their next four games after Martin's last-minute equaliser against Forest in July, the point Derby snatched undoubtedly played a part in Forest's collapse. Of minor consolation for the Reds was that their seventh-placed finish was the first time they had finished ahead of Derby – in tenth – since 2013. Yet given the circumstances, to celebrate this would be akin to grasping at the flimsiest of straws.

2020/21
That isn't a derby

With another nationwide lockdown on the horizon, residents in the Lenton area of Nottingham awoke in October to find their small corner of the world catapulted into the nation's consciousness. On Tuesday, 13 October, a mural of a girl hula-hooping with a bicycle tire appeared on a wall on the corner of Rothesay Avenue. The image sat behind a battered bike chained to a lamp-post, with the bike missing a tyre. Surinder Kaur, owner of the beauty salon next to the mural, confirmed that the bike had appeared at the same time as the artwork. Days later, the elusive street artist Banksy posted a picture of a mural of a girl hula-hooping on social media, ending speculation over whether he was behind the work. The significance of the bicycle was not lost on the residents of Nottingham, the home of the famous Raleigh.

Forest responded to the traumatic denouements of the previous season in the second most predictable manner – they signed 14 new players and two loanees in the summer window. After starting with five straight league and cup defeats, the club reacted in the most predictable manner by sacking Sabri Lamouchi and replacing him with the experienced and widely respected Chris Hughton. His first game in charge saw the Reds win 1-0 at Blackburn – excellent preparation for his third match, against Derby at the City Ground, by which time two more players had arrived on loan. Derby were also struggling and had only one win to their name, meaning they sat a mere three places from the bottom of the Championship with Forest just two places above them.

With thousands watching from their sofas on Friday, 23 October, the game was largely devoid of quality and, predictably, atmosphere. Martyn Waghorn's stunning free kick gave the Rams the lead after half an hour, yet Forest's summer signing, Lyle Taylor, scored his first for his new club in the second half from close range to level things up. If it wasn't for Wayne Rooney self-isolating at home in accordance with Covid-19 guidelines, Waghorn might not have had the opportunity to take a direct free kick from such range. Derby considered themselves unfortunate not to take maximum points as Kamil Jóźwiak's effort found the net but was ruled out as Waghorn was in an offside position and judged to be in goalkeeper Brice Samba's line of sight. 'I don't see any offside,' said Cocu. 'The goalkeeper reaches for the corner where the shot goes, so the view is not blocked. The frustration is quite big here.' As for Forest, they were becoming more solid under Hughton and harder to beat, but it was distinctly unspectacular. A week later, prime minister Boris Johnson announced a second national lockdown for England to prevent a 'medical and moral disaster' for the NHS.

Cocu oversaw another four games without a win and was sacked on 15 November with Derby bottom of the table. Rooney was tasked with overseeing training. 'I'm sorry Phillip and his staff have left the club and want to thank him personally for all his help and encouragement as part of his coaching staff,' he said. 'The most important thing now is to stabilise the club and start moving up the table.' Under Rooney's watch, Derby improved to the extent that, on 15 January, he was confirmed as manager. 'When I first arrived back in the United Kingdom, I was completely blown away by the potential of Derby County Football Club. The stadium, training ground, the quality of the playing staff and the young players coming through and of course the fanbase that has remained loyal and supportive,' said Rooney via the club's website. 'To be given the opportunity to follow the likes of Brian Clough, Jim Smith, Frank Lampard and Phillip Cocu is such an honour and I can promise everyone involved in the club and all our fans, my staff and I will leave no stone unturned in achieving the potential I have witnessed over the last 12 months of this historic football club.'

The potential was certainly there, but it remained the case that the club no longer owned its own stadium and had mortgaged its training ground in pursuit of further finance under Morris. A reported takeover by a Middle Eastern investment group failed to materialise and there was interest from Erik Alonso's No Limit Sports on the grapevine, yet in the meantime attention switched to the visit of Forest to Pride Park in late February.

A week prior to the game, Banksy's mural was sold to an Essex art gallery for a six-figure sum. It was removed by specialised workers, much to the disappointment of local residents who had grown used to, and proud of, the queues of people eager to see an original Banksy. 'It was great for the city. It arrived in the midst of Covid when we were all going through a really terrible time, and there was just this brilliant moment of enjoyment, and joy and delight,' said Simon Bristow, of the Nottingham Project city rejuvenation board. 'But now sadly it's in the hands of someone else.' In a small way, Banksy had filled the void perfectly between one East Midlands fixture and the next.

Both sides had improved and slowly climbed away from the relegation zone, Forest up to 16th and Derby to 18th. Yet it remained inescapably a game between two struggling teams scrapping for respectability. One of Forest's loan signings, midfielder James Garner from Manchester United, opened the scoring with his first senior goal after 33 minutes when his shot squirmed under Kelle Roos. Yet with six minutes remaining, Colin Kazim-Richards unleashed a powerful volley which flew past Samba, meaning the two teams contested their third successive 1-1 draw. A picture of Derby's Nathan Byrne challenging Garner for the ball with his head while prone on the floor and pulling Garner's shorts down to reveal his pants all at the same time seemed to capture the rather farcical nature of both clubs and teams at this point in time.

The lack of crowds certainly had an impact on the nature of the match. 'I watched the game this season without fans and I don't think there was a booking until the 82nd minute,' said former Rams captain Shaun Barker. 'That isn't a derby. You want someone clattering into them and that is driven by fans. I can remember Nigel [Clough] would try to get you calm beforehand because he wanted you to play your game.'

It was reasonable to assume both sides might be inwardly satisfied with a point, especially Forest since they maintained their possession of the Brian Clough Trophy and extended their unbeaten sequence against the Rams to eight games. But captain and childhood Reds fan Joe Worrall was anything but. When asked if the draw was evidence of progress, Worrall replied, 'Yeah, let's not kid ourselves, though. We didn't play Barcelona, it was Derby. Fair play to them, it was a great goal from Kazim-Richards. We are disappointed, make no bones about it. But when they smash in a goal from 20 yards out, you've got to take it on the chin.' While behind-closed-doors games may well have temporarily diluted the rivalry in the stands, it lived on in the respective dressing rooms.

A significantly more serious and distressing post-match comment came from Kazim-Richards. After his superb equaliser, he woke the next morning to find several racist messages had been sent to his Instagram account. 'I was on the phone to somebody from the club to let them know what happened,' he told The Athletic. 'I thought my son was asleep. He comes in asking who called me a n******r and a monkey. I've had my son ask me why black people in movies are bad guys. I've told them it's acting and not real, don't take it seriously. A part of my children's innocence was taken by the perpetrators.' Forest said they were 'extremely disappointed' by the abuse and 'wholeheartedly support' Derby for reporting it to the police. 'Any form of racist abuse is abhorrent and has no place in football or society,' a statement said. 'The persons involved in this hate crime do not appear to claim to be supporters of our club, but if they are, we will not hesitate in taking the firmest possible action.'

As it stood, Forest had now played 19 games and 1,710 minutes at Pride Park and led for only 171 minutes. Put another way, the Reds had enjoyed the advantage at the home of their rivals for just ten per cent of all games played.

With two games remaining of the 2020/21 season, the spectre of relegation for Derby was very real and, with Forest's next fixture against struggling Sheffield Wednesday, the age-old discussion about whether you would accept your team losing if it helped your rivals suffer was liberally bandied around. Worrall, with form for speaking about his feelings towards Derby, was adamant that winning for Forest remained his priority. 'I want to win the game. The league looks after itself. I am sure when they [Derby] were looking at us, when we beat Ipswich to stay up on the final day [in 2017] – they will have wanted the result to go the other way,' he told The Athletic. 'Whoever stays up will do it on merit. It will not be holiday mode, even though we are safe. We will go to Hillsborough and try to win. There will be no funny stuff. I would be massively disappointed if there was no East Midlands derby next season. It would be fantastic if they do go down, in one sense. But I also want to play against Derby, I want to score against Derby, I want to beat Derby. If you are asking me if I want them to go down – no, I do not.'

Former Forest midfielder Guy Moussi echoed Worrall's sentiment. 'There is a line between rivalry and hatred. The hatred comes from the fans, I think. For us, as players, when we play against Derby, we just want to beat them, because of the rivalry, rather than the hatred,' he told The Athletic. 'When new players arrive, the first thing you tell them is that *this* is the game. This is the game you want to be involved in. The excitement when you play against them; the atmosphere is just different. It is hard to explain. When you play Derby, everything just means more. Everyone wants to play in the game, everyone wants to win the game, all that matters is that you beat them. When I played in this game, there was a rivalry between the players, there was Robbie Savage, who had history with Nathan Tyson for example. There was Billy Davies, who hated Nigel Clough. There was a lot of extra meaning to the game. There will be different reasons for that now, but they will still be there.'

As it was, Forest could only draw 0-0 with Wednesday but could have won if Lewis Grabban had converted his penalty. On the same day, Derby lost at Swansea, meaning that going into the final game of the season the Rams sat one place above the drop zone, two points clear of Rotherham with Wednesday and Wycombe below them. On the last day, Derby entertained Wednesday.

When Rotherham took the lead after only eight minutes away at Cardiff, it looked like both Derby and Wednesday would tumble through the trapdoor together. From the

Millers' perspective, they needed three points while also hoping their South Yorkshire rivals would do them a favour, as they needed to also better Derby's result against the Owls. At Pride Park, nerves dominated and just before half-time they grew exponentially as Wednesday took the lead. If results held, Derby would be relegated.

The Rams sprang to life in the second half and turned it around with two goals inside the first seven minutes. But Wednesday came back and scored their own pair in the space of seven minutes, meaning they led 3-2 with 20 to go. As it stood, Derby were down. But two things happened to swing the pendulum in their favour. Firstly, Waghorn converted a penalty with 12 minutes remaining to make it 3-3 and, down in Cardiff, Marlon Pack equalised for his side against Rotherham with two minutes remaining – although the two incidents happened almost at the same time, given the Rams' game was running around ten minutes behind Rotherham's owing to stoppages and injuries. When the music stopped, Derby had a chair while Wycombe, Rotherham and Wednesday didn't. They were safe. At least for the time being anyway, as a threat of a points deduction imposed by the EFL hung over the club since it remained locked in dispute with the governing body regarding its reporting of its accounts.

The celebrations from the players poured out into the street as they mingled with fans in the pouring rain. Watching the scenes in the BBC Radio 5 Live studios, former Forest player turned coach and pundit Andy Reid said, 'I'm just looking at some of the Derby County players and some of the staff running around celebrating like they've just got promoted. The way they've been this season, I'd probably be a bit embarrassed to do that, if I'm totally honest with you. Running around the pitch and hugging each other ... I know it's a good thing that they've stayed up, I totally get that, but I wouldn't be running around the pitch celebrating, because in some ways they've stayed up by default, really.'

Wycombe chairman Rob Couhig was, like Reid, less than impressed. His club released a very pointed statement, 'To finish on 43 points, and above two other teams, is a creditable achievement given the relative tight financial restraints that the club has operated under during the 2020/21 season. We have gone into battle with teams assembled for nine-figure sums, and often fallen narrowly short. Wycombe Wanderers will always continue to compete to its maximum potential, on and off the pitch, by playing within the rules. We expect our opponents to do the same. The club trusts that the correct decision will be reached by the independent commission which has been appointed to judge Derby County's case.'

The scales of mockery among the respective sets of fans were even again as Forest supporters could delight in Derby's ecstatic celebrations at simply staying up, after they had been mocked by their counterparts for invading the pitch and celebrating survival on goal difference following their win against Ipswich in 2017. Derby fans now knew what fuelled such celebrations: pure relief and escapism from an ordeal of a season both on and off the pitch. All the while, Forest supporters watched their team slump to a miserable and meaningless 2-1 home defeat to Preston from their sofas or the pub, meaning they claimed their customary place between 14th and 17th in the table.

Days after Derby secured their status, prospective buyer Erik Alonso posted a video on social media of an expensive-looking house, possibly to reassure fans concerned about the apparent disconnect between his boasting of his grand plans for the club and his financial backing. Yet such a move had the opposite effect since it appeared that the short video was taken from another user on TikTok. Days later, the proposed sale to Alonso crumbled and Derby limped on under Morris. Surely things would be better for both clubs in the 2021/22 season as both finished in the bottom eight of the division for the first time since 2009. They simply had to be. They couldn't be much worse.

2021/22

Forest sucks

In truth, Derby surviving by the skin of their teeth was, as most surely knew it to be, just a very temporary respite from their problems as July brought confirmation that the club would not be allowed to sign players until accounts were refiled for 2016, 2017 and 2018. The dispute with the EFL regarding a points deduction raged on to the extent that interchangeable fixture lists for 2021/22 for Wycombe and Derby were published, accounting for either club to be in the Championship or League One. Even if the embargo was later softened to allow five signings, Derby were still in a sizeable pickle.

Forest stalwart Michael Dawson was certainly not an option for Derby as he announced his retirement, having returned to the City Ground for the latter part of his career. Reacting to reports that he might sign for the Rams, he put those rumours emphatically to bed, 'To go to Derby, I couldn't go over that side of the Trent as a Forest fan from a young age. At the age of 37 to go there for one year, I'd be slaughtered.' Meanwhile, Wayne Rooney inadvertently made his threadbare squad even lighter by injuring Jason Knight in training before being filmed nodding off in a hotel room with two women after a boozy night out. The chaos at Derby seemed to be getting messier with each passing day, leading to them being firmly installed as everyone's favourites for relegation.

Hughton clung on to his job as Forest manager, but changes were afoot as, after recognising that the recruitment of the previous few summers had left them no better off, they brought in a new chief executive officer in the shape of Dane Murphy from Barnsley. Forest and Derby, not for the first time, shared a common bond: both had owners who prioritised promotion above everything else and, when that failed, the response was to tear everything down and start again, creating a cycle of constant renewal with each new manager wanting a new set of players, meaning a constant churn of squads.

Rooney consulted his sizeable book of contacts and came up with some experienced and unattached players, such as Richard Stearman and Phil Jagielka, and also took a punt on Ravel Morrison who had, despite his obvious talent, consistently failed to impress at a string of clubs. To everyone's surprise, Derby started well, picking up five points from their opening four games – not promotion form, but enough to offer hope that predictions of relegation by Christmas would be well wide of the mark.

Any schadenfreude from the other end of the A52 was put firmly on hold as Forest lost their opening four league games and suffered a 4-0 reverse in the League Cup second round in midweek to Wolves before the first derby of the season, on Saturday, 28 August at Pride Park. Despite presiding over 53 games, there seemed to be no discernible improvement in the team under Hughton. In fairness to him, the squad he inherited was still alarmingly unbalanced, with particular issues in the full-back areas. With an international break following the match, it seemed highly likely that defeat for Forest would claim another managerial scalp and allow whoever they had in mind to take the job after a couple of weeks' preparation time. Their only hope was the loan capture of James Garner from Manchester United for a second time, their player of the season in the previous campaign despite only arriving in January. Another goal from him at Pride Park would be more than welcome. For Derby, they would have to make do without the injured Kazim-Richards. 'I can't wait,' said Rooney. 'I hope they [Forest] are ready because these players will be ready. Of course they haven't had a good start to the season and we have had a positive start to the season.'

Just to spice things up, on the eve of the game Forest signed Sheffield United's former Derby player Max Lowe, who was born in South Normanton and came through the academy. In the away end supporting the Reds was former striker Nigel Jemson, who scored his first goal for Forest against Derby at the Baseball Ground, and the fathers of two current Forest players: Neil Back, the former England and Leicester rugby union captain and father to full-back Fin, and David Johnson, father of highly rated striker Brennan Johnson. Among the home fans was David Nugent.

The game saw the return of the familiar early goal as Tom Lawrence smashed Derby ahead after 11 minutes of a first half in which Forest were frankly dreadful. After half-time, Derby ran out of steam and Forest's determination not to lose was evident, culminating in Johnson volleying home in the 82nd minute. Again, Kelle Roos might have thought he could have been more of a sturdy barrier. Along the way, there were the usual incidents: Craig Forsyth putting his studs in where no studs should go and strong claims for a Derby penalty when Worrall thrust out a shoulder to intercept a ball in the area.

Both managers agreed that a draw seemed fair. 'On reflection it was a fair result,' said Rooney. 'I didn't feel they were creating that many clear-cut chances, but they had the momentum in the second half.' The hugely improved second-half performance and equaliser may well have kept Hughton in his post, at least for the foreseeable future. 'Probably from where we have been, we are thinking this is not going to be our day again,' said Hughton, 'but I thought when we got our breakthrough it was deserved.' An international break gave the Forest ownership time to chew things over in terms of the rarely stable managerial situation.

An attendance of 22,000 was way below the norm for such a fixture, but this was perhaps more of a reflection of the chaotic running of the club with season tickets having only just been made available, despite the campaign being four games deep, as well as stadiums only just opening up fully again after the end of Covid-19 restrictions. In addition, season tickets were not valid for this game. Besides, acquiring tickets for this fixture from a dysfunctional ticket office added another layer of complication.

When the dust settled, it was the fourth 1-1 in succession and Derby were now without a win against Forest in nine games – the longest unbeaten streak of either team in this fixture. Once again, the Reds maintained possession of the Brian Cough Trophy, extending their ownership to 915 days. With the return fixture on 22 January, they were certain to hold it for at least 1,062 days, 11 days short of Derby's record of 1,073 days.

Despite the promising second-half performance and point, Forest lost their next game – and the one after that – making their start to the season their worst in 108 years. Unsurprisingly, Hughton paid for it with his job, his contract terminated on Thursday, 16 September, the morning after a home defeat to Middlesbrough. Frustration with the way the club was being run under Marinakis grew, fuelled by Brennan Johnson's father David tweeting, 'Just so angry and disappointed how this club is run. It's embarrassing (the whole board should have gone) they are a disgrace. The last time I said anything bad about the club, Giannis called me. I'll wait for his call, I guess, as I was right the first time.'

The Giannis in question here is Giannis Ventros, Marinakis's right-hand man, who was both listed on the Nottingham Forest page at Companies House as chief executive officer yet, at the same time, was absent from the role on the 'Who's Who' section of the club website. Just to make the situation more confusing, Forest's appointment of Dane Murphy as chief executive officer was confirmed on their website.

Confusion reigned at the City Ground as to precisely how the club was being run behind the scenes in the wake of yet another managerial casualty when things were supposed to be different under the Greek ownership. After all, when Marinakis first took over, he appointed Nicholas Randall QC as chairman, whose open letter in June 2017 promised that they were 'committed to building structures at the club which give the fans and the community a voice and the opportunity to participate with action. We will do this through the advisory board and observers at board meetings: fans and young people will play a crucial part in our project.' None of these structures yet existed. The letter also placed strong emphasis on stability, going as far as to assure supporters that the incumbent manager, Mark Warburton, would be given 'the precious commodity of time'. He was sacked seven months later and Hughton's departure now meant that Marinakis had burned through five managers in four years. Despite the arguments in favour of disposing of Hughton, the club appeared anything but stable, with over 80 incoming loan or permanent deals for players since the open letter.

While Hughton was clearing his desk, it was reported that Derby were close to agreeing a points deduction with the EFL for breaching financial fair play rules, with a nine-point punishment being mooted and perhaps a further suspended three points pending future compliance. Just 24 hours later, it got worse as Derby's steady start to the season was utterly undermined by a statement appearing on their website announcing that the club, the ultimate holding company of the group, and all of the subsidiary companies, had filed notices of intention to appoint administrators. Manager Wayne Rooney said he learned of this not from Mel Morris or anyone at the club, but from Sky Sports. The blame was laid at the Covid-19 pandemic, but fans felt that the ruinous running of the club was the sole responsibility of Morris as a 12-point deduction beckoned. On top of the possible nine points Derby were being threatened with for breaching EFL accounting rules, the club was staring down the barrel of a 21-point deduction, which would almost certainly mean relegation to the third tier for the first time since 1984.

The following day both teams chalked up league wins, giving fans some brief respite from the woes of events off the field. Forest posted their first away win on a weekend in front of fans in 24 months by beating Huddersfield Town, while Derby beat Stoke City 2-1 at Pride Park, thanks in part to a goal by Max Bird on his 21st birthday.

A day later, Morris gave an interview to BBC Radio Derby in which he doubled down on the explanation offered in the club statement, 'Had it not been for Covid, we'd have had £20m more to service our creditors, to service our debts, and the club would not be in administration. Period.' Asked if he felt he had fired managers too easily, Morris adopted hypophora, 'Did I make mistakes? Absolutely. No question. Did some of that come from a lack of experience? Absolutely.' He went on to emphasise how hard the task was and how hard he had worked to make it successful, but ultimately admitted that he failed.

Morris presided over a wage bill that had spiralled out of control to around 161 per cent of the club's turnover for the 2017/18 season. He then appointed Frank Lampard as manager, followed by Phillip Cocu and Wayne Rooney – all famous on the world's stage and none working for free. With financial fair play rules nipping at his heels, he sold Pride Park to another of his companies for an eye-watering figure of £81m – a fee contested by the EFL – allowing the club to temporarily squirm around FFP restrictions in the short term. Yet the consequences of such decisions were now coming home to roost as football creditors sought £10m in full and an American private equity firm queued up for £20m. Both would have to get behind HMRC who were owed almost £30m.

Whichever way the situation was looked at, it was an incredibly bleak one. Plunged into administration, the club didn't own the stadium or training ground and were staring League One in the face. Liquidation couldn't be entirely ruled out. All of that made the decision to turn down three summer bids from Forest for defender Lee Buchanan even more baffling. The final offer was reported to be worth an initial £1.5m with add-ons but was rejected, despite the defender being out of contract at the end of the season, meaning he would be available at a reduced fee the following January. It appeared that Morris was unable to see the wood for the trees.

At this point in the season with the state that each club found themselves in, it felt like two drunken teenagers scrapping in a pub car park having gorged themselves on cheap lager and sloppy kebabs. A few days later, Forest appointed their 22nd full-time manager in 21 years, announcing former Swansea City boss Steve Cooper, who had also led England's Under-16s and Under-17s. Significantly, Cooper's job title was head coach, not manager, hinting at a different way of doing things at the City Ground in order to maintain some much-needed continuity and stability at the club.

The day after Forest's announcement, Derby's website posted a wholly more sobering, if not unexpected, statement, 'Andrew Hosking, Carl Jackson and Andrew Andronikou, managing directors at business advisory firm Quantuma, have been appointed joint administrators of The Derby County Football Club Limited (Derby County) on 22nd September 2021.' The league table was immediately updated to incorporate the automatic 12-point deduction for entering administration, sending Derby to the foot, six points adrift of second-bottom Forest. That further nine-point deduction was still on the cards. Hosking said, 'We are in the early stages of assessing the options available to the club and would invite any parties to come forward. Our immediate objectives are to ensure the club completes all its fixtures in the Championship this season and finding interested parties to safeguard the club and its employees.'

This wasn't a blip or even a relegation, but a significant threat to Derby's existence. Forest being second from the table bottom with only one win from eight games suddenly seemed not so bad.

Over the following days, the extent of Derby's situation was laid bare. Rooney revealed how he hadn't spoken to Morris for seven weeks and at one point had even resorted to using the club doctor's phone in an attempt to get some answers, 'He [Morris] answered the phone, so obviously he could answer calls from the club doctor but not the manager. It was not ideal.' Despite this, the early signs from the administrators were optimistic. 'I do not consider, at all, that this could be a liquidation scenario like Bury,' said Hosking. Derby County Women would also be affected and lose some funding from the men's team but would not enter administration as they were a separate entity and operated on a self-sufficient hybrid funding model. 'If the main club remains in administration when the cycle of application for the [Women's] Championship comes around, I think we would not submit an application regardless of our league position,' said chief executive Duncan Gibb in reference to an application for promotion to the second tier in the Women's National League. 'That would be sensible because, ultimately, I'm the custodian of the football club so I always have to do what is right for the football club. If that means we have to keep our tinder dry for a season then so be it.' The forthcoming fixtures against Forest Ladies, to be held at the City Ground for the first, time remained very much on the cards. It was Forest's hope that it would attract a record attendance for an FA Women's Northern Premier League game, held by Derby when 2,318 saw Forest beat the Rams. The Forest website happily bought into the rivalry, 'With the demand for women's football in Nottingham, the aim is to beat that record!'

Cooper's first game in charge of Forest brought some relief with a 1-1 draw at home with Millwall. Max Lowe, formerly of Derby, equalised with a fluke goal when he saw his deep cross nestle in the net. Derby lost 1-0 at Sheffield United to a last-minute penalty converted by Billy Sharp. Actual football was only a very temporary escape from Derby's perilous situation, though, and Steve McClaren voluntarily stepped down from his position as technical director but remained involved as a senior advisor in an effort to preserve jobs. A few days later, Quantuma put out a tweet inviting 'all parties to register their interest', which had an air of desperation about it, even if that wasn't the intention.

The first Forest v Derby female fixture did take place at the City Ground and on Sunday, 3 October and, once again, the attendance record for the FA Women's Northern Premier League was broken as 4,443 sat through four seasons of weather in one afternoon to see Derby claim a 2-0 win. Derby went in a point behind their rivals in the league, but with a game in hand, having only dropped points once so far. 'Sunday is a massive game,' said Ewe Rams boss Sam Griffiths prior to kick-off. 'It [a win] would also allow the belief within the squad to grow. They are a quietly confident group overall but always have a will to keep developing and a win in the East Midlands derby over their biggest rivals is one not to be taken lightly.' The Reds themselves were just three points behind leaders Wolves.

Forest had a great opportunity to take the lead when Freya Thomas was felled and the referee awarded a penalty, yet Charlotte Clarke in the Derby goal saved well from Rosie Axten. With former Red Precious Hamilton now playing up front for the Rams, the game swung Derby's way and Emily Joyce capitalised on a defensive mix-up to give her team the lead. Minutes later and just before half-time, Ellie Gilliat's free kick found the bottom corner to put the Rams two goals clear. The game ended 2-0 and Derby leapfrogged their counterparts. They completed the double over Forest by beating them 1-0 at Pride Park in March thanks to a goal from Sherry McCue, who slotted a penalty home in the first half. Typically, the game was not without incident as, in the second half, Derby's Megan Tinsley handled a goalbound curling effort from Becky Anderson and was promptly shown a red card. Gianna Mitchell blazed her penalty over the bar and the match ended 1-0.

Given the relentless doom surrounding the precarious situation of the men's team, Derby Women's victory in Nottingham represented a proud moment for the city and another was around the corner when, in the following days, Derby was confirmed as one of the eight UK cities to be longlisted to become the next UK City of Culture. Each candidate would receive £40,000 to support the next stage of their applications. The bid, led by Adam Buss, the chief executive of the city's Quad arts venue and bid director for the 2025 campaign, told *The Guardian*, 'We've always lived a bit in the shadows – maybe people go past on the M1, or the train. But what we want to say with city of culture is "Stop! Come here."' To achieve this, the plan was to showcase Derby's industry and artistic prowess.

To temper such optimism – after all, this was Derby in 2021 – reports of Mike Ashley's interest in buying Derby County surfaced after the British billionaire sold Newcastle United to a public investment fund from Saudi Arabia. In the week that Quantuma announced its desire to appeal against the 12-point deduction, it was reported that former owner Andy Appleby was representing a client who was interested in buying Derby. As numerous rumours and counter-rumours surfaced, American businessman Chris Kirchner, founder, owner and chief executive of Slync.io, a global logistics company, wrote to supporters announcing that he wanted to take the club out of administration. The 34-year-old stated that he was 'at the beginning of procedures that must take place with the administrators and the EFL' and had 'already been in conversation with all parties to discuss where to start'. With the team picking up points, such an announcement gave everyone connected with the club real hope of overcoming the 12-point penalty and somehow avoiding relegation. The significance of the rivalry seems to have been a lesson Kirchner learned early on and used to curry favour with Derby fans on social media. When challenged about whether he had the funds to pull the deal off, Kirchner replied via Twitter with, 'I'll pass on expanding beyond saying Nottingham Forest sucks.'

The morning of 16 November brought the news Rams fans were dreading, if at least expecting. Quantuma announced that they had agreed a further nine-point deduction with the EFL, plus a further suspended three points, after the club admitted to breaches of the EFL's profitability and sustainability rules. Quantuma also confirmed that the appeal against the previous 12-point deduction for entering administration had been dismissed. This meant that Derby's total deduction for the season was 21 points, meaning they were bottom of the table with minus three points and 18 from safety. Despite Rooney coaxing some promising performances from the hastily constructed squad, relegation to League One seemed inevitable. 'This matter has been determined under the terms of an "Agreed Decision" reached between the league and the club and was formally ratified by an Independent Disciplinary Commission chair as per the requirements of EFL regulations,' said the statement on Derby's website.

Quantuma's Carl Jackson said, 'This has been a difficult matter to navigate bearing in mind the various issues concerned. Whilst point deductions are never ideal for any club, it was critical to the club's future that all matters were concluded between the EFL and the club in relation to historical issues. This conclusion allows us to proceed with our restructuring strategy for the club with prospective interested parties.' If there was a silver lining among the thickest of dark clouds, this was it – Derby were no longer fighting legal battles or sifting through admin or carrying out very public disagreements with the EFL; they had swallowed the bitter medicine and could at least start to take their first steps towards what they hoped would be a long-term recovery.

Despite the pending relegation, Derby County was still a relatively attractive proposition for someone out there, or at least the club and its fans hoped it was. Furthermore, their previous relegation to the third tier was a short stint as they won promotion back at the second time of asking and then walked off with the Second Division title the very next year. Maybe a stint in League One could be the cleansing experience the club needed.

Yet that level is now a very different beast from what it was in the mid-1980s. Traditionally, big clubs like Sunderland, Sheffield Wednesday and Ipswich Town were down there and making very hard work of extracting themselves from its tentacles. League One was favouring clubs that spent wisely and well within their means, such as Rotherham United and, indeed, Wycombe Wanderers, who themselves would justifiably wonder why such points deductions were not administered the previous season. Regardless, Derby could at least start to move on.

Days later, a statement of affairs was available via Companies House, showing that HMRC were owed north of £36m. The list of creditors ran into the hundreds, including Derby City Council, East Midlands Ambulance Service NHS Trust, Dungannon Swifts Football Club, St

John Ambulance, Derby County Community Trust and even their own supporters for advertising on the DCFCFans web forum. The team responded by promptly beating Bournemouth 3-2 at Pride Park, the Cherries' first away defeat of the season, meaning Derby were back at square one on zero points.

Embarrassed by the club owing such a substantial sum of money to St John Ambulance, Derby fan Andy Mitchell set up a fundraising page via JustGiving and within days raised over £12,000 for the charity. The sums owed to so many creditors offered a peek behind the curtain at the type of costs flowing in and out of a Championship club, perhaps raising more questions than answers. Yet not for the first time, it was fans who had to put their hands in their pockets to help fill the gaping holes created by over-spending.

By Christmas Eve, still no deal with any of the interested parties had materialised, prompting Kirchner to announce the withdrawal of his bid. He had previously aired his frustration over the whole process in an exchange on Twitter with a fan enquiring about how any proposed deal was coming along, saying, 'I do have issues with the delays and inability to keep deadlines. The only one to really blame for this situation is Mel Morris. Proper fuck job.' Such language was an obvious sign of his desire to walk away from it all, having been unable to agree a deal with either Morris or Quantuma.

'It is with real sadness that I can confirm I am withdrawing from the process to buy Derby County Football Club,' Kirchner said in his statement. 'First and foremost, I would like to apologise to the fans. As you know, I've been in talks with the administrators for about two months.

Two weeks ago, I made a formal offer to buy the club. I believe I presented a very detailed, generous and ambitious long-term sustainable business plan. It included purchasing the stadium, future funding and maintaining the academy's status. We improved that offer further today. I wanted to agree a deal that I thought was in the best interests of all parties, but, unfortunately, the last 24 hours has proven that just isn't possible. So it is with deep regret that I must now stand aside and let the administrators pursue their own course.'

Hours later, Quantuma responded, '[We] would like to put on record we disagree with that has been said. While yesterday was difficult, it provided stimulus to one of the remaining bidders who increased his offer for club. We expect to name preferred bidder status imminently.' It later transpired that any such naming of preferred bidders was nowhere near 'imminent'.

With January's transfer window about to open, Derby's situation seemed even further from any form of resolution and the likelihood of losing even more players increasing by the hour. In stark contrast, Cooper's appointment at Forest inspired a remarkable run of form. Christmas Day found Derby bottom of the table and 17 points from safety, while Forest were a point off the play-offs and top of the form table since Cooper took charge, at the same time as Nottingham's LadBaby celebrated their fourth consecutive Christmas number one in the UK Singles Chart with 'Sausage Rolls for Everyone' (featuring Ed Sheeran and Elton John).

Just eight days before the two teams met at the City Ground, Friday, 14 January turned out to be a seismic day. The Bennerley Viaduct, a Victorian railway bridge which runs between Derbyshire and Nottinghamshire, was opened to the public after five decades of disrepair and dereliction. Thanks to repair costs of £1.7m, with £560,000 coming from the Railway Heritage Trust, one could now walk or cycle across it for the first time since 1968.

Yet the situation was less rosy concerning Derby County. The day was earmarked to finally announce Quantuma's preferred bidder, with Mike Ashley and Andy Appleby known to be in the frame. Yet this failed to materialise as the EFL demanded evidence that the club had the funds to operate through the rest of the season. Progress towards any outcome was floundering on the rocks of disputed compensation claims from Middlesbrough and Wycombe Wanderers, still deeply irked that from their perspective, Derby's financial irregularities denied them a play-off place in 2019 and survival in the Championship in 2021 respectively. Quantuma and the EFL appeared to be blame each other for the impasse. On top of that, talismanic defender Phil Jagielka left for Stoke City because of the restrictions imposed on Derby without proof of funds, prompting a petition organised by Rams fans to urge the sports minister to look into the deadlock. Everything just left Wayne Rooney increasingly frustrated.

Rarely have the two teams met in recent times when both have been so beloved by each set of supporters. Derby fans fully embraced the efforts of their team by following away in huge numbers and mobilising to do what they could to both show their deep appreciation for the team's remarkable results and to challenge the existential threat to their club. Forest followers, too, fell hard and fast for Cooper's team, evolving from the bottom of the table with only a single point to fancied challengers for a play-off spot. And both sets of supporters were buoyant after the previous weekend's results: Forest gaining a hard-earned win at Millwall thanks to an added-time winner from Lewis Grabban – hard on the heels of dumping Arsenal out of the FA Cup at the City Ground for the second time in four years – and Derby beating Sheffield United at Pride Park.

The Reds sat in ninth place with 37 points in a table unbalanced by postponements owing to the Omicron variant of Covid. The Rams took a huge psychological step forward by lifting themselves off the bottom with their 2-0 win against the Blades, reaching 14 points. Reading – themselves unravelling after their own six-point deduction and on a terrible run of form – were within sight, just eight points ahead. Indeed, were one to add the removed 21 points to Derby's total, it would place them two points behind Forest and just below them in the table. Despite their wildly contrasting fortunes, the two clubs once again gravitated towards each other like moons around a planet.

Ahead of the game, it remained the case that no Rams boss without the famous surname Clough had won at the City Ground since George Jobey in September 1925. Furthermore, it was also the case that Derby held the record for most consecutive days as holders of the Brian Clough Trophy – 1,073 days. The date of the game represented 1,062 days since Forest took the trophy from Derby with their 1-0 win on 25 February 2019. Were Derby to win, they would preserve their record. Should Forest draw or win, they would break Derby's tally. On top of that, Derby's mere existence was under significant threat since they had until the end of the month to prove they could operate until the end of the season, meaning that the fixture could well be the final one between the two clubs in their current guise. Although perhaps not the most crucial game that has ever played out between the two clubs, it was arguably one of the most significant.

The noise in the week prior to the match was ceaseless. Statement upon statement was released. The EFL stressed there was no vendetta against Derby and certainly no desire to see the club liquidated. Middlesbrough dug their heels in and reiterated their stance that they lost revenue as a result of Derby's breach of the Profit & Sustainability Rules. The language they used was forthright, 'Without breaking the confidentiality of the proceedings, in simple terms, MFC allege Derby County and its directors systematically cheated under the P&S Rules and that such cheating affects the integrity of the competition.' The word 'cheat' cropped up on more than one occasion, 'In simple terms so far as MFC is concerned, had Derby County not cheated, MFC would have been in the play-offs [in 2019]. However, Derby County did cheat and, as a result, MFC lost the opportunities that arise as a result of that.'

With the EFL, Middlesbrough and Wycombe standing firm, Derby County and its administrators were running out of options. The fans mobilised and lobbied parliament via a petition and urged anybody with clout to speak out and draw attention to the seriousness of the situation, including Nottingham South MP Lilian Greenwood who wrote to government minister Nadine Dorries asking for her support in securing the club's future. 'Some of my constituents' families have supported Derby County for over 70 years,' said Greenwood, 'and this founder member of the Football League simply cannot be allowed to disappear.'

All the while, Rooney's job grew harder. Influential midfielder Graeme Shinnie was sold to Wigan Athletic for an undisclosed fee, reported to be in the region of £30,000 by various sources. Although the Scot expressed a desire to remain at the club, his being out of contract in the summer meant that any funds from a sale – no matter how small – would be better than no funds, even if the reported fee seemed alarmingly low. Millwall pursued promising forward Louie Sibley with offers that would have previously been deemed to be derisory. On top of all that, Everton sacking Rafael Benítez sparked speculation that Rooney's boyhood club might fancy offering him a shot at management in the Premier League.

On the eve of the return derby, Rooney spoke openly about how difficult managing the team was under such circumstances, unleashing his anger upon Morris. 'He is why we are in this situation,' he said. 'He did not speak to me when he was at the club. I don't like to waste my breath on that anyway. He has moved on and left us in a very difficult situation. I am sure he is enjoying his life at home.'

Yet the dark clouds receded ever so slightly in terms of Derby's predicament on the same day with the news that a wealthy US family had made a £28m bid to take the club out of administration and, in doing so, prove they had the funds to complete the season. The bid from the Binnie family, founders of the investment company Carlisle Capital, was not said to include Pride Park Stadium, which Morris still owned. There was much checking and waiting to be done before such a bid could be ratified, but the fact that a bid was on the table offered hope that liquidation could be avoided. In the meantime, there was a game of football to be contested.

Left-back Max Lowe maintained the long-standing tradition of facing his former club in this fixture by taking his place in Forest's starting XI after an enforced absence due to injury. Intriguingly, Lee Buchanan – the subject of numerous bids from Forest – was Derby's left-back. Frustratingly for Forest, Joe Worrall missed out owing to broken ribs he suffered in the win at Millwall. Given his comments after a previous meeting in which he felt frustrated not to beat the Rams, pointing out, 'We didn't play Barcelona, it was Derby,' no doubt he was as frustrated as anyone to sit this one out.

Eventually and despite the background noise, the 100th league meeting between these two enemies kicked off. Forza Garibaldi unveiled a huge display in the Trent End of the Nottingham skyline and a threatening Robin Hood figure with the slogan 'Welcome to our Forest Kingdom'. Homemade £5 notes rained down on the Derby fans from above, featuring the face of Mel Morris in homage to the ditty the home fans had been singing in mockery of the rivals' situation, 'Derby's going down with a fiver in the bank.' Disturbingly there were reports of flares being thrown into the Derby fans from the home supporters seated above them.

The away side made the better start and should have taken the lead when Tom Lawrence played a quick one-two with Colin Kazim-Richards and found himself through on goal. Convert the chance and Lawrence would become the first player to score in consecutive derbies since Matěj Vydra in 2014 and the first to score in both derbies in a season since Britt Assombalonga in 2014/15. Yet he dragged his shot wide of the post. Cooper adjusted his team's formation to counter Derby's threat and the game swung noticeably in their direction, even if the first half was, aside from Lawrence's miss and Forest keeper Brice Samaba sustaining a small moon-sized egg on his head after a collision with Lawrence, fairly uneventful and low on quality.

Just three minutes into the second half the deadlock was broken by Grabban, scoring his third goal in three games. A free kick by James Garner was headed back into the box by Scott McKenna and the ball eventually feel to the feet of Grabban who sent the Trent End into ecstasy. Flares emitting red smoke rained down on to the playing surface and a handful of fans joined them on the pitch, unable to contain their delight. The home side grew stronger and looked the more likely team to score again, which they duly did in the 82nd minute when Brennan Johnson played a ball wide to Philip Zinckernagel from his own half and then scampered upfield to convert the Dane's return ball. In doing so, Johnson did what Lawrence had been unable to do and he did indeed score in consecutive derbies and both in a single season. Spookily, it was in the 82nd minute that he had equalised against Derby in the previous fixture too. More flares. More fans on the pitch. Later in the season, on collecting his award as the Championship's Young Player of the Year and being asked about his 2021/22 highlights, Johnson recalled these goals, 'I think the goals against Derby – such a big game for Nottingham Forest and really good to do it against them.'

Lawrence was not to be outdone though and he followed in Johnson's footsteps by converting a penalty in the 88th minute after being felled by Steve Cook. The denouement was shaping up to be a tense one. Yet the home side managed the game well – including the six minutes of added time – and came away with a deserved win, which kept them in the play-off race and put a dent in Derby's hopes of pulling off a miraculous survival. The obligatory red card was brandished to Derby's Ravel Morrison for a scything challenge on Zinckernagel and, at the final whistle, it was just like old times as a scuffle broke out between both sets of players in which words were spoken and heads were grabbed, resulting in charges of failing to ensure their players conducted themselves in an orderly fashion and a fine of £10,000 for each club. On the one hand, it was a game that played all the East Midlands derby hits in the right order, but given the Rams' very real prospects of relegation (at best) and Forest looking very much upwards rather than at mid-table, it had a sense of *fin de siècle*: there was every chance that it might be the last such fixture for at least a season.

'In the second half we were good and I felt we created the real opportunities,' said Cooper. 'It was disappointing they got a goal back, because otherwise I thought we managed the game well. We were definitely good for the win. There was only one winner today, no doubt about that.'

Forest's win set a new record for unbeaten games in this fixture as they were now ten without defeat against their old foes, beating the previous record of nine held by Derby between October 1904 and September 1921. Moreover, Forest were about to set a new record for the number of days as holders of the Brian Clough Trophy. The trophy would extend its long residency at the City Ground for a little longer – perhaps a lot longer – depending upon what the next month or so held for Derby County.

The following day, Burnley gained a point against Arsenal, meaning they now had 12 points in the Premier League, ensuring that Derby's record low of 11 points was still intact. Despite the pain of their defeat at the City Ground, those connected with Derby had, for the moment at least, other things to worry about. 'The next few days are crucial. I've had assurances that I don't have to sell players,' said Rooney. 'We need preferred bidders to help this club exist. If not, we will have to see what we can do at the end of the window.'

Rooney's fears were eased with the EFL agreeing to a month-long extension of the deadline set to demonstrate proof of funds until the end of the season. 'Today's development will allow the club to meet its ongoing obligations,' read a Derby County statement, 'while giving a further four weeks to continue the discussions with the interested bidders and relevant stakeholders in respect of a sale, alongside providing additional time to seek clarity on the claims from Middlesbrough and Wycombe.' They could breathe ever so slightly easier, for the time being at least. Further encouraging news came when Rooney explained that he had turned down Everton's approach to be interviewed for their manager's job. 'Everton approached my agent and asked me to interview for the vacant job, which I turned down,' said Rooney. 'I believe I will be a Premier League manager – I believe I'm ready for that, 100 per cent. And if that is with Everton one day in the future that would be absolutely great. But I've got a job here that I'm doing at Derby County which is an important job to me.'

On the eve of the closing of the January transfer window, both clubs were thrust into the nation's footballing spotlight on Sunday, 30 January when Sky built their Super Sunday around each of their fixtures in the absence of any Premier League games that weekend owing to a brief winter break. A march from the Assembly Rooms to Pride Park ahead of Derby's match against Birmingham City was organised by supporters in an effort to bring their club's decline to the forefront of the wider footballing public. Approximately 9,000 fans marched with flags and banners pleading for a solution to the crisis before settling down to watch Derby play against the Blues in front of a capacity crowd, including Richard Keogh, and an attendance that was the highest in the Championship so far that season.

The atmosphere was somewhat punctured, though, as in only the seventh minute, Lyle Taylor, signed a few days earlier on loan from Forest, pounced to give the away side the lead. He took great pleasure in scoring, his smile seemingly as wide as the distance between Nottingham and Derby. It got worse and Derby found themselves 2-0 down until the 87th minute, at which point Luke Plange's strike reduced the arrears and offered a glimpse of hope. And then something extraordinary happened: exactly 365 days since suffering a second serious knee injury, Krystian Bielik, on his return to first-team action, produced an overhead kick to equalise in the 96th minute. Pandemonium reigned and Derby started to believe harder than they had before. They were now just seven points from safety and the team they were chasing, Reading, were imploding harder and faster with each passing game.

Forest, having beaten bottom club Barnsley in midweek, stood on the brink of finally breaking into the play-off places. A win at struggling Cardiff was all that was required, yet they fluffed their lines and lost 2-1. The bigger picture changed once again: after four games of the season, both clubs had looked in danger of relegation. Midway through, the notion that there might be a whole league between them seemed possible as Forest charged towards promotion and Derby towards League One. Yet with defeat at Cardiff and both Grabban and Worrall sidelined through injury, maybe both clubs would – once again – be contesting this fixture in the same league in 2022/23. This was, of course, assuming that Derby could continue trading.

Mel Morris finally breaking his silence and releasing a statement in which he offered to personally take over the claims made by Middlesbrough and Wycombe offered some daylight in terms of arriving at a resolution. 'I invite Boro, and in due course, Wycombe if they so wish, to take their claims to the High Court against me personally,' said Morris. He also questioned the consistency of the EFL's handling of FFP/P&S breaches, which some saw as an overt reference to Forest's relationship with Marinakis's other club, Olympiacos, 'I also question if the EFL examines player transaction between EFL and foreign clubs under common ownership with a view to ensuring "arm's length" fair value for transactions with related parties?' Forest did indeed have a history of trading players with Olympiacos, with some making minimal appearances and being transferred for undisclosed fees. There remained too many moving parts before any resolution to Derby's crisis could be entertained, but eventually some clarity was offered by Morris to complement the optimism on the pitch of the club pulling off a remarkable escape.

Forest rallied ahead of their meeting with FA Cup holders Leicester at the City Ground. Four years earlier, Arsenal came to Nottingham as holders but were defeated 4-2 in the third round by a startlingly young Forest side. Having put the Gunners out 1-0 again this time around, Forest then faced Leicester in the fourth round. The BBC screened the game live and, in their build-up, framed the game as an East Midlands derby. Comparisons were drawn between which miracle was the greater: Forest's rise from the Second Division to domestic and European champions or Leicester's 2015/16 Premier League title. Such debate and conjecture invariably still takes up just as much narrative space as the 'local derby' angle when it comes to such a fixture.

For some Leicester fans, the rivalry remains as fierce as ever as some supporters took it upon themselves to throw chairs and tables at the Fat Cats café and the Cross Keys pub in the city centre before the kick-off. But on the field, Forest once again performed their party trick of dumping the holders out as they eased to a 4-1 win, despite a Foxes fan running on to the field of play and attacking the Forest players celebrating their third goal of the afternoon. Shortly afterwards, a win at second-placed Blackburn Rovers put the Reds into the play-off places for the first time in the season, crowning Cooper's achievement of taking the side from the bottom of the table to sixth.

Things were looking rosier in Derby's garden, too, following a 3-1 win against Hull City, which drew Reading even closer into view as Barnsley and Peterborough continued to struggle. More significantly, on 11 February – the day before the Rams faced Middlesbrough at the Riverside Stadium – Derby County released a statement giving all fans the news they had been desperate to hear, 'As a direct result of private conversations between Mel Morris and Steve Gibson, both parties are pleased to announce that they have reached an accord on a resolution of the claims by Middlesbrough Football Club against Derby County Football Club, and others.' The details would remain private, but it did mean that plans to push forward in securing a sale could proceed with serious intent now that the claim from Middlesbrough was resolved and no longer an obstacle for prospective buyers. Many other snags remained, but at least one major one was no longer in play. A day later, Derby lost 4-1 against Gibson's Boro, yet as long as Reading, Barnsley and Peterborough continued to struggle, they had a chance and, given the latest developments, a growing belief that things might just turn out to be all right.

Yet the ownership issue lingered on and on and February brought three consecutive defeats. The EFL issued a statement on 28 February reminding all that the administrators had yet to provide any evidence of sufficient funding to complete the current season, thus missing the four-week extension to do so. In addition, the EFL stated that they 'await an urgent further update from them on both that and the announcement of a preferred bidder'. It took until early April for the preferred bidder to be eventually named and, despite seemingly walking away from the situation at the end of the previous year, it was Chris Kirchner.

An end to the months of uncertainty was in sight, but it would not be straightforward. Further negotiations would be required regarding Derby's continuing occupation of Pride Park, with suggestions that Kirchner would continue to rent the stadium from Morris. On top of that, Kirchner would be taking over a business that owed significant money to HMRC and various other creditors and, should he fail to pay unsecured creditors 25 per cent of what they were owed, a 15-point deduction lay in wait, be it in the current season or in League One in the increasingly likely event of relegation.

Quantuma's announcement of Kirchner being the preferred bidder sparked a flurry of interest in the historical content of his social media account. Several tweets containing misogynist and homophobic sentiments were retweeted by various users before the account was deleted. A statement given to BBC Radio Derby by a spokesperson for Kirchner said, 'The tweets took place nearly ten years ago … He was quoting song lyrics and movie quote. It is not his personal opinion. He recognises that the tweets are not suitable content. Which is why they have been deleted.' Despite all this, Derby's future was at least a step closer to being secured, while Kirchner created a new account and used it to respond to questions from supporters.

The Damoclesian sword finally fell on Derby on Easter Monday as they recorded their ninth successive away defeat, going down 1-0 at Queens Park Rangers and finally confirming their relegation. They needed to equal or better Reading's result, but predictably it was not a day without drama. Reading had taken an early lead at home to Swansea but found themselves 4-1 down with half an hour left to play, meaning there was still hope. However, a remarkable fightback by the Royals, culminating in a

95th-minute equaliser, confirmed third-tier football for the Rams. Former Derby man Tom Ince chipped in with a goal for Reading, while Tom Lawrence was dismissed around the same time as the Royals' equaliser. The scene of this miserable day for Derby was significant too: Loftus Road. This was the setting where 17 years ago, almost to the day, Forest had tumbled into the third tier. Like two planets orbiting the same sun, where one club goes, the other usually follows. After 14 years of a ram unrelentingly butting a tree trunk while enduring repeated lashes from the branches, they were finally uncoupled from this brutal ritual.

While Derby exited the Championship through the trapdoor, Forest took the express elevator. A superb run of form through March and April propelled them even further up the table, culminating in a clash at second-placed Bournemouth in the penultimate game of the season, which was effectively a decider for the second automatic promotion spot behind champions Fulham. A late goal for the Cherries denied Forest and consigned them to the agony of the play-offs, where they would meet Sheffield United, their opponents in the heart-breaking 2003 semi-finals.

On the eve of Forest's second leg, Kirchner announced he had exchanged contracts with Qauntuma and was soon to be funding Derby. Despite the contracts being conditional on the sale of the stadium, with reports saying that a local businessman was working on a deal to take ownership of Pride Park from Morris and rent it to Kirchner, he didn't anticipate any issues. The end of the most protracted, painful and difficult of takeover sagas seemed to be in sight. But there was a twist: Kirchner failed to meet multiple deadlines for completion and withdrew his offer, leaving Derby very high and dry. It got worse as Rooney then resigned, expressing the view that he felt the club needed someone with fresh energy to take it forward.

Just when all seemed lost, successful local businessman and lifelong supporter David Clowes stepped in and struck a deal to buy the club, having purchased Pride Park Stadium a few days earlier. As long as certain restrictions and the payment of outstanding debts were to be honoured, Derby could start the following season with a clean slate. Finally, the Rams were in a position to move on and out of one of the darkest periods in their history.

For Forest, another saga was unfolding. A fully earned 2-1 win at Bramall Lane in the first leg meant that Forest were in a commanding position for the return game at the City Ground, especially after Johnson gave them the lead in the first half on the night. But a spirited display and two goals from the Blades took the tie to extra time, then penalties after a 3-3 aggregate draw. Three outstanding saves from Brice Samba eventually vanquished the Blades and took Forest to Wembley for the first time since 1992, and their first trip to the new stadium, where they would meet Huddersfield Town.

The rivalry with Derby is never far away. Bobby Zamora, scorer of a last-minute goal in the 2014 play-off final for QPR against the Rams, recorded a message for the London-based Forest Supporters' Club, 'Just wanted to wish you all the best. Let's try and make Derby miserable again this time of year.' Zamora and Forest fans got their wish. An own goal settled what is often billed as the most expensive game in football and Forest achieved promotion to the Premier League for the first time since the previous millennium.

After 14 years of breathing the same Championship oxygen, hostilities – on the pitch at least – would temporarily cease as each club prepared for their very different adventures. In keeping with the tradition of this rivalry, when one club prospers, the other suffers.

* * *

Many lament the loss of the good old days when football was played on a Saturday at 3pm, when kids got passed over the turnstiles and when football clubs meant something more than being a vehicle for betting companies or cryptocurrency. Perhaps this is why such rivalries persist and, if anything, are even more important. They periodically remind us that for all the constant noise and chatter about record-breaking transfers, breakaway leagues and state ownership of football clubs propped up with petrodollars, there remains no better feeling in football than beating your local rivals.

'It's the mocking your mates, it's revelling and basking in the glory of beating them, no matter how you perform,' offered Shaun Barker. 'It could be the worst game of football ever played, but if you beat them, it doesn't matter. There is nothing more important to a fan than beating your rivals, over relegation.' If winning is everything, losing is unthinkable. 'You just don't want to bloody lose!' concurred Jamie Thrasivoulou.

Yet there is something upon which even Forest and Derby fans can find common ground. 'The one thing Derby and Forest fans will always agree on is that Brian Clough was a bloody genius,' said the poet. 'When anyone from Derby is abroad, they get asked if Derby is near Leicester or Nottingham. We do see ourselves as an underdog city.

Maybe part of that is to do with Brian Clough; I'm sure if Cloughie had stayed at Derby, Derby would have been European champions because he was just such a great manager.' Perhaps so, but the fact he went and did precisely that with Forest not dimmed Clough's standing one iota among Derby fans.

As times change, rivalries and fans change. 'It's different now,' said Steve Sutton. 'The Baseball Ground created a tremendous atmosphere because they were right above you. People were under sheds like the old Trent End. The noise that came out of there when you were stood in that goal was phenomenal. You could hear every comment. Modern grounds are less intimidating. There isn't the violence now that there was.'

Indeed, the violence has been largely transported away from modern stadia and even organised meetings on wasteland for a good old-fashioned, no-holds-barred dust-up seem antiquated. Yet the spite, bitterness and venom remain alive and well on social media. And despite the degree of sanitisation that modern football entails, 'Even now, when working on the radio [for BBC Radio Notts as a pundit], it's the first game I look for,' added Sutton.

At its most fundamental level, the mechanics of a local rivalry are very simple:

> *And there's only two teams in this town*
> *And you must follow one or the other*
> *Let us win, let them lose, not the other way round*
> *In a northern industrial town*

It's not until the finale of the song above when Billy Bragg reveals that the northern industrial town about which he sings is not Leeds or Manchester, Sheffield nor Glasgow, and not Nottingham or Derby. It's Belfast.

The point Bragg is making is not only that Belfast is like any other northern industrial town in terms of football, but also that football rivalries are found anywhere and everywhere. Like words through a stick of rock, being a fan of one team or the other cuts all the way through a community. Whether you are red or blue, or in this case, red or white, defines you. And being branded as such means carrying around with you a range of emotions from despair through to anguish and occasionally utter and unbridled elation.

Regardless of class, race, gender, sexuality or any other identity marker, willing your team to win and the other to lose transcends everything. If your team can't win, then the next best thing is for the other lot to lose.

It's a weird and all-consuming existence being so closely tied to the fortunes of your club in relation to the other, yet at the same time, it's arguably the most natural thing in the world. No doubt Neolithic farmers, while proud of the crop they produced, took just as much pleasure in the failing of the crops of that other lot just a few miles away. For all the pride enjoyed by one mob in building Stonehenge, it's a fair bet that a rival lot just down the road simply dismissed it as a bunch of badly placed stones. One likes to think that a range of 'Amesbury Forever' stickers mysteriously appeared on the side of a hulking block of one of the sarsen stones overnight back in the Neolithic era, only to be scratched off and replaced by 'West Amesbury Boys' stickers the following evening.

We define ourselves not just by our own achievements, but also by the failings of others. We measure our success in relation to others' shortcomings. We want to be better than the others – not everyone, but certainly those who are comparable. If we are doing better than them, we feel vindicated; our life has meaning. Our identity is composed of not only what moves us, speaks to or what we love, but also what we hate.

Brothers bicker: it was always thus. Adolf and Rudolf Dassler's feud led to the creation of Adidas and Puma. Liam and Noel Gallagher's simmering rage towards each other shows no signs of diminishing with age. Even football's beloved Charlton brothers seemed to be cut from different cloths. Familiarity apparently breeds contempt, even more so in the case of being so closely bound. It is a parental figure that binds such bickering brothers together, reminding them of what they have in common. When it comes to the relentless squabbling between Forest and Derby, Brian Clough is that father figure, reminding each of better times behind them, while also standing as a permanent beacon of hope for what might be achieved in the future. Yet neither can escape each other's existence, each in a permanent state of resentment towards the other for daring to exist so close by.

Acknowledgements

THANK YOU to John McGovern, Shaun Barker, Steve Sutton and Jamie Thrasivoulou who gave up their time to speak to me. I remain deeply grateful for your patience and insight. Thank you to Daniel Taylor for having an extensive collection of memorabilia and being kind enough to share parts of it. Thank you to Matt Oldroyd for your encouragement, support and steady stream of excellent historical research. Thank you to Richard Harrison for the programmes. Thank you to Ollie Wright and Blake Fallows for their Derby wisdom. Thank you to Gareth Davis for his meticulous attention to detail. Thank you to all of the authors of the books listed in the bibliography; your books are a treasure trove of insight. Thank you to anyone connected with the British Newspaper Archive website. And thank you to the podcasters, bloggers and tweeters whose thoughts have seeped into my mind, and this book. Finally, thank you to Jenny and Anya for tolerating this affliction.

Bibliography

Newspapers
Aberdeen Press and Journal
Athletic News
Birmingham Daily Post
Bolton Evening News
Burton Chronicle
Coventry Evening Telegraph
Derbyshire Advertiser and Journal
Derby Daily Telegraph
Derby Evening Telegraph
Daily Express
Daily Mail
Football News
Football Post (Nottingham)
The Guardian
Lancashire Evening Post
Leicester Daily Post
Liverpool Echo
London Evening Standard
Manchester Evening News
Nottingham Daily Guardian
Nottingham Evening Post
Nottinghamshire Guardian
Nottingham Journal
Nottingham Post
The People

Reading Observer
Sheffield Daily Telegraph
Sheffield Evening Telegraph
The Sportsman
Sports Argus
Sporting Life
Sunday Express
Sunday Mirror
Weekly Dispatch
Yorkshire Post and Leeds Intelligencer

Magazines
Punch
Forest Review
United Review
The Ram
The Rampage
Bandy and Shinty, issue two (Steve Wright)
Bandy and Shinty, issue five (Phil Juggins)
Bandy and Shinty, issue three
The Sun Soccer Annual 1972
FourFourTwo

Books
Adams, David Wallace, *More than a Game: The Carlisle Indians Take to the Gridiron, 1893–1917* (Oxford University Press, 2001)
Barrett, Michael & Sque, David, *Preston North End – The Rise of the Invincibles* (Invincible Books, 2016)
Beckett, John, and Brand, Ken, *Nottingham: An Illustrated History* (Manchester University Press, 1997)
Bickerton, Bob, *The Essential History of Nottingham Forest* (Headline Book Publishing, 2002)
Bromfield, Craig, *Be Good, Love Brian: Growing up with Brian Clough* (Mudlark HarperCollins Publishers, 2021)

Broughton, Chris, *Forest Ever Forest* (Tricky Red Publications, 2001)
Brown, Paul, *Savage Enthusiasm* (Goal Post, 2017)
Chapman, Lee, *More Than a Match: A Player's Story* (Stanley Paul, 1992)
Clough, Brian, *The Autobiography* (Partridge Press, 1994)
Clough, Brian, *Walking on Water: My Life* (Headline Book Publishing, 2002)
Craven, Maxwell, *An Illustrated History of Derby* (The Breedon Books Publishing Company, 2007)
Ellis, Andy, *Derby County Football Club 1888–1996* (The History Press, 2008)
Ellis, Andy, *Derby County FC: The History of the Baseball Ground* (JMD Media Ltd, 2012)
Gemmill, Archie, *Archie Gemmill: Both Sides of the Border* (Hodder and Stoughton, 2005)
Goldblatt, David, *The Game of our Lives: The Meaning and Making of English Football* (Penguin, 2014)
Goldstein, Dan, *English Football: A Fans' Handbook 1999–2000* (The Rough Guides, 1999)
Greaves, Jimmy, *Greavsie: The Autobiography* (Time Warner Books, 2003)
Hamilton, Duncan, *Provided You Don't Kiss Me: 20 Years with Brian Clough* (Fourth Estate, 2007)
Hartrick, David, *Silver Linings: Bobby Robson's England* (Pitch Publishing, 2021)
Henshaw, Philip, *Showdown at the Palace: The 1898 FA Cup Final* (Independently published, 2021)
Hills, Ryan, *Pride: The Inside Story of Derby County in the 21st Century* (Pitch Publishing, 2020)
Hinton, Alan, *Triumph and Tragedy: The Alan Hinton Story,* (Geoffrey Publications, 2021)
Hodge, Steve, *The Man with Maradona's Shirt* (Orion Books, 2010)
Imlach, Gary, *My Father and Other Working-Class Football Heroes* (Yellow Jersey Press, 2005)

Juson, Dave and Bull, David, *Full-Time at The Dell* (Hagiology Publishing, 2001)

Kuper, Simon, and Szymanski, Stefan, *Why England Lose: Why England Lose and other Curious Phenomena Explained* (Harper Sport, 2009)

Lawrence, D.H., *Sons and Lovers* (Heinemann Educational Books, 1963)

Lawson, John, *Forest 1865–1978* (Wensum Books, 1978)

Matthews, Stanley, *The Stanley Matthews Story* (Oldbourne Book Co. Ltd, 1960)

McGovern, John, *From Bo'Ness to the Bernabéu* (Vision Sports Publishing, 2012)

McKinstry, Leo, *Jack and Bobby* (CollinsWillow, 2002)

McMinn, Ted, *The Tin Man* (Black and White Publishing, 2009)

Morris, Terry, *Vain Games of No Value? A Social History of Association Football in Britain During its First Long Century* (AuthorHouse 2016)

Murray, Scott, *The Title: The Story of the First Division* (Bloomsbury, 2017)

Pearce, Stuart, *Psycho: The Autobiography* (Headline Book Publishing, 2000)

Pearce, Stuart, *Never Stop Dreaming: My Euro 96 Story* (Hodder & Stoughton, 2020)

Preston, John, *Fall: The Mystery of Robert Maxwell* (Viking, 2021)

Rippon, Anton, *Derby County: The Story of a Football Club* (North Bridge Publishing, 2013)

Rippon, Anton, and Ward, Andrew, *The Derby County Story* (The Breedon Books Publishing Company, 1998)

Rippon, Nicola, *Derby, The Fifties and Sixties* (North Bridge Publishing, 2014)

Robertson, John, *Super Tramp: My Autobiography* (Mainstream Publishing, 2011)

Seddon, Peter, *Steve Bloomer: The Story of Football's First Superstar* (The Breedon Books Publishing Company, 1999)

Shilton, Peter, *The Autobiography* (Orion Books Ltd, 2004)
Soar, Philip, *The Official History of Nottingham Forest* (Worth Press Ltd, 2015)
Taylor, Peter, and Langley, Mike, *With Clough by Taylor* (Sidgwick and Jackson, 1980)
Torvill, Jayne, and Dean, Christopher, *Torvill and Dean: Our Life on Ice: The Autobiography* (Simon & Schuster UK Ltd, 2014)
Wilson, Jonathan, *Brian Clough: Nobody Ever Says Thank You – The Biography* (Orion Books, 2011)
Wright, Don, *Forever Forest* (Amberley, 2015)

Websites
Blackpast.org
Bostonunited.co.uk
Britishnewspaperarchive.co.uk
Casualculture.co.uk
Dcfc.co.uk
Eastmidlandsbusinesslink.co.uk
Eurogamer.net
Hartlepoolunited.co.uk
Mumblingnerd.com
Nottinghamforest.co.uk
Sportchippers/youtube.com/channel
Theathletic.com
Torvillanddean.com
Thesparrowsnest.org.uk

Podcasts
Buxton, Adam, EP151, 'Torvill and Dean', 3 March 2021, *The Adam Buxton Podcast*
Humphreys, Rachel, 'The Life and Death of Robert Maxwell', 1 March 2021, *Today in Focus*
Talk Derby to Me
Radiolab, 'Ghosts of Football Past', 4 February 2018